How to Do *Everything* with Your Camera Phone

John Frederick Moore

McGraw-Hill/Osborne

New York   Chicago   San Francisco   Lisbon
London   Madrid   Mexico City   Milan   New Delhi
San Juan   Seoul   Singapore   Sydney   Toronto

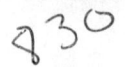

McGraw-Hill/Osborne
2100 Powell Street, 10th Floor
Emeryville, California 94608
U.S.A.

To arrange bulk purchase discounts for sales promotions, premiums, or fund-raisers, please contact **McGraw-Hill**/Osborne at the above address. For information on translations or book distributors outside the U.S.A., please see the International Contact Information page immediately following the index of this book.

How to Do Everything with Your Camera Phone

Copyright © 2004 by The McGraw-Hill Companies. All rights reserved. Printed in the United States of America. Except as permitted under the Copyright Act of 1976, no part of this publication may be reproduced or distributed in any form or by any means, or stored in a database or retrieval system, without the prior written permission of publisher, with the exception that the program listings may be entered, stored, and executed in a computer system, but they may not be reproduced for publication.

234567890 CUS CUS 01987654

ISBN 0-07-225764-4

Publisher	Brandon A. Nordin
Vice President &	
Associate Publisher	Scott Rogers
Editorial Director	Roger Stewart
Acquisitions Editor	Marjorie McAneny
Project Editor	Jenn Tust
Acquisitions Coordinator	Agatha Kim
Technical Editor	Joni Blecher
Copy Editor	Sally Engelfried
Proofreader	Susie Elkind
Indexer	Valerie Haynes Perry
Composition	International Typesetting and Composition
Illustrators	International Typesetting and Composition, Melinda Lytle
Cover Series Design	Dodie Shoemaker

This book was composed with Corel VENTURA™ Publisher.

Information has been obtained by **McGraw-Hill**/Osborne from sources believed to be reliable. However, because of the possibility of human or mechanical error by our sources, **McGraw-Hill**/Osborne, or others, **McGraw-Hill**/Osborne does not guarantee the accuracy, adequacy, or completeness of any information and is not responsible for any errors or omissions or the results obtained from the use of such information.

Dedication

For Ellen and Livingston Moore

About the Author

John Frederick Moore has covered technology since the early 1990s. He has been a staff editor and writer for *PC Magazine* and *Home Office Computing* and was the senior technology reporter for CNNfn.com, for which he covered the Microsoft antitrust trial among other major tech-related breaking news events. Currently a freelance writer, Moore is a regular contributor to CNET.com, for which he frequently reviews cell phones and MP3 players. He wrote CNET's *Quick Guide to Camera Phone Services,* as well as the site's "Ultimate Cell Phone Headset" roundup. An avid jazz fan, Moore is a contributing writer for *Jazziz* magazine. His work has also appeared in Salon.com, *Poets & Writers, The New York Press,* and *Bookmarks.*

Contents

Foreword xi
Acknowledgments xiii
Introduction xv

PART I	**Getting to Know Your Camera Phone**

CHAPTER 1	**Learning Camera Phone Basics** 3

How Camera Phones Work 4
    How a Camera Phone Is Different
        from a Digital Camera 5
What You Can Do with a Camera Phone 5
    Instant Electronic Postcards 5
    Photo Caller ID 6
    Shopping 6
    Law Enforcement 7
    Professional Applications 7
Terms You Should Know 10
    Pixel 10
    Megapixel 10
    Resolution 10
    VGA 10
    MMS 11
    Compression 11
    JPEG 12
    Kilobyte 12
Shopping for Camera Phones 12
    Which Camera Phone Is Best for You? 13
    Style Considerations 13
    How Do You Want to Connect? 13
    Online Storage 14
    Should You Buy a Separate Camera Attachment? 15

	Know the Brands	16
	Handspring (Palm One)	16
	LG	17
	NEC	17
	Nokia	18
	Samsung	18
	Sanyo	19
	Sony Ericsson	19
	Toshiba	19
	Supported Carriers	19
	Choose the Right Service	20
	Factors to Consider	21
	What Other Services Do You Need?	22
	Moving On	23
CHAPTER 2	**Getting Started**	**25**
	A Guided Tour of the Device	26
	The Screen	26
	The Lens	29
	The Buttons	31
	The Menus	32
	The Card Slot	34
	The IrDA Port	35
	Using Your Camera for the First Time	35
	Charging the Battery	35
	Accessing the Camera Mode	36
	Taking Your First Picture	36
	Saving Your Pictures	36
	Viewing Your Pictures	37
	Sending Your Pictures	37
	Setting Preferences	39
	Resolution	39
	Image Quality	40
	Brightness/Contrast/White Balance	40
	Picture Effects	42
	Moving On	44
PART II	**Shooting Great Pictures with Your Camera Phone**	
CHAPTER 3	**Taking Good Pictures**	**47**
	Capturing Great Shots	48
	Framing Your Shot	49
	Adjusting for Lighting Conditions	50
	Understanding Depth of Field	54

Contents **vii**

Taking Self-Portraits	57
Taking Continuous-Action Shots	59
Using High and Low Resolution	61
Web Publishing	61
MMS/E-mail	62
Photo Caller ID	63
Printing	65
Moving On	65

CHAPTER 4 **Saving and Managing Your Pictures** — **67**

Move Pictures to Your PC	68
Use a Data Cable	69
Use IR	70
Use Bluetooth	71
Use Your Carrier's Messaging Service	71
Use E-mail	75
Image Management	77
Working with Windows	77
Image-Management Software	82
Adobe Photoshop Album 2	84
JASC Paint Shop Album 4	89
Microsoft Digital Image Library	92
Apple iPhoto	94
Create Photo Archives	96
Moving On	99

CHAPTER 5 **Editing Your Photos** — **101**

Working with an Image Editor	102
Adobe Photoshop Elements 2	103
JASC Paint Shop Pro 8	104
Microsoft Digital Image Pro 9	106
Performing Common Editing Functions	106
Align a Crooked Picture	108
Crop a Photo	109
Adjusting Brightness and Contrast	113
Sharpen Your Photos	116
Eliminate Specks	118
Change the Image Size	119
Change the File Format	124
Moving On	126

How to Do Everything with Your Camera Phone

PART III	**What to Do with Your Photos**	
CHAPTER 6	**Sharing Your Photos**	**129**
	Multimedia Messaging	130
	Sending an MMS Message	131
	Picture Messaging Websites	132
	How Much Will I Pay?	144
	Third-Party Online Services	146
	E-mail Your Pictures	150
	Moving On	156
CHAPTER 7	**Printing Your Photos**	**157**
	Choosing a Printer	158
	Memory Cards	159
	Bluetooth and IrDA	160
	Other Features	161
	Making the Print	162
	Adjust the Size	162
	Beware of Running Costs	165
	Online Print Services	166
	Using In-Store Kiosks	170
	Moving On	172
CHAPTER 8	**Creating a Moblog**	**173**
	What's a Moblog?	174
	Individual vs. Community	174
	Buzznet.com	176
	Mobog.com	179
	Textamerica.com	182
	Upload to Community Moblogs	190
	Moving On	195
CHAPTER 9	**Other Fun Stuff for Your Photos**	**197**
	Set Up Photo Caller ID	198
	Photo Creations	199
	Create a Photo Album	199
	Create a Slide Show	205
	Make a Movie	207
	Create Greeting Cards	209
	Digital Frames	212
	Moving On	214

PART IV — Get the Most Out of Your Camcorder Phone

CHAPTER 10 — What Your Camcorder Phone Can Do for You ... 217
- Get to Know Your Camcorder Phone ... 218
  - Terms You Should Know ... 219
- Issues to Consider ... 221
  - Time and Size Constraints ... 221
  - Remember Your Memory ... 223
- Shopping for a Camcorder Phone ... 225
  - Look for More Memory ... 225
- Choose a Model ... 230
  - Nokia 3620 ... 231
  - Samsung VM-A680 ... 232
  - Sony Ericsson P900 ... 233
  - Toshiba VM4050 ... 234
- Camcorder Phones at a Glance ... 235
- Moving On ... 235

CHAPTER 11 — Capturing, Sharing, and Editing Video ... 237
- Shooting Video ... 238
  - Work with Strong Natural Light ... 239
  - Get Close ... 240
  - Let the Action Come to You ... 241
  - Using the Camcorder Function ... 241
- Share Your Video Clips ... 243
  - Sprint PCS Picture Mail ... 244
  - Textamerica ... 247
  - Move Clips to Your PC ... 247
- Acquire Video From Third-Party Sources ... 250
  - MobiTV ... 252
  - RealOne ... 253
  - 1KTV ... 254
  - Verizon Wireless GetFlix ... 256
- Use Video Editing Software ... 258
  - U-Lead VideoStudio 8 ... 259
- The Future of Video ... 269
  - Video Calls ... 270
  - TV Tuners ... 270
- Moving On ... 271

PART V	**Appendixes**	
APPENDIX A	**Working with a Megapixel Phone**	**275**
	What to Look For	276
	The Lens	278
	Memory Expansion	279
	Data Cables	279
	Consider an Extra Battery	280
	Minding Your Messaging	280
	Picking a Data Plan	281
	Warning Your Recipients	281
	A Few Megapixel Models	281
	Audiovox PM-8920	282
	Kyocera Koi	282
	LG VX8000	283
	Motorola V710	284
	Nokia 7610	284
	Getting Great Pictures	286
	Using the Highest Settings Possible	286
	Using Bright Light	287
	Cropping Your Images	287
	Print Your Pictures	288
	Moving On	291
APPENDIX B	**Privacy, Security, and Copyright**	**293**
	Privacy	294
	Private Parts	295
	Security	297
	The Spy Who Robbed Me	297
	Camera or No Camera?	298
	The Perfect Score?	298
	Copyright	299
	Fair Use	300
	Be Fair, Have Fun	301
	Index	**303**

Foreword

When I first started covering cell phones they were just beginning to shrink—becoming small enough to fit in your pocket, instead of your briefcase. No one even thought about incorporating a camera, let alone a 262,000-color display. The issues of the day were paltry battery life, how to master text messaging, and what to do with wireless data. People thought receiving stock quotes on your phone was the killer app.

A lot's changed since then. Cell phones are still small, they still let you make and receive phone calls, but a device that was designed to keep you in touch anywhere at any time recently got a lot more personal and a lot more fun. Now you can use your mobile to capture candid and not-so candid moments. The best part is that you don't have to fork out a lot of cash to own such a device. In fact, at least a third of all handsets offered by carriers include a camera and are available at a range of prices from the low- to high-end.

Whether you're an early adopter and have had a camera phone for quite some time or are just getting your first handset, this book's for you. John Moore, veteran cell phone reviewer, has packed it full of tips on how to find and take advantage of all the features packed into your camera phone; how to get great-looking pictures, no matter what model you have; what to do with those captured memorable moments; how to maximize your phone's memory to store more pics; clever ways to send and receive images without having an expensive service bill; shooting video and adding a soundtrack to it; and even the essential privacy facts surrounding camera phones.

You'll be amazed at just how sophisticated your camera phone is and the myriad of fun things you can do with it. If you have a camera phone, whether it offers megapixel or VGA resolutions, shooting pics of friends and family for photo caller ID is just the beginning. Remember, life's happening all around you—don't just talk about it, use your phone to photograph it and share it with the world.

Joni Blecher
Cell Phone Diva
CNET.com
http://cellphones.cnet.com

Acknowledgments

As much as I'd like to say this book is solely the result of my efforts, that simply isn't true. No one, certainly not myself, could complete such a project without plenty of help. First, I must thank the folks at Osborne, especially Acquisitions Editor Margie McAneny, who was an enthusiastic champion of this book from the start and whose unflagging optimism and positive energy helped erase many doubts on this end. To Jenn Tust, project editor, and Sally Engelfried, copy editor, by far the best copy editors I've had the pleasure of working with, thank you for saving me from looking foolish. And thanks to Agatha Kim, who flawlessly handled the constant copy flow and somehow managed to stave off chaos.

I couldn't have written this book without the help of several people in the camera phone industry who were gracious in lending their products and providing information: Keith Nowak of Nokia; Brad Shewmake of Kyocera; Jackie Bostick and Jennifer Stevens of Sprint PCS; Jennifer Bowcock and Angelia Langston of Cingular Wireless; and Brenda Raney of Verizon Wireless.

A quick thank you to David S. Rubin for his photography tips (and his Rolodex). A special tip of the hat to Joni Blecher: aside from serving wonderfully as technical editor, she's a great friend who was kind enough to point Osborne in my direction. She, more than anyone else, made it possible for me to write this book.

As for my beautiful wife, Nancy, she makes everything possible.

Introduction

There's one complaint I often hear from friends who own digital cameras: "I feel like my pictures are being held hostage." The *Midnight Express*–like connotations of that statement notwithstanding, their complaints are valid. They have all these great photos stored on the device, but they have no idea what to do with them. That feeling is even more true with owners of camera phones.

So many of us—about 65 million—purchased camera phones in 2003. That number is expected to rise to 100 million by end of 2004. Soon, half of all cell phones sold in the United States will feature integrated cameras. Not bad considering handsets with integrated cameras hit the U.S. market in early 2003. Impressive, yes, but what about all those pictures trapped in our cell phones?

That's where this book comes in. Part I helps you become familiar with the ins and outs of your camera phone by explaining key terms, reviewing common features, and comparing the various camera phone brands and cell phone carriers.

When camera phones first hit the market, skeptics pointed out that the inferior picture quality would hold it back from widespread adoption. That prediction, of course, has turned out to be false. And although camera phones still lag behind their digital camera counterparts in terms of image quality, they are getting better. By the end of the year, you'll find several camera phones that take pictures at 1 megapixel or more (don't worry, I'll explain what that means soon enough). By next year, camera phone image quality should be on par with that of low-end digital cameras. (Although camera phones use digital technology, for simplicity's sake, we will refer to traditional digital still cameras as digital cameras.)

Even if you don't plan on moving to a higher-end unit soon, Part II is all about making the most out of your pictures. You'll learn how to take the best picture possible, as well as get tips about storing and editing your pictures.

But, you ask, what do I do with all these pictures? Part III has that covered, showing you how to share your photos with other cell phone users and send them via e-mail. You'll also learn about fun options, such as adding audio messages to your pictures and sending your shots to camera phone Weblogs—sites that collect pictures taken from camera phones. You'll even be surprised to find out how many printing options you have—or will soon have—at your disposal.

Because technology is always moving forward, Part IV covers the newest trend in cell phones—video. It explains what you can do with your cell phone's video features, including the basics about shooting short video clips, how to share your videos, where to find video content, and what new offerings are on the horizon.

The final section, Part V, is comprised of two appendixes. Appendix A offers a glimpse into the world of megapixel camera phones: what to look for, tips about messaging, what types of phones are out there, and guidance on taking great pictures with these phones. And just so you don't think I'm glossing over the more controversial aspects of camera phones, Appendix B serves as a primer on security and copyright issues. I want you to have fun with your camera phone, not get arrested.

And as a gift to you, you'll find a special Spotlight section in the middle of the book that shows you how to "Create Your Own Moblog." You'll learn how to submit pictures to the Web and contribute to the community moblog created for this book. Because Textamerica is the only moblog optimized for viewing on your cell phone, you'll discover how to save the site as a Bookmark on your handset.

This book is organized in a way that you can either read it cover to cover or pick it up at any point and get the information you need. You'll find step-by-step instructions, illustrations, and figures to guide you through key processes. Other special elements to help you get the most out of this book include:

- **Tips** Show easier ways to accomplish certain tasks and how to get more out of your camera phone

- **Notes** Highlight additional information you may need regarding the topic being discussed

- **Cautions** Help you steer clear of common pitfalls for camera phone users

- **How To** Sidebars that summarize key tasks explained more generally in the chapter

- **Did You Know** Sidebars that offer interesting tidbits of information about the subject at hand

I hope this book will shine a light on things you didn't know or never thought you could do with your camera phone. With new and improved technologies hitting the market at a rapid pace, there's no doubt that you'll be able to do everything—and more—that you can do with a standard digital camera.

I'd love to get your feedback, whether it's relating interesting uses you've found for your camera phone or what improvements you'd like to suggest for future editions. You can reach me at cameraphonebook@hotmail.com.

Thanks, and happy reading.

Part I: Getting to Know Your Camera Phone

Chapter 1: Learning Camera Phone Basics

How to...

- Use your camera phone for various tasks
- Explain important terminology
- Choose a camera phone
- Pick the right service

Let's face it, technology makes us impatient. The more technology enters our lives, the more we want stuff done immediately. Only in the last few years have cell phones become ubiquitous tools for the general population, as more and more people have discovered the need to be available anytime, anywhere. Digital cameras, with their ability to display the captured image almost immediately, brought a sense of instant gratification to photographers of all stripes—no more waiting until you got your pictures back from the drugstore to discover that photo of your daughter playing T-ball was blurry and underexposed. You can see how well (or poorly) your pictures come out immediately just by looking at the screen.

But even that sense of immediacy isn't always enough. With a digital camera you can instantly see how great that picture you took of the sunset while you were strolling on the beach came out, but you can't immediately send an e-mail to one of your friends to brag about what a wonderful time you're having on vacation while they're toiling away at work (not that I condone such gloating!). Nor can you quickly add an audio message to a photo and send off an electronic birthday message to your wife's cell phone. It *is* possible to accomplish all that, however, with a camera phone.

You'll learn how to perform these and many other tasks in the pages to come.

How Camera Phones Work

Like digital cameras, camera phones capture images on image sensors. Most use complementary metal oxide semiconductor (CMOS) chips, though more and more are now integrating the higher-quality charged-coupled device (CCD)—a silicon chip about the size of a fingernail. Either chip can include millions of sensors, each of which registers the brightness of a color. A CCD or CMOS chip with a million sensors captures a megapixel of data.

Also, like their digital camera counterparts, camera phones store images in memory as JPEG files, which utilize built-in compression to enable small file sizes.

How a Camera Phone Is Different from a Digital Camera

Unlike digital cameras, camera phones don't feature a viewfinder. Instead, you frame and view your subjects on the main phone display. Also, the image quality you get with most camera phones is decidedly inferior to what you'll get with even a low-cost digital camera. For now, that is. Most camera phones feature sensors with less than 1 megapixel of data, whereas an entry-level digital camera will offer 2 megapixels. Earlier this year, however, the first megapixel cameras became available in the U.S. By the end of 2005, you should be able to find some camera phone models with 2-megapixel sensors, so the gap is closing quickly.

One advantage, camera phones offer flexibility and convenience that digital cameras don't. For starters, they're small. Many models will easily slip into a shirt or pants pocket. And unlike digital cameras, you can immediately zip off your pictures to a friend's cell phone, e-mail them to your family, or send them to a website for storage.

What You Can Do with a Camera Phone

With the immediate gratification they offer, camera phones can be highly flexible tools. When used as a supplement to your digital or film camera, you'll find camera phones to be a convenient means of capturing photo opportunities in unexpected moments.

Instant Electronic Postcards

During a recent visit to the top of the Hancock Building in Chicago, I spotted people taking pictures of the spectacular views of the city and the lakefront. Through casual observation I determined that about half of the people taking pictures were using camera phones, including myself.

It's not hard to imagine many of them sending their pictures to friends as an instant electronic postcard, either via e-mail or through their carrier's messaging service, as shown in Figure 1-1.

FIGURE 1-1 Use your camera phone to dash off electronic postcards immediately after taking a picture.

Photo Caller ID

One of the advantages the cell phone has over its landline counterpart is the ability to customize. Cell phone users love to personalize, whether it's their ring tone or the color of the faceplate. Camera phones add to that level of personalization. Most phones with integrated cameras allow users to associate a picture with a contact stored in the phone's memory. When you get an incoming call from that person, the photo you've linked to that contact—a picture of the person, for example—will appear in the display (as shown in Figure 1-2). That's true whether your phone sports a flip cover with an external display or is a "candy bar"–style unit (some of the early Samsung models, however, do not include this feature).

Shopping

With convenience comes fun, as well as more practical applications. Shopping, especially when doing so for another person, can be a trying experience. A camera phone enables you to snap a quick photo of an item of clothing, a car, or just about any object and immediately send it to another person to get their opinion.

CHAPTER 1: Learning Camera Phone Basics

FIGURE 1-2 Associating an image with a phone book listing allows you to establish photo caller ID.

Law Enforcement

Camera phones have been increasingly cited as tools to help law enforcement officials capture criminals. Some recent examples, according to news reports, include:

- An Atlanta woman using her phone to take pictures of a man exposing himself to her. The images led police to his capture.

- In Japan, police set up an e-mail address for citizens to submit camera phone shots of suspicious activities.

- In Sweden, a convenience store owner snapped a picture of a robber, which was later used to help identify and arrest the suspect.

Professional Applications

Though they seem mostly like fun toys to play with, camera phones are making inroads into professional uses. Although the image quality isn't yet on par with digital cameras, the quality is acceptable for web use. Some professional applications include:

- Car dealers attending auto auctions and sending pictures to their bosses or potential buyers.
- Construction workers sending photos to supervisors for advice about problems on the site.
- News organizations encouraging journalists to capture newsworthy events when professional photographers are not available.
- Interior designers taking pictures of merchandise to attach to reports that they show to clients.
- Real estate agents taking quick shots of properties and posting them on Internet sites or sending them to clients (Figure 1-3).

FIGURE 1-3 Some real estate agents use camera phones to take pictures of property, which they can later post on the Internet or send directly to their clients.

Voices from the Community

An Editor's Picks

Although it barely existed just two years ago, the camera phone has quickly become a must-have gadget. Camera phones now extend to almost every manufacturer and carrier. We've just begun to see a few models with a resolution of 1.3 megapixels, which is on par with the first digital cameras. In addition to being popular among consumers, camera phones have even sparked legislation at the federal level that aims to limit their use.

At its core, the camera phone is simply an innovative technology and an undoubtedly fun device to use. Mobile customers in the United States can now join their counterparts in Asia and Europe in taking and sending pictures to their friends via their carriers' wireless data networks. These on-the-fly shots bring a whole new meaning to the expressions "wish you were here" and "you had to be there." Sharing vacations, fun moments with friends, or family outings are a snap, and a picture really can tell a thousand words.

The selection of camera phones has grown quite large. Personally, I think flip phones are better suited for cameras. The ergonomics are more comfortable, and some have swiveling lenses, which makes it easier to take self-portraits. Nonetheless, some manufacturers, such as Sony Ericsson, are making candy bar–style phones that even resemble actual cameras from the back.

My personal favorites:

- **Samsung VM-A680**   A CNET editor's choice winner, this compact flip phone for Sprint PCS service comes with a small flash for darker situations. The camera has extensive options and features and it even takes 15 seconds of video.

- **Motorola V600**   This stylish flip phone for AT&T Wireless service takes some of the best quality photos I've seen to date. Plus, a convenient meter lets you keep track of how much space is left in the handset's memory.

- **Siemens SX1**   The camera on this smart phone actually is incorporated into one of the integrated games. Using the viewfinder screen you shoot down buzzing wasps flying in front of whatever the camera is seeing.

—Kent German
Associate Editor
CNET.com

Terms You Should Know

When it comes to using new technology, people (especially nontechies) are often more intimidated by the vocabulary than the device itself. Camera phones come with their own lingua franca. Here are a few terms you should be familiar with when buying or using a camera phone.

Pixel

These are the building blocks of digital images; *pixels* mean "picture elements." They are single points in a graphic image, arranged in a checkerboard pattern.

Megapixel

One million pixels. The more pixels represented in a graphic image, the more finely detailed the image appears. Most camera phones sold in the U.S. feature about 0.3 megapixels, but Sony, LG, and other manufacturers have released 1.3 megapixel models.

Resolution

This refers to the sharpness and clarity of an image, but how it's expressed can be confusing. In the strictest sense, resolution refers to the density of pixels—that is, how many pixels fit into an inch. That's why you'll often see such terms as 96dpi (dots per inch) when referring to a digital image. Things get confusing when camera phone manufacturers say their images support resolutions up to 640 × 480. This actually refers to the image size, or the number of pixels displayed in rows and columns. In other words, a 640 × 480 image contains about 300,000 pixels, or 0.3 megapixels, which is the maximum provided by camera phones manufactured before mid-2004. The higher the resolution, the more the image maintains its sharpness when displayed at larger sizes. Figure 1-4 illustrates the difference in quality between low- and high-resolution pictures. Most camera phones will offer options to take pictures at low-, medium-, and high-resolution settings.

VGA

VGA means video graphics array. Designed by IBM, it's become the de facto standard graphic display system for PCs. You'll notice some camera phones referred to as being VGA-quality. That means they support a maximum resolution of 640 × 480

CHAPTER 1: Learning Camera Phone Basics   11

FIGURE 1-4   The picture on the left was taken at the highest possible resolution, 640 × 480 pixels; the same image taken at 320 × 240 pixels (shown on the right) will appear distorted if viewed at larger sizes.

(with 16 colors) or 320 × 200 (with 256 colors). If you plan to use your pictures for more than just sharing with other cell phone users, it's best to look for a phone that's at least VGA-quality.

MMS

Multimedia Message Service (MMS) is a method for transmitting graphics, video clips, sound files, and short text messages over wireless networks. It's most commonly used for communication between mobile phones. Camera phone users can send pictures via MMS directly to other cell phones if the recipient's phone supports MMS and uses the same wireless provider. If you plan to share lots of pictures with friends or family members, it's best to look for a phone that supports MMS.

If the recipient is on the same carrier but doesn't have an MMS-capable phone, they will receive a text message with a website link to view the picture.

Compression

Compression refers to a method of storing data in a format that requires less space than usual. It's useful in the realm of camera phones because it allows for small color images, which is necessary given the memory constraints of the phones and the relatively slow speed of wireless networks for transmitting images.

JPEG

JPEG is the graphics file format used by camera phones. After transferring an image from your phone to your computer, you'll notice the extension .JPG after the file name. JPEG employs lossy compression, which attempts to eliminate redundant or unnecessary data. It can reduce a file to about 5 percent of its normal size, but lossy compression can also result in the loss of some image detail.

Every time you modify and save a JPEG file, the image is degraded slightly. That's the effect of the format's lossy compression scheme. This isn't a problem if you simply open and view your photographs, but to preserve as much image quality as possible, try to keep your modifications to a minimum.

Because JPEG files degrade with each modification, it's a good idea to keep a master, or unedited, version of your favorite images.

Kilobyte

A *kilobyte* is a unit of measurement for data files, designated by the abbreviation KB. Technically, it refers to 1,024 bytes of data, although in general usage it refers to 1,000 bytes. Your camera phone may produce images as small as 5KB (in low resolution) and as large as 80KB (in high resolution). The smaller the size in KB, the less detail the image contains. A 5KB image may be appropriate for photo caller ID, but it's inappropriate for printing or web use. It's also worth determining how much internal memory your phone supports. Twenty 50KB images equal approximately 1MB of memory. That amount on a PC is hardly worth worrying about, but many camera phones come with 1MB of memory or less, some of which will be occupied by your contact list, ring tones, and other common elements. Be mindful not only of how many pictures you keep stored on your phone, but how large those images are.

Shopping for Camera Phones

With all the basic information out of the way, it's time to start looking at the devices themselves. Choosing a camera phone and service to fit your needs can be a difficult task. I'm not going to make specific product recommendations. Rather, I'll explain some of the various options at your disposal and leave the decision making to you.

Which Camera Phone Is Best for You?

This is a tough question, especially because so many models are available to choose from. Besides, all you're going to do is make phone calls and take a few pictures, right? Well, you need to consider several criteria.

For starters, think about resolution. If you plan on posting a lot of photos on the Web, you'll want a phone with a VGA-quality camera. On the other hand, if all you care about is sending picture messages, a handset that supports a lower maximum resolution will suit you just fine.

There's also the matter of style. Although this is the most superficial concern, you won't be happy walking around with a phone that you find unattractive. Also, you need to think about how you're going to get your pictures from your phone to your computer.

Then there are special features. Specifically, do you need them and, if so, are you willing to pay extra?

Most important is the type of wireless plan you choose. If you're going to be sending lots of pictures, you'll need to investigate what type of data plan works best for you.

Style Considerations

We try hard not to be shallow, but difficult as it can be to admit, style matters. If it didn't, every cell phone would come in the most utilitarian design possible. A quick scan of your surroundings will tell you that people want their phones to reflect their needs or personality.

Style can be as simple as determining whether you want a camera phone with a flip-down cover or one that is candy bar–style (as shown in Figure 1-5). Candy bar–style phones tend to be smaller, but unless you're the type who's diligent about locking the keypad when not using your phone, there is the issue of accidentally pressing certain buttons when taking it out or putting it away. If you prefer a flip phone, then you'll probably require a unit with a fairly large external display. After all, you won't be able to use such camera phone niceties as picture caller ID without it.

How Do You Want to Connect?

One of the key tasks you'll accomplish with your camera phone is liberating those images from the device and moving them onto a computer. You have several options in this regard, and the handset you choose depends on the type of computer equipment you'll be working with.

If you plan to use your carrier's photo messaging service as much as possible, then you should have little to worry about because you'll be downloading your

FIGURE 1-5   Samsung's SPH-a620 flip phone (left) features an external screen large enough to display photos; the Sony Ericsson T610 candy bar–style unit (right) is more compact than a flip phone, *and* it features a larger external display.

pictures to a website directly from your phone. But if you're looking for a more direct route, you'll want to consider other options.

For example, if you're looking to move a few pictures directly to a personal digital assistant (PDA), such as a Sony Clié, you may want to consider a phone with built-in Bluetooth technology, such as the Sony Ericsson T616. Though it sounds like some sort of mythological creature, Bluetooth is a technology that lets wireless devices communicate with each other.

If you prefer a direct wireless connection with your PC, then you may want to consider a phone that features an infrared port (IR). That will only work, however, if your computer also has an IR port. Otherwise, you'll want to invest in a set of data cables that plug into your computer's universal serial bus (USB) port.

I will discuss these options and others in further detail in Chapter 4.

Online Storage

In a relatively short time, camera phones have become more sophisticated in terms of the features they offer. The early models offered little more than the ability to take pictures at different resolutions. Now, you get options on flip phone such as a swivel display, which lets you twist the flip cover 180 degrees to make it easier to take self-portraits by using the phone's display (this can be found on Samsung's SPH-a600 and SPH-a610). In that same vein, more cameras are offering self timers, which let you get in on group photos.

Some units, such as the Samsung e715, come with a built-in flash, while others, such as the Sony Ericsson T616, offer flash attachments at an extra cost.

More Megapixels

By the end of 2004, you should be able to choose from a variety of megapixel camera phones. Several models, if not already available, will be released throughout the year, including the Nokia 7610, the Sony Ericsson S700, and the LG 8000. Some of these megapixel cameras will feature CCD sensors, which means better-looking photographs, giving you even more options in terms of printing and web publishing. Appropriately, because these higher-resolution images will occupy more space, these units will also feature more on-board memory or options for separate memory cards.

> **TIP** *To get the best image quality from a megapixel camera phone, make sure it features a CCD sensor. Some models, like the Nokia 7610, retain the CMOS sensors used in lower-resolution camera phones.*

Whatever options beyond the basics you consider, be sure to determine whether you'll use the features enough to justify any extra cost that may be involved.

Should You Buy a Separate Camera Attachment?

Some phones, such as the Sony Ericsson T226, don't come with integrated cameras but do work with optional camera attachments. These small units snap into the jack at the bottom of the phone, such as Sony Ericsson's MCA-25 CommuniCam Mobile Camera (Figure 1-6).

One advantage of buying separate camera attachments is that they usually come with a standard optical viewfinder, which gives you a more familiar camera experience—something you don't get with built-in camera phones. Generally speaking, however, these attachments don't work quite as well as integrated cameras. They also add bulk to your phone and can be awkward to handle. If you already have a phone and think you'd like to add photo capabilities, you'll have to decide whether or not it's worth spending $50 for a separate attachment, which you'll have to lug around and which may deliver inferior-quality pictures, or shelling out possibly hundreds of dollars for a new phone with the more convenient built-in camera.

FIGURE 1-6   Camera attachments allow you to add camera features to a standard cell phone.

Make sure your phone supports a camera attachment before you buy an attachment.

Know the Brands

If you're shopping for a camera phone, you won't encounter a shortage of options. Wireless providers love to tout their latest and greatest from a variety of brands. In this section, I'll look at some of the more popular offerings by the top manufacturers.

The cell phone industry moves quickly, and new models will be available by the time this book is published.

Handspring (Palm One)

Although this company's Treo 600 is touted more for its seamless marriage of cell phone and PDA functions, it also sports a digital camera. Because it features an integrated full QWERTY keypad, you'll find it easier to zip off a quick picture with text message. The 2.5-inch display is also larger than the screens you'll find on standard camera phones, which should ease the strain on your eyes. (www.palmone.com)

LG

You've probably seen this brand more on such products as refrigerators and washing machines, but this Korean manufacturer also produces the popular VX6000 camera phone for Verizon Wireless. The three colored dots that scroll across the external LCD recall those old-school, handheld video games. LG's VGA camera lets you save 20 images to the phone's memory and includes five Fun Frames, which let you place a headshot image and place it in a variety of templates, such as a magazine cover. (www.lge.com)

NEC

With its 525HD model for AT&T Wireless (shown in Figure 1-7), NEC proves that smaller isn't always better when it comes to cell phones. At 4.28 by 1.88 by 1.06 inches with the cover closed, this handset is a bit larger than similar units. But if you plan on sending a lot of picture messages, you'll appreciate the fairly large (2.2 inches diagonally), very vibrant color display, as well as the roomy keyboard with a wealth of buttons that provide one-click access to specific functions within

FIGURE 1-7 NEC's 525HD features a large, vibrant display.

the menu context. For example, you can access your contact list with a single click when you want to send a photo message. The 525, however, produces pictures at only 160 × 144, so you'll have to decide whether you can live with the limitations that come with such a small image size. (www.nec.com)

Nokia

The top dog among cell phone manufacturers, this Finnish company offers a selection of uniquely designed camera phones. The 3650, shown in Figure 1-8, features a keypad with the numbers in a circular arrangement, sort of recalling the old rotary phones. It also features a slot for adding a MultiMedia Card (MMC) for extra memory, which will come in handy if the pictures begin to accumulate, and the ability to shoot 30 seconds of video. (www.nokia.com)

Nokia's 3200 model allows you to create your own custom phone covers, including ones made from pictures taken with the integrated camera.

Samsung

With a reputation for sleek and clean product designs, this Samsung offers several options for multiple wireless carriers. The SPH-a600 model features a screen that rotates 180 degrees, which makes for easier self-portraits. Although this particular

FIGURE 1-8   The Nokia 3650 includes a slot for adding extra memory.

handset doesn't feature an external LCD, Samsung's a620 does include that as well as a selection of photo effects, including black and white, sepia tones, and ultra-violet images. (www.samsung.com)

Sanyo

This company's line of camera phones for Sprint PCS is highly regarded for its combination of style and substance. The SCP-5300, the first camera phone sold by a carrier in the U.S., features a built-in flash and the ability to close the cover and use the smaller external LCD to take self-portraits. The 8100 does away with the flash but is a bit smaller and less expensive than the 5300. (www.sanyo.com)

Sony Ericsson

If you want points for style, you'll want to consider Sony Ericsson's T616. This candy bar–style unit is small and sleek and the handset features a four-way joystick-type button just above the keypad, which makes for easier navigation through your photo gallery and menu options. The T616 also features an IR port and Bluetooth connectivity, so if your computer supports such connections, you can wirelessly transfer your pictures to a PC. (www.sonyericsson.com)

Toshiba

This company offers the VM4050 for Sprint PCS, which is both a camera phone and video phone. This handset offers a 2.2-inch display, an auto-focus lens, an integrated camera/video light to illuminate low-light environments, and 17 different frames. (www.toshiba.com)

Supported Carriers

Table 1-1 lists the companies that manufacture camera phones along with their corresponding wireless providers. I did not include prices in this chart because the cost of your camera phone will vary depending on your mode of purchase. You can usually find great deals and rebates by purchasing your phone directly from your carrier when signing up for a new plan.

 *Some of the best deals require a two-year commitment. Be sure to read the fine print of any promotional offer.*

Brand	Supported Carriers
Audiovox	Verizon Wireless
Handspring	AT&T Wireless Cingular Sprint PCS T-Mobile
LG	Verizon Wireless
NEC	AT&T Wireless
Nokia	AT&T Wireless Cingular T-Mobile
Panasonic	AT&T Wireless
Samsung	AT&T Wireless Sprint PCS T-Mobile Verizon Wireless
Sanyo	Sprint PCS
Sony Ericsson	AT&T Wireless Cingular T-Mobile
Toshiba	Sprint PCS

TABLE 1-1 Camera Phone Manufacturers and Their Wireless Carriers

Choose the Right Service

An important step in freeing images from your phone is choosing the wireless service that's most appropriate for your needs. With camera phones, this is a two-step process:

- First, you need to determine which provider offers the calling plan that best suits your needs. Frankly, this is the *more important* factor in choosing a provider—your camera phone is a phone first, and factors such as reception affect both the quality of your phone calls and your ability to send multimedia messages.

- Once you've narrowed down your choices based on calling plans and carrier coverage, you need to decide whether that carrier's MMS or data plan matches well with your photo messaging demands.

CHAPTER 1: Learning Camera Phone Basics 21

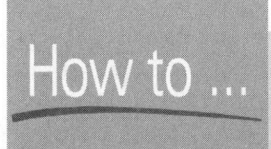

How to ... Determine the Most Cost Effective à la Carte Option

Sending pictures from your cell phone, whether via e-mail or MMS, to another cell phone user results in an extra charge on top of your standard bill. If you're the type who sends only a handful of picture messages a month, you may prefer to pay for each message rather than pay for a flat-rate plan. However, not all à la carte plans are alike.

First, you should determine what types of messages you're sending. If most of the pictures you send are destined to end up on a friend's cell phone, then you can get away with taking photos at a lower resolution. Although this results in a less-detailed image, your pictures will be perfectly suitable for viewing on another cell phone. The main advantage, however, is that it also results in a smaller image size, perhaps as little as 3KB. If you go with a carrier that charges a penny a kilobyte, such as Sprint PCS, then your message costs only 3 cents. That's much cheaper than a plan, such as T-Mobile, that charges 25 cents per message sent or received.

If, however, you plan on sending images via e-mail, you'll probably want to deliver the best image possible to your recipients. Depending on the phone, high-resolution images can run between 30KB and 80KB. In that case, you're better off paying by the message rather than by the kilobyte.

These prices can change at any moment, so you should ask your carrier for details before making a final decision.

Whatever plan you choose, know that sending and receiving pictures will cost extra. If you plan to take and send pictures from your phone only occasionally, you might be fine with paying for messaging services as you go along. Some carriers charge by the kilobyte while others charge per message. If you're only going to send three or four pictures a month, you'll have to determine whether it's more cost effective to pay, say, 2 cents a kilobyte or 25 cents a message. But if you plan on using the camera and messaging features on a regular basis, it's worth investigating what type of flat-rate plans the carriers offer.

Factors to Consider

Picking the right camera phone service goes beyond which provider offers the most messages for the least amount of money. You'll want to know, for example, whether

Did you know?

Why Camera Phones Aren't More Expensive

When you browse through a carrier's selection of cell phones, you'll notice that camera phones aren't necessarily more expensive than handsets that lack integrated cameras. That's because the carriers subsidize the cost of the phones they offer. It's a variation of the old strategy of giving away the razor so you can make money by selling lots of blades. This is especially true with camera phones, since carriers anticipate customers spending more money on data services, such as picture messaging, than on a phone.

the carrier you're considering offers online storage. Some carriers, such as Verizon Wireless, offer online storage as part of their monthly fees. Others, however, either charge extra or only offer it through third-party providers.

CAUTION *Carriers that offer online storage may set a limit, such as a maximum of 1MB of files. If that's the case, be sure to periodically move your images from the online storage site to your computer's hard drive or external media, such as a CD-ROM.*

What Other Services Do You Need?

It's worth investigating what types of features beyond sending and receiving images that you'll receive from your provider, such as the ability to send your images as greeting cards to any e-mail address or create photo albums that you can share with others. You should also consider what type of editing functions—if any—you're able to perform on your pictures.

The five carriers that cater to camera phone users (listed in Table 1-2) each have unique offerings. Chapter 6 will explore in further detail the services each provider offers.

NOTE *Nextel, which caters mostly to business customers, does not offer camera phones or photo-messaging services.*

Carrier	Key Benefits/Features	Monthly Cost
AT&T Wireless	Greeting-card selection Links to third-party online photo services	$2.99 for MMS, plus $2.99 for mMode Internet Service
Cingular Wireless	Online storage Greeting-card catalog	$2.99 for 20 photo messages
Sprint PCS	Online access to contact lists Basic editing functions	$15 for PCS Vision Pictures Pack
T-Mobile	Inexpensive	$4.99 for unlimited picture messaging
Verizon Wireless	Upload photos from PC to online album Share albums via e-mail	$4.99 plus airtime for 40 messages

TABLE 1-2 Picture Messaging Services at a Glance

Moving On

That was a nice way to ease into things. Now it's time to delve into specifics. In the next chapter, I'll go over your camera phone's features with a fine-tooth comb, including how to navigate the menus, set preferences, and send your first picture.

Chapter 2 Getting Started

How to...

- Identify your camera phone's components
- Use your camera phone for the first time
- Take your first picture
- Save and send your pictures
- Use the menu settings

Now that you've gotten the overview, it's time to delve into specifics. The following pages will guide you through the ins and outs of camera phones. Each model is unique, of course, and where appropriate I'll point out some of the differences. For the most part, however, the general concepts are the same across the different brands.

A Guided Tour of the Device

I know what you're thinking: *I know what a cell phone looks like and how it works. What could you possibly tell me that I don't already know?* Plenty, I hope. Remember, your camera phone has to be functional as both a phone *and* a camera. Certain features that may be convenient for one use may not be so for the other, so it's worth your time to investigate what you need from both.

The Screen

When it comes to camera phones, the screen is one of the most important features. You'll notice that your camera phone doesn't have a viewfinder, which means you have to use the screen to frame your pictures (camera attachments, on the other hand, do feature viewfinders). Not all screens, however, are created equal.

> **TIP** *Although cell phone screens are typically resistant to scratches, they are prone to heavy smudging. Use a soft, dry cloth to clean it.*

Clamshell

This type of display flips open to reveal the phone's keypad and activates the internal display. If you want to take a self-portrait, you have to turn the phone around so that the screen is facing away from you. Some phones, such as the Audiovox CDM-8900, will display your image on the external LCD (which will be facing you during a self-portrait), allowing you to frame the shot better. The LG VX6000, on the other hand, features a small mirror next to the lens that lets you see yourself while taking a picture. With some units, you'll have to use your best guess.

A high-resolution display, like the Toshiba VM4050 has, is a nice feature but be aware that your pictures will look much better on the phone than they will on your computer monitor. That's because a high-quality computer monitor displays up to 2,048 × 1,536 pixels, whereas even a quality camera phone screen, such as the Samsung SCH-a610, displays only 128 × 160 pixels (see Figure 2-1). Pictures taken at 640 × 480 will look especially sharp on such a screen.

Candy Bar

This style of cell phone doesn't include a cover. Instead, the unit is flat with the screen and keypad on one side, as in Figure 2-2. Candy bar–style phones are more compact than their clamshell cousins (with the cover open, that is), so you may have an easier time holding the camera steady when taking pictures, especially if the button to take pictures is located just below the screen, as in Figure 2-3.

FIGURE 2-1   The Samsung SCH-a610 features a clamshell design.

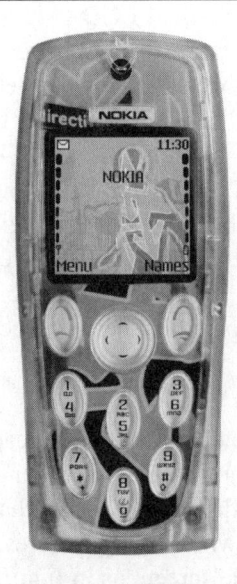

FIGURE 2-2 Nokia's 3200 candy bar–style phone

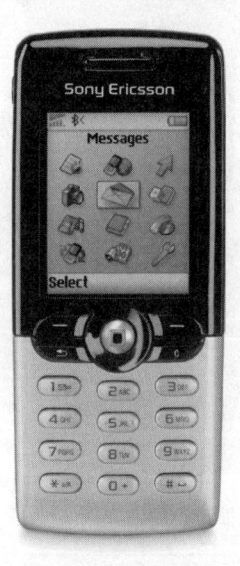

FIGURE 2-3 Sony Ericsson's T610 features a button for taking pictures directly below the screen.

Swivel

This type of display was created with camera features in mind. These are flip phones with a lid that rotates 180 degrees when opened. That not only makes it easier to take self-portraits, but it also means you don't have to move as much to position the camera (see Figure 2-4). Swivel screens also eliminate the need for an external display, since you can close the lid with the screen on the outside or the inside. If you choose to keep the screen on the outside, pictures saved as caller photo ID will appear larger than they would on an external display.

The Lens

As with any camera, it's important that you take special care with your camera phone's lens. Camera phones employ a CMOS lens. The important thing to know about CMOS is that it allows for small designs and consumes less power, which is why they're widely used in camera phones. With the newer megapixel-plus models, however, more camera phones are using CCD lenses, which provide better image quality.

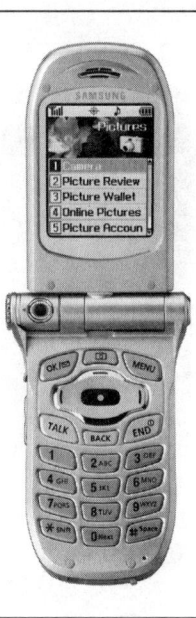

FIGURE 2-4 With Samsung's SPH-a600 swivel-style phone, the lens sits on the hinge between the cover and the keypad, which allows you to rotate the screen to the most convenient angle.

NOTE *If you have a multimegapixel camera phone that uses a CMOS lens, your pictures will come out with a larger print area, but the quality of the image may be inferior to pictures taken with CCD lenses.*

On a candy bar–style phone, you'll find the lens on the back of the device. On clamshell-style handsets, it's usually located either on the top or bottom of the flip cover (see Figures 2-5 and 2-6) although it also can be found on the back of the phone's main body.

CAUTION *When the lens is positioned on the top of the cover while closed, opening the lid places it close to the phone's main body. Because of this, it's easy for your index finger to block the lens while you're holding the device. The same holds true for candy bar–style phones.*

There's one other thing you should know about camera phone lenses. When manufacturers list the lens' zoom capability, they're talking about digital zoom as opposed to optical zoom. With a standard camera lens, the zooming capabilities are optical, meaning the adjustments are made by the optics of the lens to bring the subject

FIGURE 2-5 The lens on this candy bar–style phone is housed on the back of the device.

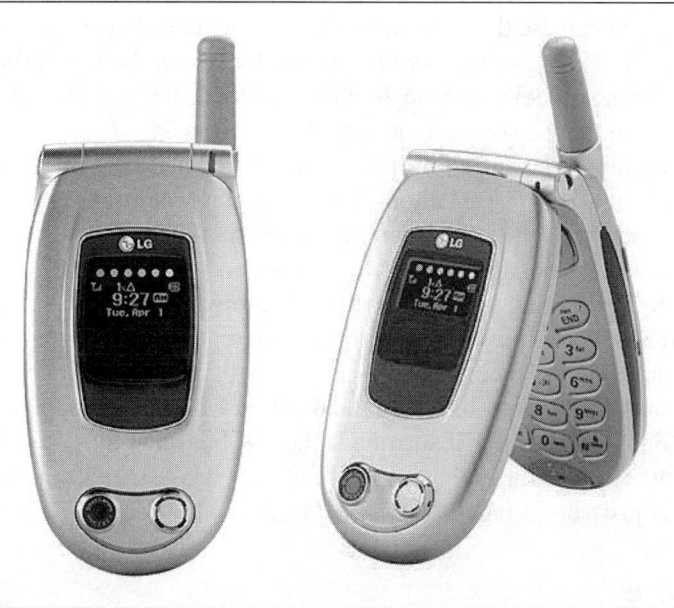

FIGURE 2-6 With a flip phone, such as the LG VX6000, you'll find the lens on the flip cover.

closer. Digital zoom, on the other hand, isn't really zooming in the strictest sense. Rather, it crops a portion of the image and enlarges that portion to full size. This results in a loss of image quality, something you can ill afford with camera phones. So when you see that your camera has listed 2X zoom capabilities, that means it doubles the size of a particular portion of the image in the frame. I recommend staying away from the digital zoom feature.

> **TIP** *Although most camera phones feature a plastic cover over the lens to prevent scratching, you'll want to keep the cover free of smudges or debris.*

The Buttons

Button placement is important for ease of use in taking and managing your pictures. Some models feature a dedicated camera button, which takes you either to the camera menu options or directly into picture-taking mode in a single click. Others, however, require you to access camera features through the phone's main menu, which is a more tedious process.

32 How to Do Everything with Your Camera Phone

Typically, you can use the same button to take pictures that you use to access the camera mode. You can also use the OK button, located at the top of the keypad, to snap photos. Some models, like the Toshiba VM4050, include a separate camera button located on the side of the unit to perform this task.

On many phones you'll find Soft Keys on the upper corners of the keypad, as illustrated in Figure 2-7. These buttons link to menu options displayed on the lower corners of the screen. While in camera mode on the LG VX6000, for example, you'll find menu selections for Gallery on the left and Options on the right. Pressing the left Soft Key will bring you to all the photos stored on the device. After pressing the right Soft Key, you're presented with options to set the self timer; adjust resolution, brightness, and white balance; and take pictures with color effects and frames. You'll find that the navigation buttons above the dial pad will come into play frequently. This is the four-way button that surrounds the OK button at the top of the keypad. You'll use this to move through your photo gallery, make menu selections, and in some cases adjust your images.

The Menus

The menu structure varies from phone to phone. There are, however, enough common camera mode menu selections, as shown in the following list.

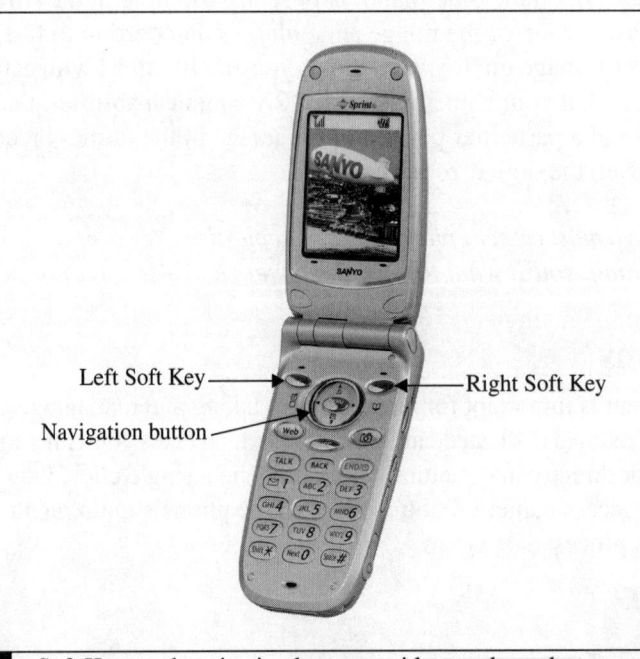

FIGURE 2-7 Soft Keys and navigation buttons guide you through camera menu options.

- **Take Picture**   This, I hope, is self explanatory.

- **View Gallery**   Here you can view all the pictures saved in the phone's memory. From here, you can also send messages, upload pictures to an online album, assign pictures to contacts for photo caller ID (if your phone supports it), set pictures as the phone's wallpaper, or perform basic editing functions.

- **Send Picture Message**   This is where you can send an MMS message to another cell phone with the same carrier that also supports MMS or attach a photo to an e-mail message. Some phones make this process easier than others by providing easy links to your contact list.

- **Settings**   This is for establishing such preferences as the size and quality of the pictures you take, whether you want to include effects such as black and white or sepia tones, and whether you want to make adjustments to brightness and white balance. With some phones, you'll find some of these options when in picture-taking mode rather than in standard camera menu mode. In this case, click the appropriate Soft Key to access Options or Menu.

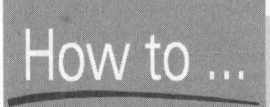

How to ... Change Your Shortcuts

Your camera phone comes with shortcuts assigned to the Soft Keys or navigation keys, but with some handsets, you can change these settings to suit your tastes. The LG VX6000, for example, allows you to assign a shortcut to the left navigation button. If you'd like to press this button for instant access to your image gallery, use the following steps:

1. Go to the main menu, then choose Tools.

2. Select My Shortcut, then select Gallery.

The process will differ according to phone model. With some phones, for example, you change the shortcuts through the Settings menu. Consult your manual to determine whether you can change your shortcuts and for the exact steps required to do so.

The Card Slot

If you plan on taking lots of pictures and don't want to go through the process of uploading them to a website or your computer, you'll want to check out camera phones that feature a slot for memory-expansion cards. You'll typically find the slot either at the base or the top of the phone. Nokia's 3650, for example, comes with a 16MB memory card that holds more than 1,000 VGA-quality photos taken with the camera phone. Not only do you get extra storage, but you also can use the card to print directly from HP Photosmart 130, 145, and 245 model printers.

NOTE *The Nokia 3650 camera phone stores the memory card behind the phone's battery, so it's not easily accessible.*

CAUTION *Not all memory cards are the same. The Nokia 3650 uses a Multimedia Card (MMC), while the Handspring Treo 600 uses memory cards in the Secure Digital (SD) format. The Sony Ericsson P900 works with the company's MemoryStick Duo. If you plan on using memory cards for printing, make sure your printer supports the right format.*

Voices from the Community: A Family Affair

My husband, Jim, and I never seemed to have a camera with us when we really needed one, but we always had our cell phones with us. Given that we have two small kids, it just made sense to get camera phones.

Now, Jim and I both have LG VX6000 phones and we really like them. I like the size of it—nice and small—and I like that it has voice dialing, which is very important while driving. As for the camera features, when I'm out with the children, if something comes up all of a sudden that would make a great picture, I'll take a quick shot and send it to Jim's phone or e-mail it to my family in Philadelphia.

The camera phone really came in handy recently when my mom bought a new car. Jim happened to be in Philadelphia at the time, and he took a picture of the car and sent it to my phone, so I was able to get a look at it and know that she'd bought something decent.

I'd like to see the clarity of the images improve. The pictures get a little grainy when you enlarge them. When the picture quality improves, I'll use it a lot more.

—Maureen Juhas
Naperville, IL

The IrDA Port

If you're lucky enough to have a camera phone with an infrared (IrDA) port, you'll be able to transfer pictures wirelessly from your handset to another device that accepts infrared data transfers, such as a PDA or a PC. You can even print your pictures without the hassle of first transferring images to your computer if you have an IrDA-compatible printer.

The IrDA port is a small, dark, rectangular piece of plastic, usually located on or near the top of the device on either corner or on the spine of the handset. If you're going to beam your photos wirelessly between devices, make sure the path between the two is unobstructed and that the ports line up.

Using Your Camera for the First Time

Now that you know where everything is, it's time to use your camera phone. That means charging the battery, getting to your phone's camera mode, and working with pictures for the first time.

Charging the Battery

When you first get your camera phone, it's important that you charge it fully before you begin using it. This is particularly important with camera phones because the camera features are an extra drain on the battery. The first charge should take three or four hours, even if the indicator says it's fully charged after only an hour or so. All new batteries require a "break-in" period and must be slow-charged prior to initial use. After charging your phone fully the first time, you won't ever have to wait as long to bring it to a full charge again.

Some units come with a travel charger, which you simply plug the AC adapter directly into the phone and insert the plug into a wall outlet. Others come with a desktop charging cradle. With these devices, you plug the cradle's power cord into a wall outlet, then position the phone into the cradle.

NOTE *Make sure the phone is turned off the first time you charge the battery.*

TIP *To get the most out of your battery, recharge it only after completely draining it. That is, leave your cell phone on until the battery is dead. Also, avoid overcharging the battery. Be sure to follow the manufacturer's instructions for proper battery care.*

Accessing the Camera Mode

As I mentioned earlier, many phones come with a dedicated button for accessing the camera mode. This button is represented on the keypad or on the side of the unit with a small camera icon. If your camera has a dedicated camera mode button, in most cases you'll be presented with options to take a picture, view the gallery, send a picture message, or adjust picture settings. With some models, pressing the camera button will immediately take you to picture-taking mode, meaning you'll have to access the menu if you simply want to view your saved pictures.

If your phone doesn't include this one-click access, you'll have to go through the phone's main menu. Press either your phone's dedicated menu button or, if the word Menu appears on the bottom corner of the screen, press the appropriate Soft Key to call up the system menu. Once there, you'll find selections such as Contacts or Phone Book, Call History, Messaging, and so forth. Press your phone's navigation buttons, located above the dial pad, to find a selection called Camera or Pictures. Once that's highlighted, press the OK button to access the camera mode.

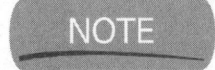

> **NOTE** *Some phones don't allow you to receive calls while in camera mode. Any incoming calls will go directly to voice mail. Also note that you'll always have to exit the camera mode to make calls.*

Taking Your First Picture

Once you're in camera mode, you're ready to take your first picture. Some phones automatically bring you to picture-taking mode, while with others you need to select the Take Picture option. Once there, the phone's screen changes into a video display, which you will use to frame your shot. When you're satisfied with the composition, click the Camera button or the OK button to take the picture.

> **NOTE** *Some phones display borders and center marks to help you frame your picture.*

Saving Your Pictures

After taking the picture, you'll most likely be presented with options to save or discard the image. If you're happy with the picture you just took and want to save it in the camera's memory, click the OK button or the appropriate Soft Key under the Save option displayed on the screen. The picture is then added to the camera's photo gallery.

Some models feature an Auto Save option that automatically saves every picture you take to the gallery. In this case, after taking the picture, you will be given the option to erase the image before taking another picture.

Viewing Your Pictures

Now that you've gotten a few shots under your belt, you'll want to be able to browse through your collection. You access the phone's gallery by entering camera mode, then selecting an option called Gallery or My Pictures. You not only can view pictures you've taken, but also shots you've downloaded from websites or received from other camera phone users.

You'll first be presented with a series of thumbnails, or miniature versions, of your pictures. Use your phone's navigation buttons to move through these thumbnails. When you've highlighted the picture you want, click the OK button to see a full-frame view of the image. Once you're in full viewing mode, you should still be able to browse through the collection, with each image presented at full size.

Whether in full view or thumbnail mode, you can choose to send a picture message, upload it to an online album, assign the image to a contact for photo caller ID, or erase the image from the camera's memory. Some camera phones offer an option to lock or protect images, which prevents selected images from being erased.

> **CAUTION** *Be sure you really want to delete your picture before doing so. Unlike a PC, camera phones don't have an Undo button or Recycle Bin to retrieve erased files.*

Sending Your Pictures

One of the biggest advantages camera phones offer is the ability to share your pictures with others immediately after taking them. This is easier to accomplish with some phones than others, although this is largely dictated by the carrier rather than the phone manufacturer.

Verizon boasts about making it possible for users to send a picture with just a few clicks. Sending picture messages from the LG VX6000, for example, is straightforward:

1. Take the picture.
2. Click OK to send.
3. Press the left Soft Key to access your contact list.

How to Do Everything with Your Camera Phone

4. Select a contact.
5. Select a phone number (for picture message) or e-mail address.
6. Press the left Soft Key to send.

NOTE *After selecting the contact, you can add such elements as a sound clip or a text message to the file.*

The picture-sending process just described is generally similar across carriers and product lines. After sending an e-mail, your recipients will receive a message like the one shown in Figure 2-8. From there, they will be directed to a website to view the picture and listen to attached sound memos.

NOTE *With some camera phones, when you receive a message you can click on the website link to view and download an image directly to your handset, then save it as photo caller ID, wallpaper, and so forth.*

FIGURE 2-8   Recipients of picture messages from Sprint PCS will see a sample of the image, along with a link to Sprint's Picture Mail site to view the picture.

Did you know?

Messaging May Cost You Airtime?

We're accustomed to paying a fixed price for an unlimited amount of web surfing and e-mailing, but that's not always the case when it comes to your camera phone. If you only plan to send occasional picture messages or e-mail attachments from your camera phone, you may be charged airtime minutes, which come out of your calling plan, as well as messaging fees. Verizon Wireless deducts airtime from its MMS and basic data plan subscribers. Because carriers alter their plans often, be sure to check whether airtime charges apply to your picture messaging and web browsing.

Setting Preferences

Like digital cameras, camera phones provide you with a variety of picture-taking options, including settings for the size and quality, as well as adjustments for lighting conditions and how you'd like your images to look. In the next few pages, you'll learn where to find those features and how they're useful. Chapter 3 will discuss in more detail how to put these settings to use.

Resolution

When camera phones refer to resolution, they're referring to the image size. This relates more to how large your image's print area will be than the image quality. That is, you'll be able to make a larger, clearer print of an image measuring 640 × 480 pixels compared to one measuring 160 × 120 pixels.

Nonetheless, making the appropriate resolution setting is important as it depends on what you wish to use your photos for. A picture used for caller ID will look just fine at a low resolution. Also, because it's an image that will be stored in your phone's memory, the smaller image size will save space. If you plan on posting your pictures to a website, however, you should use the phone's highest resolution setting, since these images will be viewed on computer monitors, which have a much higher resolution than your camera phone's display.

Here's what you need to do to set the resolution:

1. Enter picture-taking mode.
2. Select the Options menu with the appropriate Soft Key.

3. Use the navigation button to scroll to the Resolution option and click OK. Your phone may have an option for Picture or Camera Settings. If that's the case, select that option then scroll to the Resolution option.

4. Use the navigation key to select a resolution setting and click OK.

Your phone should display a brief message confirming your selection.

> **NOTE** *Some phones allow you to make this adjustment without having to go through the Options menu. With the Audiovox CDM-8900, for example, you simply press the Up/Down navigation buttons to toggle through the resolution settings.*

Image Quality

This setting allows you to adjust the sharpness of the image rather than the size. With camera phones, the quality of the image is determined by the amount of compression used to process the JPEG file. A high image quality setting uses less compression, which results in a more finely detailed image that occupies more memory. Pictures taken at a low image quality setting, conversely, may appear slightly more pixelated but will occupy a bit less disk space. Your choices are usually low, medium, or high, or sometimes economy, normal, or fine. With the LG VX6000, a picture taken at 640 × 480 saved in high-quality mode comes in at about 50KB, while one at the same size taken in economy mode is only 28KB. It doesn't, however, change the density of pixels or dots per inch (dpi). Whether taken in high- or low-quality mode, 640 × 480 images register as 96dpi. The difference is often negligible when it comes to low-resolution pictures, but for web use or printing, a high-quality setting is paramount.

Not all camera phones offer this option. If you plan on multiple uses for your images, it's worth seeking out a phone with different image quality and resolution settings.

Brightness/Contrast/White Balance

Camera phones, even those with built-in flashes, are best suited for pictures taken outdoors in the daytime or in well-lit indoor environments. Nonetheless, it's important to make adjustments for lighting conditions. You'll find these settings under the Options menu while in picture-taking mode.

Brightness

When looking at the screen to display your shot, if you find the image presented is a bit dim or excessively bright, you should adjust the brightness control. After selecting this option from the menu, you'll see a slide bar near the top of the screen. A small red bar will sit at the zero position. Use the Left/Right navigation keys to make the adjustments. Sliding it to the right (+1 or +2) will increase the brightness, while moving it to the left (–1 or –2) will decrease the brightness level. Figure 2-9 and Figure 2-10 present the same image with slight adjustments to the brightness level.

Contrast

This setting is used to adjust the balance of light and dark elements in an image. Camera phone sensors can't represent the infinite range of contrast in a given scene. Therefore, you have to consider what the most important part of an image is. When photographing light-toned elements in a bright environment, for example, the image may appear washed out, making it necessary to increase the contrast.

White Balance

White balance refers to the ability to adjust the color based on the lighting situation. The camera uses white as a reference and adjusts the color balance to make white as true as possible. This, in turn, corrects all the other colors. If your subject is

FIGURE 2-9   This picture was taken indoors with a moderate amount of sunlight coming through the window.

FIGURE 2-10 Increasing the brightness level intensified the light reflecting off the flower petals.

wearing a white shirt and it appears to be a shade of yellow, you'll need to adjust the white balance to compensate for the lighting conditions. These are the typical white balance settings on your camera phone:

- **Auto**   Automatically adjusts the color balance to lighting conditions. This generally works in outdoor light or when there are multiple light sources.
- **Sunny**   Balances for natural daylight.
- **Cloudy**   Adjusts for overcast conditions. This will produce a bluish tint in other conditions.
- **Tungsten**   Corrects for the reddish/orange cast of tungsten light bulbs.
- **Fluorescent**   Corrects for the green cast of fluorescent light bulbs.
- **Night or Darkness**   Allows for taking pictures in dark settings. Because this increases the exposure, it's tougher to hold the camera still enough to take a sharply focused picture.

Picture Effects

Now the fun begins. If you're feeling adventurous and would like to show a little more creativity, you can take pictures with a variety of special effects, as discussed next.

Black and White

This effect setting takes pictures in monochrome. Pay particular attention to the contrast when taking pictures in this mode because light and dark elements are more prevalent in black and white than in color photographs.

Sepia or Antique

This effect casts a brownish tone to your images, giving them the look of old photographs associated with Civil War veterans.

Negative

This effect gives images the appearance of an X-ray by making the light elements dark and the dark elements light, as shown in Figure 2-11.

Watermark

This effect setting places a cross-hatching effect to give images the texture of U.S. currency.

Glitter

This effect places elements that resemble sparkles around the image, lending the appearance of flashbulbs popping in the background.

FIGURE 2-11   The negative effect provides an eerie, X-ray type effect.

CAUTION: *Some cameras don't allow you to apply these effects for high-resolution images. If that's the case, you may have to change the resolution setting first. Some camera models will automatically reduce the size for you. The disadvantage is that the effect you selected may not be as striking because of the smaller image size.*

Moving On

Now that you've become intimately familiar with your camera phone, it's time to start taking some pictures. In the next chapter, I'll review some basic photography techniques that will help you capture the best images possible. I'll also look at some of the special features in your camera phone and how they help, or don't help, you get that great shot.

Part II
Shooting Great Pictures with Your Camera Phone

Chapter 3

Taking Good Pictures

How to…

- Frame your shots
- Adjust for lighting conditions
- Work with depth of field
- Take self-portraits
- Adjust the resolution to suit your purpose
- Preserve battery life

I hope this doesn't come off as insulting, but it's a safe bet that you're no Annie Leibovitz when it comes to photography skills. Not too many people are and that's okay, because you don't need such prodigious talent to get the most from your camera phone.

In some ways, taking pictures with your camera phone is a different experience than taking pictures with a film or digital camera. Nonetheless, some similarities to traditional photography do exist, and there are steps you can take to ensure that you take the best pictures possible. With megapixel-plus cameras hitting the market, it's becoming even more important to employ standard photography techniques. After all, how many times can you stand hearing your friends say, "That would've been a great shot."

In this chapter, I'll cover photography fundamentals, as well as how to take great shots in the context of how you plan to use your pictures.

Capturing Great Shots

One of the reasons people leave their pictures imprisoned in their camera phones is that they're disappointed with the pictures they've taken. The images are too blurry or too washed out or the perspective is distorted. That's because they're not taking the same care to take a good picture as they would with a standard film or digital camera.

There's also the fact that most people were never taught the proper way to judge a potential photograph. What we see with our eyes often differs from what comes out of the camera, and that's especially true with camera phones because of their inherent limitations. Film cameras and digital cameras are more limited than what the human eye can detect, and camera phones are more limited than both film and digital cameras.

CHAPTER 3: Taking Good Pictures 49

For that reason, you not only need to apply basic photographic principles to get the best-looking pictures possible, but you need to be aware of and know how to compensate for your camera phone's deficiencies.

Framing Your Shot

The camera phone is a great way to capture a spontaneous or otherwise unexpected moment. With that in mind, many people attempt to snap a picture without thinking about the composition of the shot. That's the wrong approach if you actually want to display your pictures in some fashion.

Use the Entire Frame

Any photographer will tell you that one of the most basic techniques is to use the whole frame. Many people tend to focus their attention only on the center of the frame, or the main subject of the picture, while ignoring the rest of the scene. When you take the whole frame into account, you pay close attention to objects in the background or on the periphery of the image. If you merely focus on the subject, you may find unwelcome surprises when you see the finished result. In the image on the left in Figure 3-1, I paid too much attention to the subject and not enough to the rest of the frame. As a result, the lovely fountain in the background appears to be coming out of the woman's head. When I took the rest of the scene into account, the result was a more balanced picture without any unintentional and embarrassing effects.

FIGURE 3-1 In the image on the left, the fountain appears to sprout from the woman's head; the image on the right takes the background into account.

NOTE *With some phones, the frame that appears on the screen doesn't exactly represent what the photo will look like. You might think you have someone's entire head in the shot, only to find out the top was cut off in the actual picture. Take some sample shots first to get a perspective on how your phone's display frames an image.*

Place Subjects Off Center

Another classic rule is to avoid placing the main subject in the center of the frame. Placing the subject slightly off center gives a more interesting sense of space, as you can see in the difference between the two images in Figure 3-2.

TIP *You may find it easier to frame your subjects properly with a camera phone if you use the phone's display as a guide rather than a viewfinder.*

TIP *Because you use the screen to frame your shots, your hand may have a tendency to move more than if you were looking through a regular viewfinder. That's because your hand moves more when your arm is extended. Holding the camera phone as close to your body as possible with your elbow tucked in toward your rib cage will minimize your hand movements.*

Adjusting for Lighting Conditions

It would be nice if the lighting conditions for taking photographs were always optimal, but that's not the case. Many of those buttons and dials you find on traditional

FIGURE 3-2 Placing the main subject slightly off center (shown right) provides a more interesting perspective when setting up a photograph.

cameras deal specifically with this problem. Unlike 35mm film cameras or digital cameras with manual settings, however, camera phones don't offer a wealth of user controls for manipulating the lens to adjust to lighting conditions. With that in mind, you'll have to do your own compensating for less-than-ideal lighting conditions.

Avoid Low Light

Camera phones have difficulty capturing details in low-light environments. Even a unit with a built-in flash will provide minimal support, since the range is only about two or three feet, compared with the 10- to 15-foot range you get with a midlevel digital camera. As you can see in Figure 3-3, the difference between using a flash and not using a flash in a dimly lit room is negligible, at best.

Camera phones automatically make adjustments to the shutter speed based on the amount of light available. That is, when there is ample light, such as outdoors in bright sunshine, the shutter speed is relatively fast. In low-light scenarios, the shutter is open longer. As with any camera, when the shutter is open for a longer period, it's tougher to hold your hand steady enough to take a clear picture. Taking pictures in bright environments provides a faster shutter speed and a deeper depth of field. Therefore, the more light in your environment, the sharper the image.

FIGURE 3-3 The photo on the left was taken in a dimly lit room without a flash; the photo on the right shows that using a flash delivered no discernible advantage in this case.

Did you know?

Shutter Speed

Shutter speed refers to the amount of time light is allowed to pass through the lens aperture, or opening. Single lens reflex (SLR) cameras, the type professional photographers and amateur enthusiasts use, employ mechanical shutters that open and close for an amount of time—1/125th of a second, for example—that's set by the user to expose the film to light.

Digital cameras, on the other hand, use digital shutters, which set the exposure of the image sensor. Some digital cameras allow you to set the shutter speed manually, but most consumer-level units make the adjustments automatically based on lighting conditions. The same holds true with a camera phone.

When you make adjustments to compensate for low light, such as using Night or Darkness modes, the camera automatically sets a long shutter exposure to let as much light reach the sensor as possible. With any camera, the longer the shutter is open, the harder it is to capture a clear image when holding the camera in your hand.

Most photographers recommend using a tripod if the exposure is set below 1/60. A camera phone's shutter speed will be much slower than this in low-light environments, which is why it's best to place the phone on a steady surface if you're going to use low-light settings.

Adjust the Brightness Level

If the image on your display seems too dark or too light, try adjusting the brightness level before taking the picture. You'll be able to see the difference on the screen as you make the adjustment, especially when taking pictures of subjects that have light-colored elements. Figure 3-4 illustrates the difference a simple brightness adjustment can make.

Adjust the White Balance

In some cases, it's not so much a matter of having enough light as it is what kind of light you're dealing with. In these instances, adjustments to the white balance can improve your pictures. Different light sources have different color temperatures.

CHAPTER 3: Taking Good Pictures   53

FIGURE 3-4   The photo on the left is too dark and grainy; however, by boosting the brightness level and activating the Night white balance setting the subject becomes much more visible.

Experienced photographers use blank white or gray cards to help judge the white balance. Not everyone will have the time or the inclination to go through this procedure to take a quick snapshot. If that's the case, you can simply keep the white balance set at Auto. But if this setting doesn't properly compensate for lighting conditions, and if you have a couple of minutes to spare, you can use the same technique the professionals use:

1. Place a white sheet of paper or card in front of you.
2. Go to picture-taking mode.
3. Look at the white card through the screen.
4. If the card appears off-color (too yellow or red, for example), go to your camera phone's white balance settings and toggle through the selections until the card appears as close to white as possible.

NOTE *Your camera may feature a white balance setting called Darkness, which is designed for dark environments. Because the shutter is open for a long period in this setting, it can be difficult to take a picture in focus when holding the camera phone in your hand. If you choose this setting, be sure to set your camera phone on a desk or other stationary location and, if your camera has one, use the self-timer.*

Avoid Backlighting

Before snapping a picture, think about where your light source is coming from. When the light source is behind your subject, it will appear too dark, almost like a silhouette. That's because the camera reads the brightness behind the main subject and sets its internal meter to expose properly for the extra light. Cameras with fill flash options can compensate for this, but camera phones, even those with built-in flashes, have no such feature. Backlighting is often used to good effect in nature photography, but VGA-quality camera phones don't provide the detail necessary to use this lighting technique to its full effect. Unless you actually want your subject to appear as a silhouette, it's best to stand with the light behind you, not your subject.

Understanding Depth of Field

Another basic photography concept worth knowing is depth of field, which is the distance between the nearest and farthest points that appear in sharp focus in a photograph. Film and, to some extent, commercial digital cameras make depth

FIGURE 3-5   Because the sun is behind the focal point, in this case, the baseball field, the objects appear in silhouette.

CHAPTER 3: Taking Good Pictures   **55**

> **How to ... Determine Whether You Have Sufficient Light**
>
> Basic point-and-shoot digital and film cameras feature auto flash modes when the sensor determines there isn't enough light to capture an image naturally. Even if your camera phone features an integrated flash, odds are it doesn't include an auto flash mode (the flash is fairly useless, anyway). And let's face it, not many of you are going to carry around white cards and spend take the time to judge white balance. So how do you determine whether the lighting in your scene is sufficient?
>
> Your camera phone's display won't provide a fully accurate representation of what the final image will look like, but you'll have a fairly good idea if the lighting on your subject is too dim. If the image on the screen appears grainy, that's a good indicator that the lighting is insufficient to capture a crisp, detailed image.
>
> Another indicator: When taking a picture of a person, check his or her eyes. If you can see small, white reflections in their eyes, that means at least a fair amount of light is directed onto the subject. If you don't see those white dots, you may have to do a little tinkering with your phone's settings, or move to an area with better lighting.

of field adjustments with the lens aperture and focal length settings. Your camera phone, unfortunately, has settings for neither of these. (Don't complain too much. It does have a phone, after all.)

Keep Your Subject Close

Camera phones use fixed focal length lenses, and the focal length—the distance between the optical center of the lens and the place where it focuses the image—is very short (the LG VX6000's focal length, for example, is 3.3mm; for a 35mm camera lens, 50mm is considered a normal focal length). That means the lens can capture details in a wide area but not a deep one. If your subject is too far away, it will appear very small. In Figure 3-6, for example, I stood about 10 feet away from the subject, and the detail in the picture is limited. It's best if you keep your subject within three or four feet of the camera.

FIGURE 3-6 Camera phones have trouble capturing details in distant objects, even when that object is only a few feet away.

Did you know?

The Difference Between Fixed Focus and Auto Focus

Most of us are accustomed to working with auto focus cameras, whether in 35mm or digital format because most consumer-level cameras use auto focus lenses. The lens does just what the word says—it automatically focuses on the subject to be photographed by calculating how far away an object is and adjusting its optics for a sharp focus.

Camera phones, however, use fixed-focus lenses, in which the camera's focus is preset to a distance at which most objects will be in focus. The optimal focus of a typical camera phone lens is set to about four feet. This method is less precise than auto focus because the lens is unable to make any adjustments. Although objects in the distance will be in focus, they will appear small.

Avoid Zooming

Camera phone makers, like manufacturers of digital cameras, love to tout their products' digital zoom capabilities. Digital cameras at least have some optical zoom capabilities, which actually uses the optics of the lens to bring the subject closer, but camera phone users are stuck with digital zoom options only (if your phone offers them at all). Given the limited focal range of camera phones, you may be tempted to use this feature to capture faraway objects. Not only will this degrade the image quality, but as shown in Figures 3-7, you may only be able to use it when the camera is set to take pictures in a lower-resolution setting, which will result in a smaller image.

Taking Self-Portraits

Nobody's accusing you of being narcissistic. Of course you're not. But at some point you'll probably want to use your camera phone to take a self-portrait. One of the more popular uses of camera phones is the ability to show friends who are far away what you're doing at a given moment. ("Look at me! I'm at a Cubs game while you're slaving away at work!")

FIGURE 3-7 The Toshiba VM-4050's digital zoom simply crops a portion of the full frame and only takes pictures in lower-resolution settings.

Generally speaking, taking a self-portrait is easier with a camera phone than a standard camera. That's because that fixed-focus lens, the one with the wide angle that I just got through disparaging, is well suited for taking pictures of fairly close subjects. But there are a few tricks to keep in mind.

Extend Your Arm

I know, I know. I said earlier that you should keep your arm close to your body. But it's that fixed-focus lens that's bugging me again. If the camera is too close to your face, you'll get a "fish-eye" effect in which your head will appear distorted, as demonstrated in the oh-so-attractive picture in Figure 3-8. Extending your arm (but keeping your elbow slightly bent) will result in a more balanced perspective.

Find Your Focal Point

Some phones provide helpful tools for taking self-portraits. The LG VX6000 and the Sony Ericsson Z600, for example, each feature a small mirror next to the lens that you can look into to frame your self-portrait. But the best type of device for self-portraits is the swivel-style camera phone, because you can turn the screen toward you and see your face as it is actually displayed. If you use a candy bar–style handset or a flip phone without any special self-portrait tools, you should look directly into the lens while holding the camera at eye level or slightly above. Holding the camera too low can make your face look, well, fat.

FIGURE 3-8   Extending your arm and keeping the lens above eye level during a self-portrait will prevent image distortion, as shown on the right.

Using the Self Timer

Sometimes you'll want to get from behind the camera and be part of a group shot when there's no one around to take the picture for you. Some phones feature a self timer specifically for such occurrences. Use the following steps to select the timer:

1. Go to picture-taking mode.

2. Select Options.

3. Select Self Timer.

4. Choose the time interval (you usually get a choice of 2, 5, or 10 seconds).

5. Click OK or the camera button to start the timer.

Unlike 35mm or digital cameras, camera phones aren't designed to sit on a tripod. When using the self-timer, you'll need to lay the phone on its side. It's interesting that many people never think to turn a standard camera 90 degrees vertically. With camera phones, because you're accustomed to holding the phone upright, you might not think to take shots horizontally.

Taking Continuous-Action Shots

A common complaint among digital camera users is the time between pressing the button to take a picture and the camera actually processing the image, a phenomenon known as "shutter lag." This is especially true when attempting to capture spontaneous moments. My friends often lament that they missed the too-cute-for-words look on their kids' faces simply because they couldn't snap one picture after another the way they can with a film camera.

Guess what? It's even worse with a camera phone. When you press the button to take a picture, the camera needs to measure the ambient light, calculate the best exposure, and set a shutter speed. Not only does the chip take time to process the image, but you're presented with a list of options immediately after you take a picture. Even more so than digital cameras, camera phones are designed for one shot at a time. Unless, that is, your phone features an option for continuous-action images (this is sometimes called a multishot option).

This option lets the camera take a series of pictures at the click of a button, simulating the effect of a 35mm camera's automatic film advance feature. While the LG VX6000 features a multishot option, it only captures two frames at a time,

Voices from the Community: Never Miss a Precious Moment Again

With camera phones, you now have the ability to never again miss the opportunity to capture a precious moment. I've been using camera phones for the last couple of years, and I have very important memories that I'm keeping. It may not be multi-megapixel image captures, but the fact that I've got my device with me, and the fact that I can capture that moment is much more precious than the quality of that image.

The act of capture isn't going to be the most important thing. Pressing the shutter isn't important, it's what you then do with that image. The ability to instantly share those memories you have is going to be a much more important part of people's lives. Because your mobile phone will always be with you, you'll always have the chance to capture and share that memory. What we're doing in the imaging business will ultimately revolutionize the current camera market. The quality of the captured image will obviously improve over time. In the near future, people will not want to purchase a camera that doesn't have connectivity options.

We're already seeing this put to use in professional applications. In Scandinavia, we have paramedics out in the field taking photographs of accident victims and sending them back to the hospital so that people can assess the needs before they arrive, because that picture is much more illustrative then a voice call or a text message can be. We consider these people informative illustrators—people who want to describe or demonstrate something, and the picture will do so much more for them.

—David Watkins
Director of Imaging
Nokia/Europe and Africa

as you can see in Figure 3-9. The Samsung e715, on the other hand, lets you take a series of 6, 9, or 15 shots with a single click in either normal or high speeds. That phone also gives you the option to save each shot individually or as a group. The more frames you choose, however, the lower the image quality.

NOTE *Using the high-speed setting in multishot mode is a good tool for fast-moving sequences, such as sporting events, but it degrades the image quality.*

CHAPTER 3: Taking Good Pictures   61

FIGURE 3-9   The multishot option is handy for taking action pictures.

> **TIP** *When taking pictures in multishot mode, resist the urge to follow the action with the camera phone. This will cause excessive blurriness. Hold the camera steady and let the action unfold in front of you.*

Using High and Low Resolution

With the basics of camera phone photography under your belt, it's time to match those skills with best practices. To get the most out of your images, you need to think ahead about how you'll be using them. For one thing, your camera phone has a limited amount of memory, and there's no sense in amassing a collection of larger, high-resolution images when you don't need to.

Also, you need to think about the recipients of your picture messages. Most of the time, you'll be sending them pictures they didn't ask for, so you need to minimize their burden as well.

Web Publishing

If you plan on posting your pictures to a website, it's best to go with the highest resolution your camera phone offers. That's because your target audience will be viewing pictures on their computer monitors. Low-resolution images taken at 160 × 120 will display at roughly the size of a postage stamp on a computer monitor (see Figure 3-10).

FIGURE 3-10   Low-resolution images are unsuitable for viewing on computer screens.

If you try to zoom in or enlarge a low-resolution image, all detail will be lost and your picture will resemble something closer to a mosaic than a photograph, as you can see in Figure 3-11.

Because you're posting to a website, you may also want to use an image editor for cropping, retouching, or other enhancements. With that in mind, the more resolution the better, since JPEG files degrade slightly with each modification.

MMS/E-mail

At this point you may be asking yourself, "Why would I ever want to use the low-resolution setting?" It's reasonable to want the best-quality image all the time, but it's not always appropriate, particularly when sending photos to other cell phone users as a multimedia message.

You should keep images small for a number of reasons. For starters, you want to minimize your upload time and your recipient's download time, especially if you're not sure whether your MMS recipient has a data-plan subscription on their cell phone service. If the recipient pays by the kilobyte, it's better to receive a 5KB picture than a 50KB image.

FIGURE 3-11 Zooming in on a low-resolution image won't help display any additional detail.

Also keep in mind that wireless data transmission speeds are only now beginning to match the rates found on broadband Internet connections, and it still isn't yet widely available. Sprint uses the 1xRTT network, which doesn't approach broadband speeds but is considered fast for a wireless network. It took me about 25 seconds to send an 83KB file. However, you shouldn't assume that your recipient's phone supports the same transmission speeds. Adding a sound clip or text message also adds to the total size of the file you're sending. Besides, a 640 × 480 resolution is wasted if the ultimate destination is your cell phone's screen, on which low-res images look just fine.

If you're sending pictures via e-mail, however, you may want to use a higher-resolution setting, since it won't take long for your recipients to download the message, even if they still use dial-up Internet access. Also, because they'll be viewing the image on their computer, your recipients would have to strain to view a smaller, low-resolution picture.

Photo Caller ID

For linking pictures to names in your phone's contact list, you should use the smallest resolution possible. Not only are you only going to view the images on your phone,

Did you know?

High-Speed Wireless Data Networks

There's been a lot of talk in the past couple of years about third-generation (3G) wireless networks, which will bring broadband-type speeds to cell phones. The U.S. has mostly been wading in the 2.5G world, a bridge between the older, slower wireless networks and the high-speed technology that will open the door for new applications, such as video transmission. (Please excuse all the acronyms I'm about to use, but there's no way around it. Just know that whenever you see these acronyms elsewhere, they all mean "really fast.")

The 1xRTT network that Sprint PCS and Verizon Wireless use is an example of a 2.5G network. The network delivers data at speeds up to 144 kilobits per second (Kbps), about the equivalent of an Integrated Services Digital Network (ISDN) line. The actual transmission speeds you get, however, are usually closer to 40 to 80Kbps.

Verizon Wireless recently introduced its next-generation high-speed network, Evolution-Data Optimized (EV-DO), which is designed to deliver speeds at an average of 300 to 500Kbps, about what you get from a wired digital subscriber line (DSL) connection in your home. Verizon plans to make EV-DO available in all major markets by the end of 2005.

AT&T Wireless and Cingular Wireless, meanwhile, sport their own high-speed service with a name that just rolls off your tongue: Enhanced Data Rates for Global Evolution (EDGE). The carriers say the network allows users to transfer data with average speeds of 100 to 130Kbps, though you'll more likely end up with speeds of approximately 56Kbps.

Just because your carrier supports these networks, however, doesn't mean your phone will be able to take advantage of them. Be sure to check with your carrier to make sure your camera phone will support high-speed data access.

but those images must be permanently stored on the phone. If you plan on having pictures associated with, say, 10 names in your address book, it's best to have the smallest file size possible for each image. If you have 10 pictures at 5KB each, that's only 50KB of memory occupied by pictures designated for caller ID. If you use high-resolution images that measure 30KB to 80KB, you'll quickly run out of room that you may need for taking more pictures. Please see Chapter 9 for details on how to set up photo caller ID.

Printing

Until megapixel-plus models began hitting the shelves, the idea of printing pictures from your camera phone seemed laughable. So who's laughing now? Printer makers and online photo services, that's who—because they'll see an increase in business as more people start to print the fantastic pictures they captured with their camera phones.

Not that you can't print pictures taken with VGA camera phones, but the best result you could hope for from a 640 × 480 image is a passport- or wallet-sized photo. If you try to blow it up to 4 × 6, the pixels will become increasingly evident. With a 1.3 megapixel camera phone, however, it's not unreasonable to print a picture to 4 × 6 paper. And when camera phones that support 2 megapixels and up begin appearing in 2005, your printed photos will look just as good as those from a basic digital camera.

If you plan to print your pictures, you should use the highest resolution as well as the best image quality available because this provides the most color depth. This is especially important because you may be retouching or cropping your pictures before printing them, and you'll want those JPEG files to retain as much information as possible.

I'll discuss specific printing tips and techniques in Chapter 7.

Moving On

With some photography basics under your belt, you've probably been out shooting as many pictures as possible. It's great that you've been working on your technique and that you're so eager to put your knowledge to work, but just where are you going to store all of those images? Your camera phone only has so much room, and you'll need a way to save all those wonderful pictures you've been snapping.

In the next chapter, I'll review the different methods for storing and managing the pictures you've accumulated.

Chapter 4
Saving and Managing Your Pictures

How to...

- Move your pictures to a PC
- Use data cables
- Beam your pictures wirelessly
- Organize your files in Windows
- Work with image-management software
- Archive your photos

At this point, you should be feeling pretty good about yourself. You've taken some well-composed photographs, maybe dashed a couple off to your friends. Perhaps you've had a little too much fun and you've run out of room on your phone to store additional pictures. Now what?

There comes a time in every digital photographer's life when they must move their photos to a computer. For you, that time has come. Some of you may believe that dealing with your computer to handle photographs is more trouble than it's worth. It's not like going to the drugstore and picking up your prints an hour later, after all. The truth is that moving your images to a PC offers you more flexibility. In fact, you can even have those prints made professionally directly from your computer.

In this chapter, I'll go over the various methods at your disposal for transferring files from your camera phone to a PC, as well as an overview of some of the top software programs designed to help you manage the glut of photos that will eventually accumulate on your computer.

Move Pictures to Your PC

In many ways, your camera phone behaves like a small computer. A very small computer. Although the file sizes of the pictures you take are miniscule in PC terms, they quickly eat up your camera phone's memory.

Handset manufacturers are beginning to offer more internal storage space. The Samsung e715, for example, comes with 4MB of onboard memory. Other camera phones, such as the Nokia 3620, include a slot for memory cards on which you can store photos, audio and video clips, and other files you may have downloaded from the wireless Web. With megapixel-plus models now available, more storage space is essential.

I've already mentioned some space-saving tips in the previous chapter, but eventually you'll have to move your images to a PC for long-term use. Fortunately, you have a few options for accomplishing this task.

Use a Data Cable

Using a data cable is the easiest and most cost-effective method for transferring your images to a computer. Unless you purchased a hybrid cell phone/PDA—or smart phone—such as the Treo 600, odds are your phone didn't come with a data cable, so you'll have to buy one separately. Fortunately, they're not expensive, typically about $29.99.

You'll have to match your cable and corresponding software (typically sold in a package) to your phone. Most packages clearly label what brands and models their cables are designed to work with. You connect the cable to your phone's data port, usually located on the bottom of the phone, and connect the other end to your computer's USB port.

Some phones already support mini-USB (it can be found on Motorola models) so it makes transferring data that much faster—not that you're transferring large files to begin with.

> **NOTE** *Make sure your cable plugs into a USB port and not a serial port. Many newer computers don't include the older, slower data connection.*

These cables serve multiple purposes. Aside from transferring pictures to and from your PC, cables allow you to transfer or synchronize contact lists and schedules. They also provide dial-up access to the Internet, in effect turning your cell phone into a portable modem, provided your phone is capable of performing this function.

You'll need some kind of software application to perform these tasks. If you purchase a cable from your carrier, it will come with a basic data kit that will allow you to perform certain file transfers. Motorola camera phone users will want to check out the company's Mobile Phone Tools package, which includes a data cable and software for transferring images between your phone and PC. The software, which lists for $59.99 directly from the company (a downloadable version goes for $29.99 from motorola.handango.com/entertainment), also lets you send MMS messages from your PC over the wireless Web.

CAUTION *Most software packages don't offer the ability to move pictures between your phone and PC. Make sure the software does exactly what you want before you buy it.*

If you're looking for a way to move edited images back onto your cell phone, FutureDial (www.futuredial.com), which also sells data cables for a variety of cell phone brands and models, offers SnapMedia. The program lets you perform basic editing functions (cropping, zooming in and out, rotating) on your pictures. You can preview the image in a window that replicates your phone's screen size before loading it to the phone.

NOTE *FutureDial's website lists the phones it supports both by carrier and manufacturer. With newer models coming to the market all the time, the list is frequently updated.*

Use IR

One of the reasons people love their mobile phones so much is that they don't have to hassle with wires and cables. Depending on your camera phone, you may not have to either, when it's time to transfer images directly to your PC. One method for achieving this is through your phone's infrared (IR) port.

This isn't something included in every phone, or every PC for that matter. But if both devices feature such a port, you might as well take advantage of it.

To activate your phone's IR port:

1. Go to Menu.
2. Select Connectivity, then Infrared or IR.
3. Select Turn On.

To move pictures to the computer, make sure the camera phone is no more than three feet from the PC's IR port and that there are no line-of-sight obstructions between devices. After selecting a picture from the phone's gallery, click Send, then select Via Infrared. You'll see a message on the phone that the data has been sent.

If your computer doesn't feature an IR port, you can find cables that will take care of the problem. You plug the cable into your PC's USB port and line up the other end with your phone's IR port. DataPilot (www.datapilot.com) offers an IR USB cable for select Nokia, Samsung, and Sony Ericsson models. The company's DataPilot software lets you transfer images to your PC, perform basic image editing, and transfer the pictures back to your camera phone.

Use Bluetooth

The other method of direct wireless transfers between your camera phone and PC is an industry standard called Bluetooth. This technology connects to a variety of wireless devices, including PDAs, headsets, and cell phones, as well as an increasing number of computers and printers.

Some PCs, such as the Apple PowerBook line of notebook computers, feature built-in Bluetooth support. Alternatively, you can purchase PC cards or USB adapters from companies such as Belkin (www.belkin.com) and D-Link (www.dlink.com) that will allow your computer to connect with a Bluetooth-enabled cell phone.

Make sure Bluetooth is activated on the computer, then use the following steps to activate Bluetooth on your camera phone:

1. Go to Menu.
2. Select Connectivity, then Bluetooth.
3. Select Turn On.
4. Click Go to My Devices.
5. Click Add New Device.

Your phone will detect your computer and add it to the list of recognized devices. Next, select the picture you wish to transfer. Click Send and select Via Bluetooth. Select the device (in this case, the PC) to which you wish to send the picture. Your phone will display a message notifying you that the picture has been sent.

CAUTION *Turn off Bluetooth when you don't need to use it. When Bluetooth is activated, it's possible for others with Bluetooth-enabled devices in the vicinity to steal any information you have stored on the phone. This is called Bluesnarfing. Also, other Bluetooth users in range can send anonymous text messages to your phone, which is known as Bluejacking.*

Use Your Carrier's Messaging Service

If you haven't already done so, this is a good time to explore your wireless provider's photo messaging service. Aside from sharing your pictures with others (which I'll cover in Chapter 6), three of these services offer ways to transfer images to your hard drive.

Sprint PCS

The carrier's Picture Mail service (Figure 4-1) not only allows you to upload images to the site from your phone, but lets you download pictures to your PC as well.

Use the following steps to move photos from the site to your computer:

1. Go to pictures.sprintpcs.com.

2. Log in using your phone number and password (you will have created this password the first time you attempted to upload to Picture Mail from your phone).

3. Under Upload Options on the right side of the screen, select Download.

4. Select the pictures you want to download by clicking on the box underneath the thumbnail image (or you can choose Select All or Deselect All).

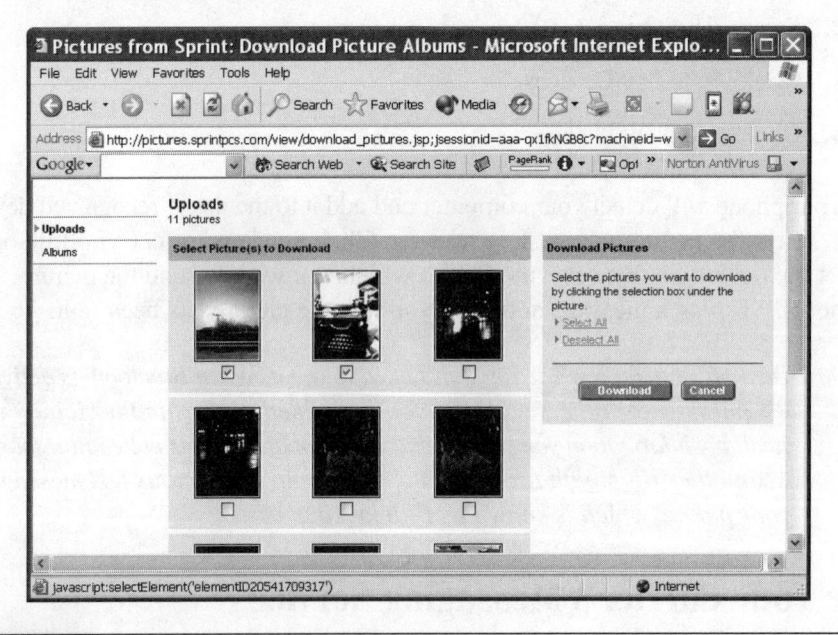

FIGURE 4-1 Sprint PCS' Picture Mail lets you download pictures to your hard drive.

CHAPTER 4: Saving and Managing Your Pictures

5. Click Download.

6. Click Save in the File Download pop-up window.

7. Select the folder in which you wish to save your images, then click Save.

Did you know? Zip Files

When downloading images from Sprint PCS, the site sends the images as a Zip file. Zip is a format that compresses several files into smaller components, allowing you to send a collection of files as a single attachment. In order to save and view the files, you must extract, or decompress, the files from the folder.

Windows XP comes with built-in support for handling Zip files. After downloading a Zipped file, use the following steps to extract a single file:

1. Locate the folder in Windows Explorer.

2. Double-click the compressed folder to open it.

3. Drag the file from the folder to a new location.

If you want to extract all the files in a compressed folder:

1. Right-click the compressed folder.

2. Click Extract All.

3. In the Compressed Folders Extraction Wizard, specify the location you wish to store the extracted files.

If you're using earlier versions of Windows, you'll have to purchase an unzipping program, the most popular of which is WinZip. You can download a free 21-day trial version from www.winzip.com. After the trial period, you will have to purchase the program for $29 to continue using it.

T-Mobile

The latest carrier to offer online picture messaging, T-Mobile's MyAlbum service lets you store up to 25MB of pictures on its site. Although you can upload pictures to the site from your PC, the site doesn't provide a method for downloading pictures from the site to your PC. However, you can always use Windows' file management conventions to your advantage.

Let's say you've uploaded a few pictures from your camera phone to the site. Once in MyAlbum, click on the thumbnail to enlarge the picture. If you have Windows XP, when you move your cursor over the picture, you'll see four small icons in the top left corner of the image. Clicking the first icon, an image of a computer disk, calls up the Save Picture dialog box. From there, you choose the folder in which you wish to save the file.

If you're running Windows 98, right-click the image, then choose Save Picture As, which will bring up the Save Picture dialog.

Verizon Wireless

Like Sprint's Picture Mail, Verizon's Pix Place lets you move images stored on the site to your computer's hard drive. The difference is that instead of a direct download, you e-mail the picture to yourself from the site (Figure 4-2). Not only does this mean extra work for you, since you have to save the pictures after receiving the e-mail, but it also means you're at the mercy of your Internet provider. Depending on traffic between the carrier's site and your e-mail system, you may not receive that message for a couple of hours.

The other downside is that whereas Sprint sends a Zipped file, which allows you to extract the full image, Verizon sends a compressed image as an attachment. In my case, a 640 × 480 image that was 43KB came through as a 160 × 120 image at 3KB.

1. Go to www.vzwpix.com.
2. Log in using your phone number and password.
3. Click Inbox to view images uploaded from your phone.
4. Select an image by clicking the box above the thumbnail, as shown in Figure 4-3.

CHAPTER 4: Saving and Managing Your Pictures

5. Click Send.
6. Enter your e-mail address.
7. Click Send.

Use E-mail

The other carriers don't provide the full range of photo messaging services that Sprint PCS and Verizon Wireless offer. In this case, if you don't have the proper data cables or are unable to move your pictures wirelessly, you can e-mail pictures to yourself.

This isn't exactly cost-effective, as it cuts into your photo messaging plan. With Cingular Wireless, for example, you pay $2.99 a month to send and receive 20 messages. Every image you e-mail to yourself is one fewer that you can send to a friend. Nor is this method as swift as a direct transfer, and it doesn't offer the flexibility you get with using an online messaging service.

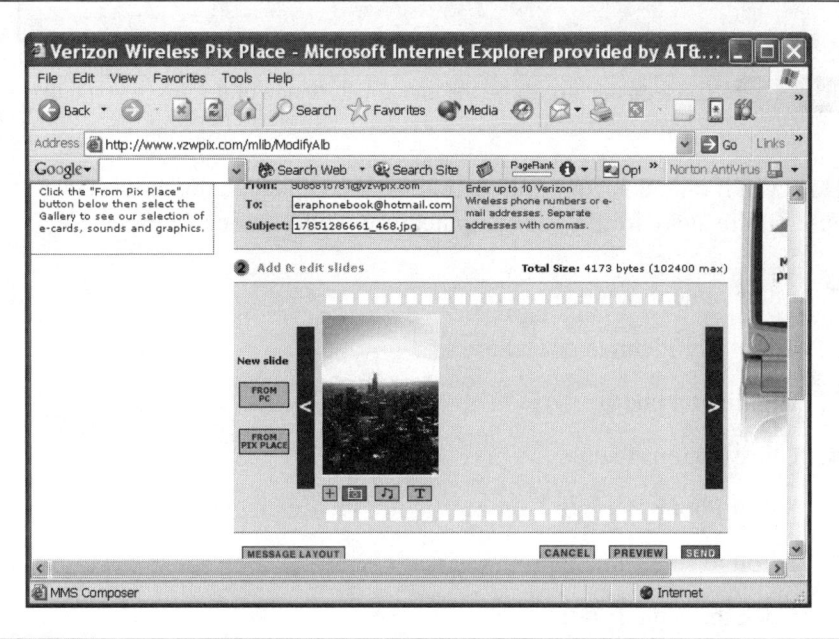

FIGURE 4-2 To move photos from Pix Place to your computer, you must send the file as an e-mail attachment.

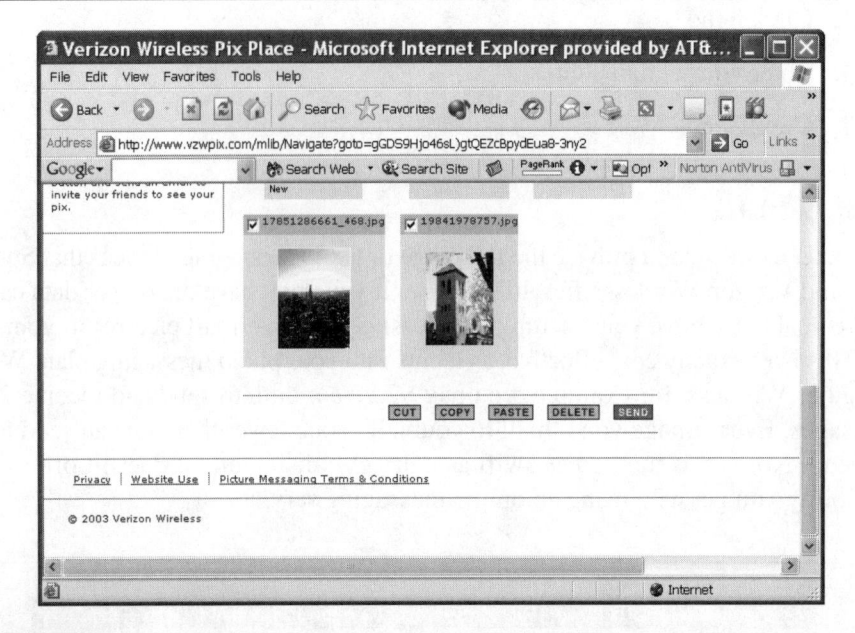

FIGURE 4-3 Click on the box above the thumbnail version of the image you'd like to send.

However, if e-mail is your only option, or if you plan on doing this occasionally because you're away from your computer, use the following steps:

1. Enter camera mode.
2. Select My Pictures or Gallery.
3. Highlight a photo.
4. Click Options | Send.
5. Select Phone Book or Contacts.
6. Scroll to select the appropriate name.
7. Click the e-mail address.
8. Choose options to add a text message, voice attachment, or subject heading.
9. Click Send.

> **TIP** *It's best that you enter the contact information, including e-mail address, onto your phone ahead of time. That way, you won't have to spend time double- and triple-tapping the alpha-numeric keypad to enter an e-mail address when it's time to send a picture.*

> **NOTE** *To send a picture immediately after taking it, begin at Step 4.*

Image Management

Those images you've amassed on your computer can quickly become disorganized. The image-management tools included in Microsoft Windows are sufficient for small collections, but as your pictures begin to compile, Windows leaves a lot to be desired. I'll provide you with some tips for working with Windows' image-management options, as well as take a close look at some popular software programs designed to organize your photos.

Working with Windows

If you have a recent version of Windows (Me, 2000, or XP), you'll find tools designed to organize photos. These tools will probably suffice if you plan on dealing with a relatively small collection (less than 50 pictures). Still, there are a few pointers that will help ease the burden.

Storing Your Images

Recent versions of Windows contain a folder called My Pictures for storing images. If you're working with a small collection (50 files or fewer), your best bet is to use this folder to store your camera phone images. For larger collections, it's best to use an image-management program like the ones described later in this chapter. If you're working with an older version of Windows (Windows 98 or earlier), use the following steps to create a My Pictures folder:

1. Open Windows Explorer.
2. From the File menu, choose New | Folder. A new empty folder will appear.
3. To rename the folder, click the New Folder text under the folder icon, type My Pictures and click Enter. Alternatively, you can right-click the folder, choose Rename from the menu, then type the new name of the folder.

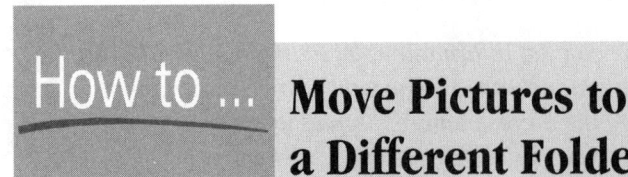

How to... Move Pictures to a Different Folder

Windows' My Pictures folder is good for managing small photo collections, but once the images begin to pile up, you'll want to place them in separate folders. If you have a collection of pictures from a recent vacation and you want to move them to a folder you created called "Cancun," use the following steps in Windows Explorer if your computer runs on Windows XP:

1. Go to My Pictures.

2. Select the photos you want to move. If you want to move a continuous series of files, click the first file in the sequence, then hold the SHIFT key, then click the last file in the sequence. To select non-continuous files, hold the CTRL key as you click on each file.

3. Click the Move this File in the File and Folder Tasks pane on the left side of the screen.

4. In the Move Items dialog, select the Cancun folder, then click Move.

If you want to organize your images by category, you can create subfolders within My Pictures to simplify finding certain types of images. For family photos, for example, you can create a subfolder called Family.

Rename Your Files

One thing you'll notice after you've moved images from your camera phone to your computer is the unruly filenames assigned to them, as shown in Figure 4-4. To make it easier to find specific files, you can rename the files with something more descriptive using the same method to rename folders, as described earlier.

Alternatively, you can rename your pictures as you transfer them to your computer. When saving a picture sent as an e-mail attachment, do the following:

1. Double-click the attachment in your e-mail program.

2. Click Save in the dialog box.

CHAPTER 4: Saving and Managing Your Pictures

3. Select the folder in which you wish to save the file.
4. Under Filename, type a new, more descriptive title, as shown in Figure 4-5.
5. Click Save.

> **TIP** *Because of unruly filenames, some spam filters will keep the pictures out of your inbox. If you know a picture is on the way, adjust the filter in your e-mail application. Alternatively, you can set up a free online e-mail account to handle those images.*

Searching for Photos

Now that you have a basic file-naming and organizational structure for your pictures, you should be able to find the photo you want with relative ease. If you'd rather not

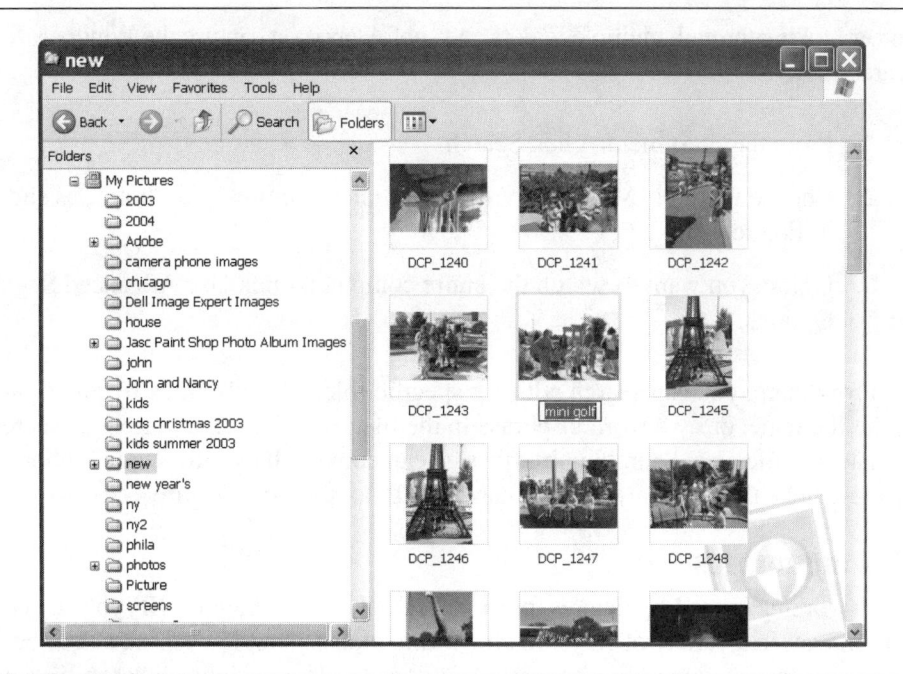

FIGURE 4-4 The default file names of camera phone images can make it difficult to find a particular photo.

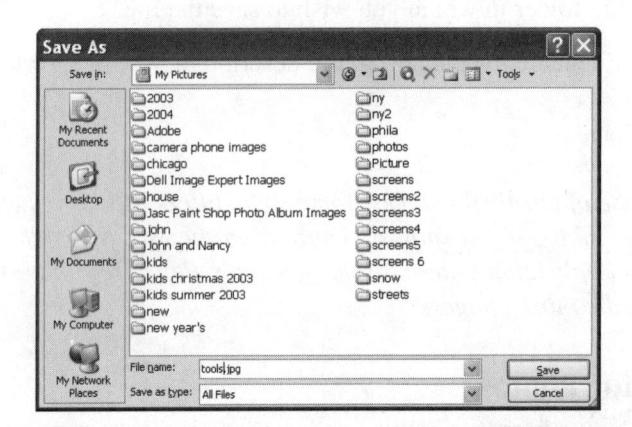

FIGURE 4-5 Organizing your photos with descriptive titles allows you to more easily find them when you need them.

bother looking through multiple folders and subfolders, you can use the Windows XP search tool:

1. From the Start menu, click Search.

2. Choose Pictures, Music, or Video, then click Pictures and Photos, as shown in Figure 4-6.

3. Unless you want to search the entire computer, click Use Advanced Search Options.

From there, you can search within a specific folder or subfolder, by all or part of the filename, or by a word or phrase in the file. You also have options to search by date and file size. Searching by file size can come in handy for camera phone images, since they'll likely be less than 100KB, as shown in Figure 4-7.

Viewing Images

When working in the My Pictures folder and subfolders in Windows XP, you can view your images in a variety of ways. In all viewing modes, double-clicking a thumbnail or icon opens the image in a separate Window. Or, if you right-click the file and select Open With, you can choose a program in which to view the image.

CHAPTER 4: Saving and Managing Your Pictures   81

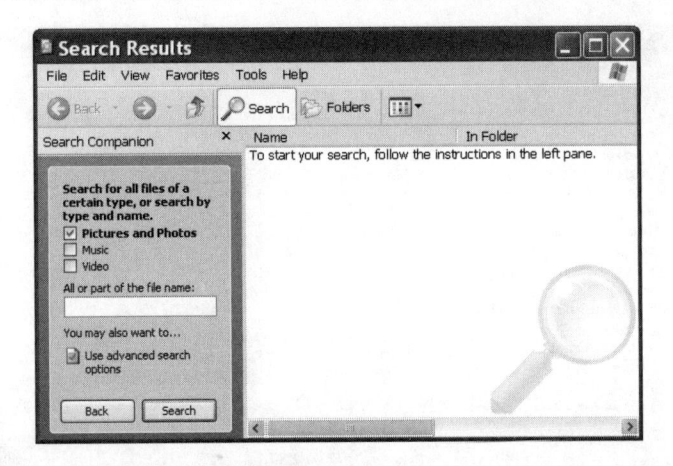

FIGURE 4-6   Windows' Search feature helps you find photos quickly.

Filmstrip   Figure 4-8 shows photos in the filmstrip format. Pictures appear in a single row of thumbnail images at the bottom of the screen. As you scroll through the thumbnails using the left and right arrow buttons or dragging the slider at the bottom of the window, the image is displayed in a box above the other pictures.

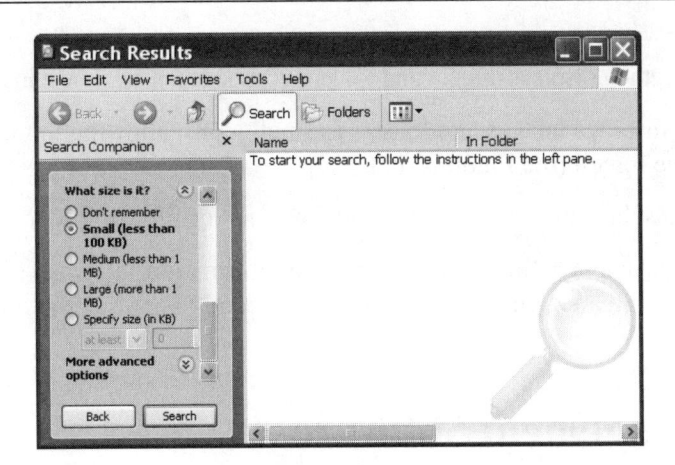

FIGURE 4-7   Searching by size is one of the options available to narrow your search.

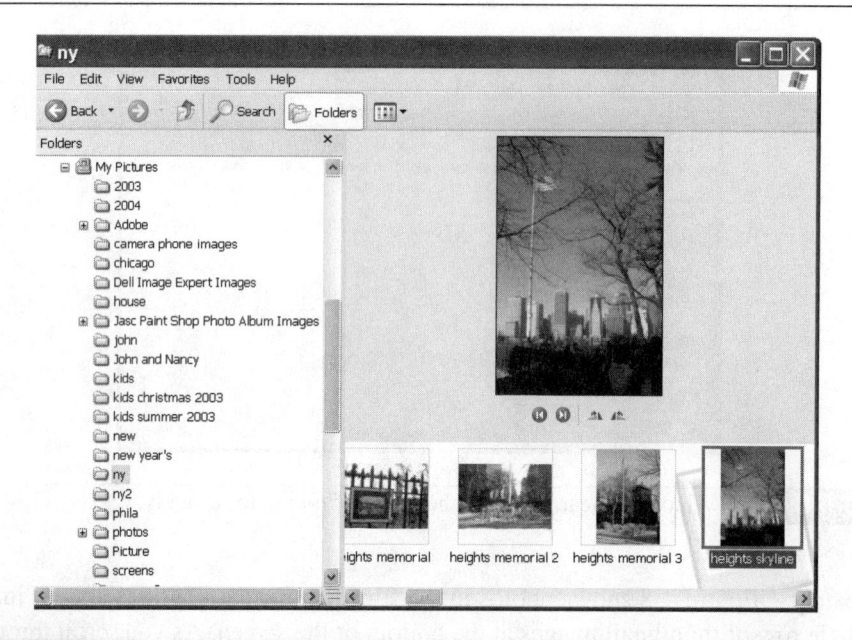

FIGURE 4-8   View your images like you were still in grade school, via filmstrip.

Thumbnail   Figure 4-9 shows that the Thumbnail setting displays thumbnails of the pictures.

Tiles   This setting displays images and folders as large icons, as shown in Figure 4-10.

Icon   This displays images and folders as small icons, allowing more files to be shown on the screen (see Figure 4-11).

List   This displays the contents of a folder as a list of files or folder names.

Details   This displays files with their related information: file size, file type, date modified, date created, and the date you most recently accessed the file, as shown in Figure 4-12.

Image-Management Software

Windows does a good job of performing rudimentary image-management functions. But as your photo collection grows, you'll want a program that can keep up with your expanding needs without having to worry about Windows naming conventions

CHAPTER 4: Saving and Managing Your Pictures

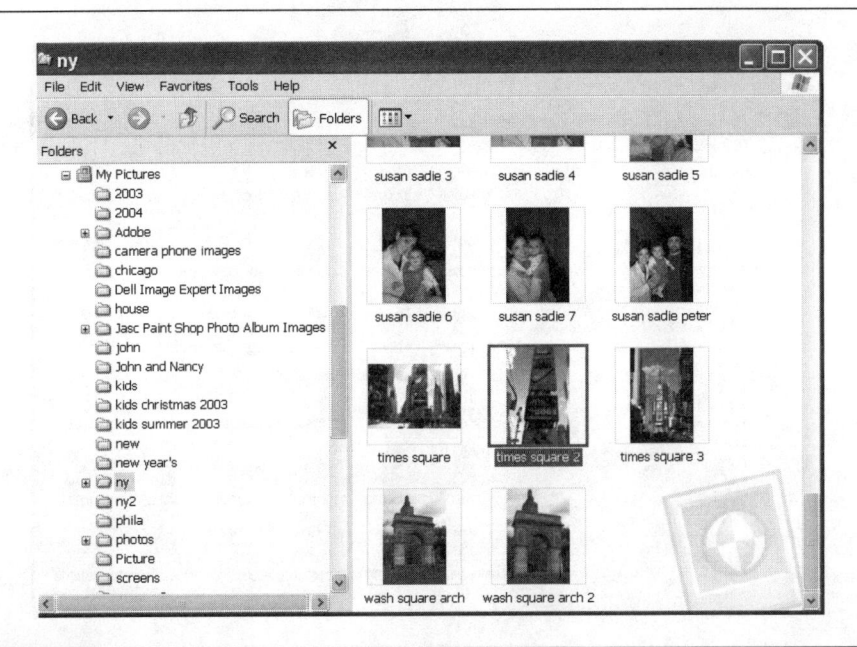

FIGURE 4-9 Thumbnails make it easy to find that pic you can't remember the name of.

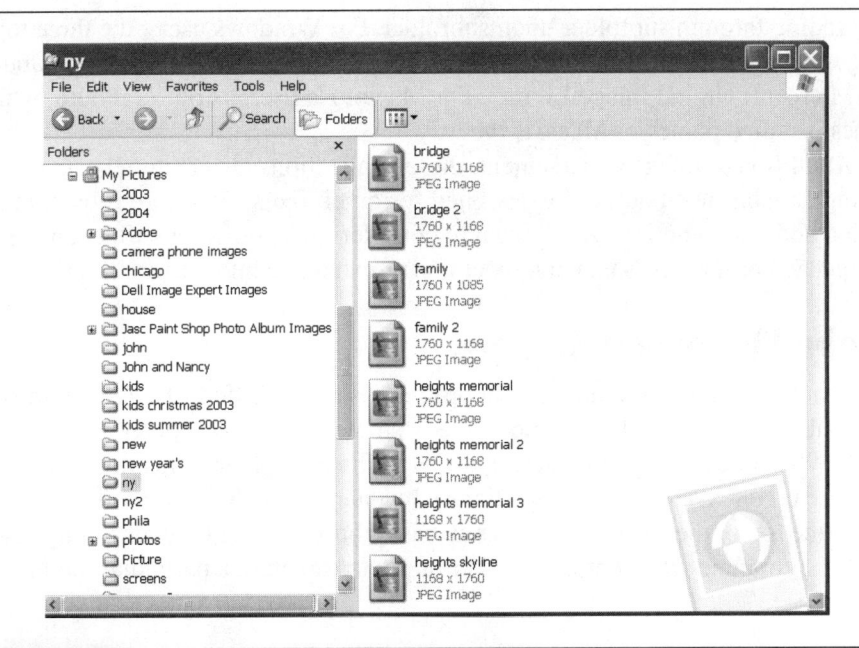

FIGURE 4-10 Your photos displayed in tile format.

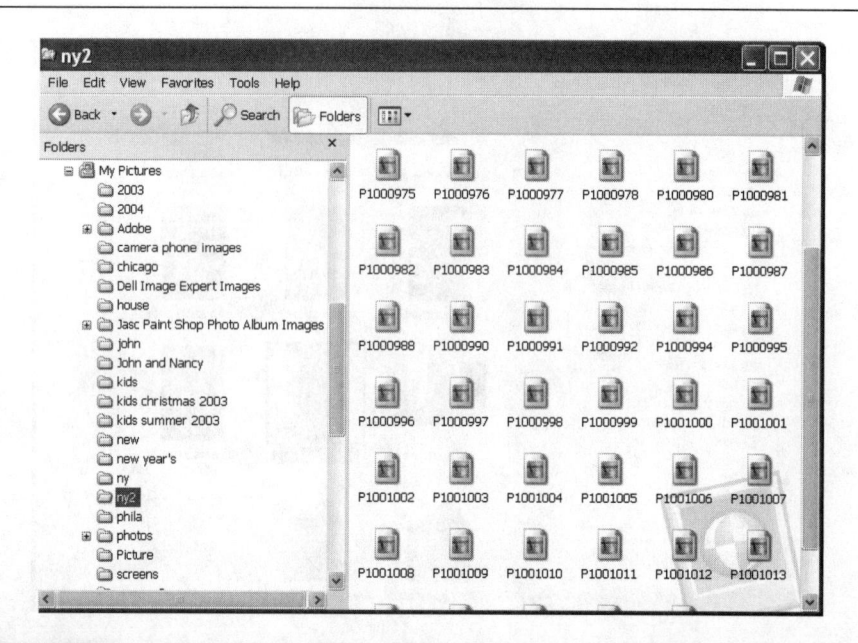

FIGURE 4-11 Like applications on the Windows desktop, you can view your images and folders as small icons.

and wading through subfolder upon subfolder. For Windows users, the three top image-management tools are Adobe Photoshop Album, JASC Paint Shop Album, and Microsoft Digital Image Library. For Macintosh users, Apple's iPhoto, which comes installed on newer Macs, is the way to go.

In addition to image management, these applications also feature basic image-editing capabilities, but they're designed for quick fixes. For more robust image editing and manipulation, you'll want to consider the applications I'll examine in Chapter 5. For now, let's take a look at image-management software.

Adobe Photoshop Album 2

The beauty of an image-management program is that you don't have to go through the trouble of renaming lots of files already stored on your computer. For starters, Adobe Photoshop Album will scan your hard drive for photos, then immediately organize pictures imported to your library by date. A timeline with a sliding bar across the top of the Photo Well lets you easily browse through your library. Bars along the timeline represent the number of photos taken in a particular month, as

CHAPTER 4: Saving and Managing Your Pictures 85

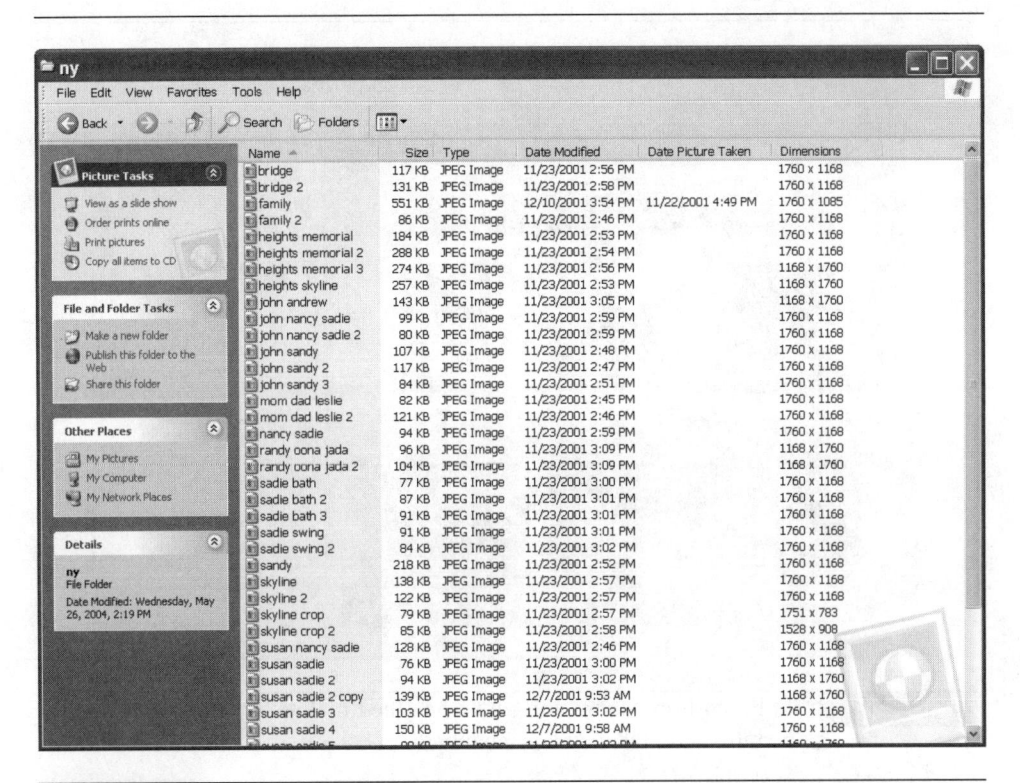

FIGURE 4-12 All the info is easily viewable when you display using Details.

illustrated in Figure 4-13. So if you went on vacation in July and took a lot of pictures, you'll see a large bar for that month.

To simplify searching for a particular image, Photoshop Album lets you create "tags," or categories, that you can drag on to your pictures in the Photo Well, as you can see in Figure 4-14. To create tags, follow these steps:

1. Click the Get Photos button on the toolbar and select From Files and Folders to move images to the library.

2. On the sidebar on the right side of the screen, click New | New Tag in the appropriate category (People, Places, and so on).

3. Type in a name for the tag.

4. Drag a selection of thumbnails to the tag name in the sidebar or drag the tag name to a thumbnail in the library. Tagged items will feature an icon in the bottom left corner of the thumbnail box.

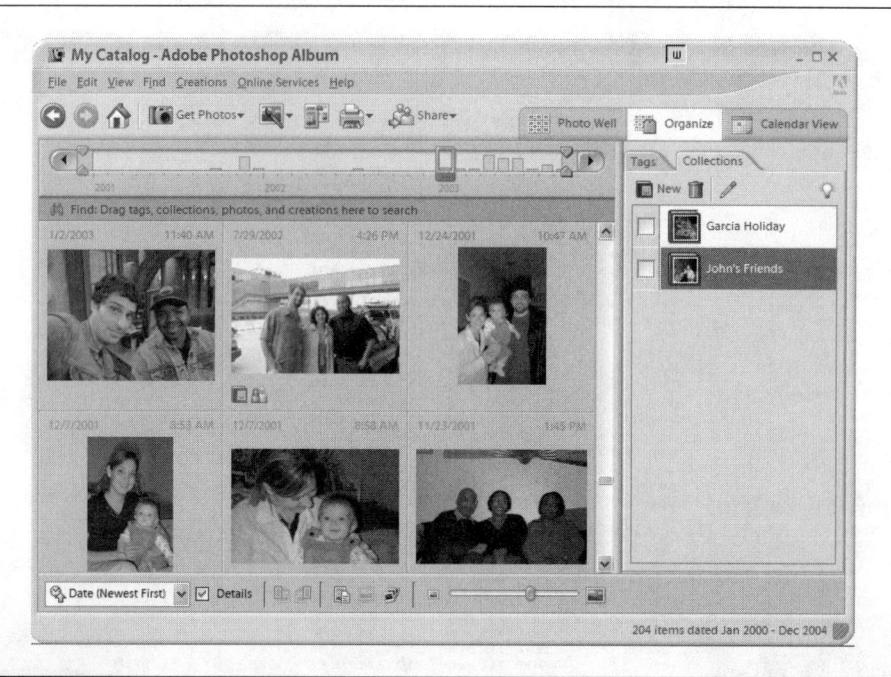

FIGURE 4-13 In Photoshop Album, the bars along the timeline represent how many pictures were taken in a given month.

> **TIP** *If you have multiple files that you wish to tag, simply select the images and drag them to the appropriate tag in the Tags pane.*

Adding tags to multiple pictures, however, can get tedious. Perhaps the best feature in Photoshop Album is its ability to create virtual collections. You can add pictures to a collection labeled Vacation, for example, and not have to worry about tagging each picture. You can include any picture in multiple collections.

You'll find the Collections tab next to Tags on the side pane (Figure 4-15). Adding photos is simply a matter of naming a new collection, selecting a group of thumbnails, then dragging them with your mouse to the appropriate collection. You can also drag the collection name to individual thumbnails.

Photoshop Album provides a variety of search options when the time comes to find a particular photo. If you added captions or notes to your images in the library, you can search for text included in those fields. You can also search by history. If, for example, you know you e-mailed a particular picture to a friend, you can search only pictures you sent via e-mail.

CHAPTER 4: Saving and Managing Your Pictures   87

FIGURE 4-14   Photoshop Album's tags feature assigns categories to your photos, which simplifies searching.

Another interesting search option lets you find pictures that share similar colors with a selected photo. If you're looking for a particular beach photo, for example, you can use another beach photo as a source.

The updated version of this popular program includes tools specifically geared toward camera phone users. If you routinely store your camera phone pictures in the same folder in Windows, you can import them to Photoshop Album by clicking Get Photos | From Mobile Phone Folder. If your camera phone uses a removable memory card—and if your computer includes a memory-card slot into which you can plug a card—you can import images directly to Photoshop Album:

1. Click the Get Photos button in the shortcuts bar and choose From Camera or Card Reader.

2. Choose File | Get Photos | From Camera or Card Reader.

How to Do Everything with Your Camera Phone

3. Select the name of the connected device from the Camera pop-up menu.

4. Browse to select a folder in which you wish to store the photos.
5. Click OK.

Imported photos will be displayed in the Photo Well.

FIGURE 4-15   With Photoshop Album's virtual collections, you can assign categories to large groups of similarly themed photos.

CHAPTER 4: Saving and Managing Your Pictures 89

> **TIP** *With some photo printers that accept memory cards, such as the Hewlett-Packard Photosmart 7550, Windows XP will recognize the card as an external storage drive when the printer and computer are connected. That means you can still use Photoshop Album's memory-card import function even if your PC doesn't feature a card slot.*

JASC Paint Shop Album 4

With its familiar Windows Explorer-like interface (see Figure 4-16), Paint Shop Album will likely appeal to novice users. The pane on the left side of the screen displays your hard drive's folders and subfolders. Clicking the appropriate directory, such as My Pictures, will display all of the folder's contents as thumbnails in the album window.

Every new album you create will appear as a subfolder on your hard drive (see Figure 4-17). Though this method will be familiar to Windows users, it's not as elegant as Photoshop Album for those who'd rather not deal with the Windows-like directory structure.

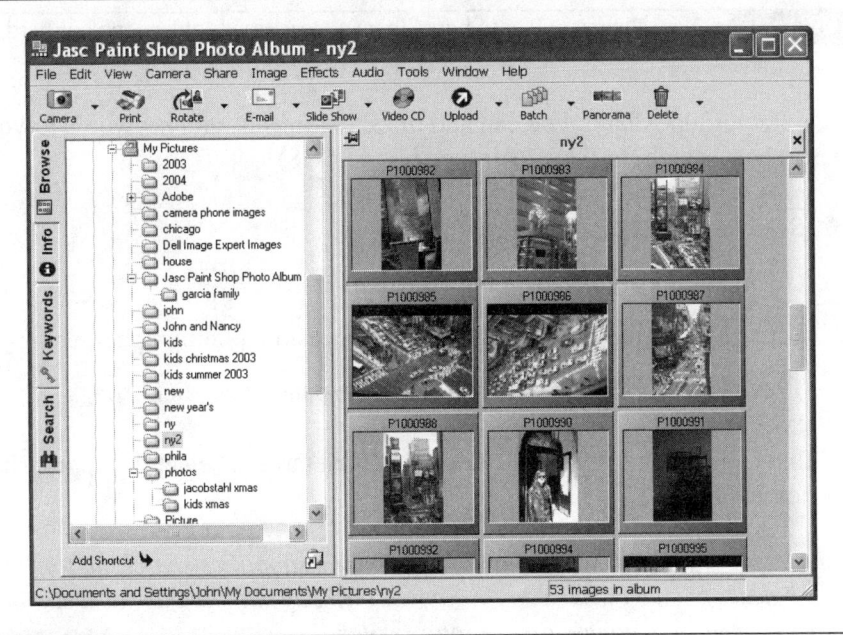

FIGURE 4-16 Paint Shop Album uses the familiar Windows directory tree for organizing your photo collection.

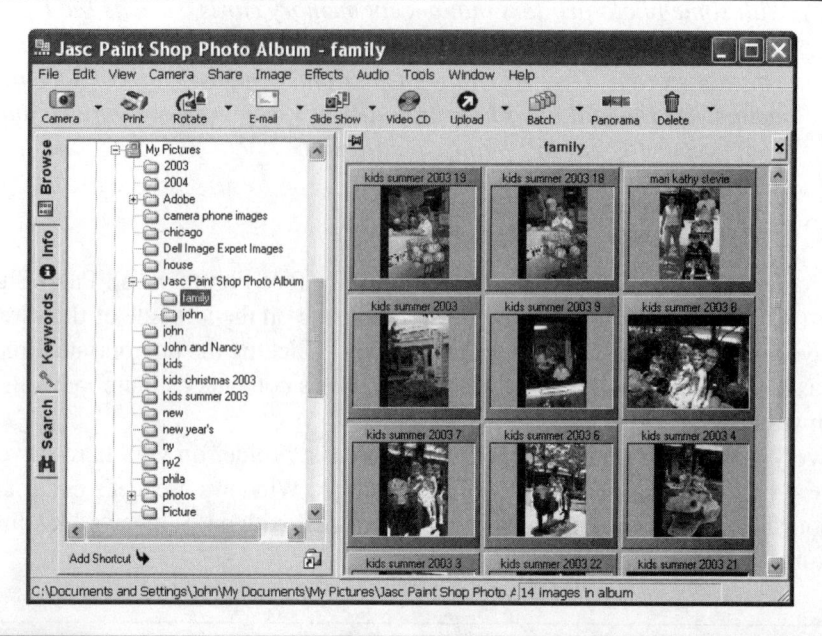

FIGURE 4-17 New albums in Paint Shop Album appear as subfolders on your hard drive.

Like Photoshop Album, you can add titles, comments, and keywords to your images to help search for them later (see Figure 4-18).

1. Select a thumbnail or group of thumbnails.
2. Click the Keywords tab on the left pane.
3. Select a description based on location, occasion, photographer, or subject.
4. Type in a description at the bottom of the pane, then click Add.

To find an image by keyword, click the Search tab and select the appropriate categories and terms.

> **TIP** *Adding keywords to a group of thumbnails simplifies searching for large batches of images, such as vacation or birthday party photos, as it eliminates the need to rename a large group of files.*

CHAPTER 4: Saving and Managing Your Pictures 91

FIGURE 4-18 Category-based keywords help you locate hard-to-find pictures in Paint Shop Album.

Like Photoshop Album, Paint Shop Photo Album also lets you directly import pictures stored on a removable media card:

1. Click the Camera icon on the toolbar at the top of the screen, as shown in Figure 4-19.

2. In the Select Album dialog, shown next, click Browse to select a folder in which to store the files.

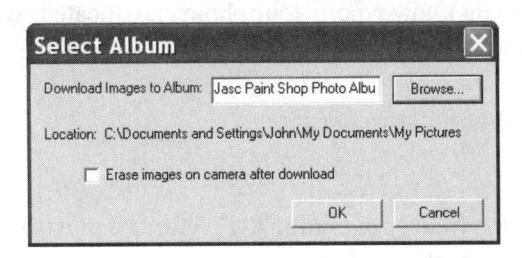

3. Click OK.

FIGURE 4-19 Paint Shop Photo Album lets you import pictures stored on external memory cards.

Microsoft Digital Image Library

It shouldn't come as a surprise that this image-management application is tightly integrated with Windows. Remember when I said earlier that it's a good idea to store small photo collections in the My Pictures folder? It's especially true with this program, which automatically loads all images stored in My Pictures and its subfolders. If your images are scattered around your hard drive, Digital Image Library will scan for them (however, this can take quite a while).

Alternatively, if you know where your photos are located, you can add pictures manually from different locations:

1. Click File | Add Pictures to Library.
2. Click Browse.
3. Navigate to the folder containing the pictures you wish to add, click the folder, then click OK.
4. Click Done.

CHAPTER 4: Saving and Managing Your Pictures

Unlike the other image-management programs, Digital Image Library doesn't create albums, so you're stuck working with the Windows directory structure. However, the application does simplify the task of associating keywords with images, which can help you find images. The Keyword Painter feature lets you select one or more keywords that you can associate with an image (Figure 4-20).

1. Click the Keywords button on the toolbar at the top of the screen.

2. Select a keyword or multiple keywords (your choices are Birthday, Family, Friends, Holiday, and Travel, or you can add your own categories).

3. Go to the folder containing the pictures you wish to mark with the keywords. A paintbrush icon and the keyword you selected will appear in place of the cursor.

4. Click on the thumbnails to which you wish to assign a keyword.

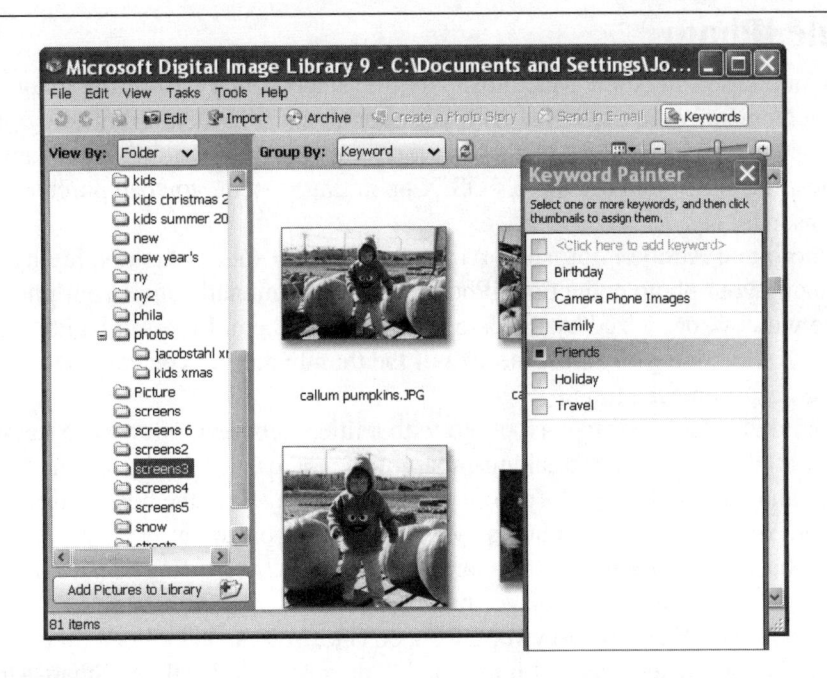

FIGURE 4-20   Digital Image Library's Keyword Painter makes it easy to assign keywords to a large collection of photos.

TIP *To assign keywords to an entire folder, select the keyword and press CTRL-A to select all thumbnails in the folder. If you wish to edit or delete a keyword later, right-click the thumbnail, click Edit Keywords, then change your selection in the Keyword Editor dialog box.*

TIP *To delete keywords assigned to an entire folder, press CTRL-A to select all of the thumbnails, right-click any thumbnail, click Edit Keywords to access the Keyword Editor dialog, and deselect your keyword. The changes will apply to all of the images in the folder.*

Unlike Photoshop Album or Paint Shop Album, Digital Image Library doesn't offer a dedicated search function. Instead, you can set the program to display thumbnails in the library based on the keyword. Click the Group By button above the thumbnail viewer and choose Keyword. Other viewing options include by date taken, event, file size, or folder.

Apple iPhoto

If you purchased an Apple Macintosh anytime since January 2002, the image-management software that came with your computer, iPhoto, is a fantastic option. If you have a slightly older Mac, don't worry—as long as your computer runs on the most recent version of Apple's OS-X operating system, you can purchase iPhoto separately.

iPhoto and Adobe Photoshop Album use similar means for displaying and organizing your photo collection. iPhoto displays thumbnails of all your photos in a large window, organized by the date you imported them. Like Adobe Photoshop Album, a slider lets you adjust the size of the thumbnails, so you can view several at once or just one at a time.

iPhoto also lets you tag each photo with a title, comment, or up to 15 keywords of your choice. For further tracking capabilities, you can set ratings of one to five stars to any picture. It's a helpful tool for, say, marking only the best pictures for printing. You can search for photos by keyword, text, or rating.

The best way to keep track of a large collection is by creating Smart Albums, which let you organize your images based on several criteria: Album, Rating, Text, Comments, Date, Filename, Keyword, Roll, or Title. You can tell iPhoto, for example, to find all photos taken between June 1 and September 1 and call that Smart Album Summer 2004. As you import new photos, iPhoto will automatically place pictures taken in that date range in the Summer 2004 album. To create a Smart Album, follow these steps:

CHAPTER 4: Saving and Managing Your Pictures

1. Click File | Smart Album.
2. Type a name for the album in the Smart Album Name field.
3. Make criteria selections from the pop-up menus. If you want to add additional criteria, click the Add (+) button.
4. Click OK.

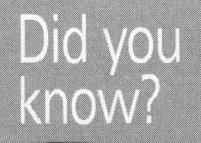

Did you know?

Online Management Options

If your photo management needs are simple and you'd rather not bother with installing additional software on your computer, there are plenty of online photo management sites at your disposal. The main benefit of these is that, in most cases, you don't have to store pictures on your hard drive. Some sites, however, limit the amount of data you can store.

If you use Sprint PCS or Verizon Wireless, these carriers offer picture messaging sites on which you can create photo albums (more on this in Chapter 6). Sprint lets you keep an unlimited amount of photos in your Picture Mail account, while Verizon Wireless has a 1MB limit (these figures are always subject to change, so be sure to check with the carrier first).

If your carrier doesn't offer a dedicated picture messaging site, you can choose among a variety of third-party sites. AT&T Wireless offers subscriptions to RUNpics (www.runpics.com) and My Photo Gallery (photogallery.aspiro.com) for $1.99 a month. Cingular Wireless has a deal with Kodak Mobile (www.kmobile.com) that lets Cingular subscribers store their images on Kodak's site for $2.99 a month. From there, you can order a sheet of four wallet-sized prints for $1.79. Other third-party sites include Snapfish Mobile (www.snapfish.com), Ofoto (www.ofoto.com), and Fuji Film (www.fujifilm.net).

When you sign up for such services through your carrier, you'll be able to upload pictures to the site directly from your camera. If you subscribe to a service not affiliated with your carrier, you'll have to download the pictures to your computer first, then upload them to the site.

Create Photo Archives

When you begin to amass a large collection, it often makes sense to archive your images to removable storage media such as a CD-ROM or DVD-ROM. For starters, this frees up room on your hard drive. Also, while you may want to save those older or seldom-used images, there's no sense in keeping them on your hard drive if you don't need to. Finally, storing images on removable media allows you to create slide shows and presentations, which I will describe in detail in Chapter 9. The image-management programs described earlier feature their own unique archiving methods.

Adobe Photoshop Elements includes a Burn option in the File menu, which takes three steps to move files to a CD or DVD. After selecting a folder or a group of thumbnails from the Photo Well:

1. Copy or move the files to a disk, as shown in Figure 4-21.

2. Determine whether you want to copy edited files only, which will leave the original files in Photoshop Album, or if you want to copy edited and original files.

3. Select a destination, as shown in Figure 4-22.

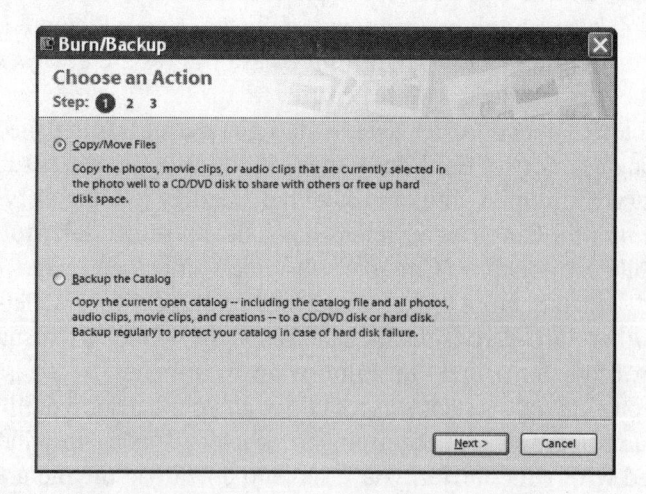

FIGURE 4-21 Photoshop Elements' Burn option lets you copy or move your photos to a CD or DVD.

CHAPTER 4: Saving and Managing Your Pictures 97

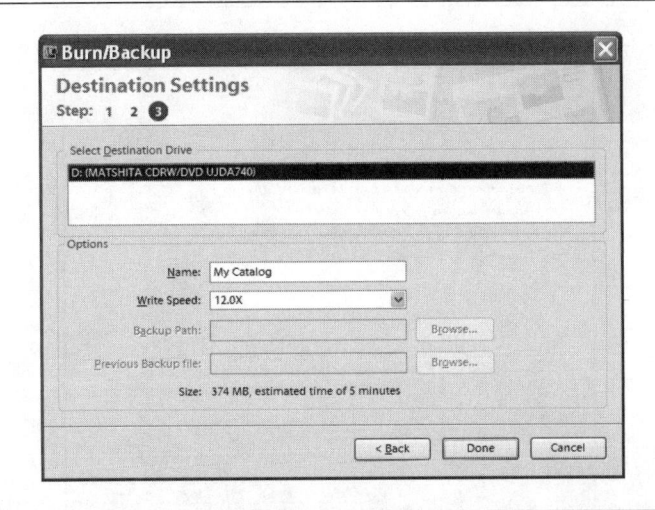

FIGURE 4-22 Choose your CD or DVD drive letter (usually D:) as the destination to burn your pictures to a disc.

NOTE *If you choose to move your files to a disk, Photoshop Album deletes the images from the hard drive but leaves a small thumbnail behind. If you click the thumbnail to access the photo, the program will prompt you to insert a disk.*

Paint Shop Album takes the simplest approach with its Catalog option. Select Tools | Catalog, choose a source (CD-ROM or Picture CD, for example), then click Start. After the cataloging is complete, you can enter a new name in the Label field.

Microsoft Digital Image Library offers the deepest set of archiving tools with its Archive Pictures Wizard (see Figure 4-23). Its best feature is its ability to archive only pictures that you added since the last archiving session. You can set the program to archive:

- All the pictures in the library
- Pictures selected when you entered the wizard
- Pictures added since the last archive (excluding modified pictures previously archived)
- Pictures added since the last archive, as well as modified pictures that were previously archived

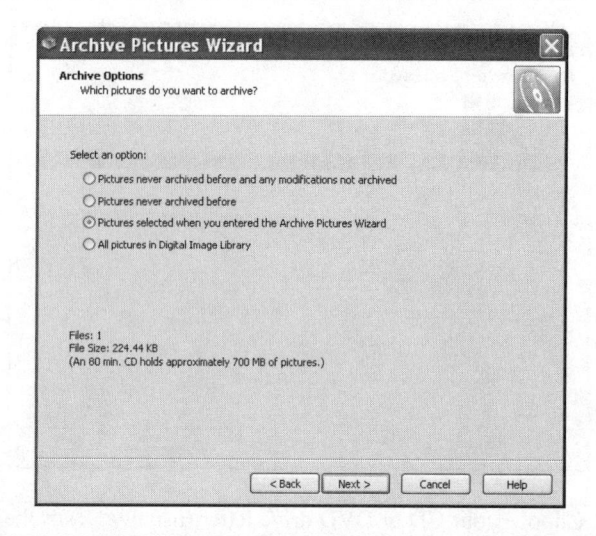

FIGURE 4-23 Digital Image Library's Archive Pictures Wizard offers a variety of options for saving your pictures to an external storage medium.

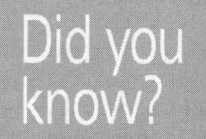

Did you know?

The Differences Between CD-R, CD-RW, and Picture CD

You have three options for archiving your images to a compact disc: CD recordable (CD-R), CD rewriteable (CD-RW), and Picture CD. CD-Rs are closest in nature to audio CDs (in fact, you can also use them to burn audio CDs on your computer). Once you copy data, it's stored permanently, which is why CD-Rs are so inexpensive (you can find them for as little as 30 cents per disc).

You can treat CD-RWs, on the other hand, just as you do a floppy disk, by adding and deleting files as you wish. The problem with this format is that different PCs often have problems reading CD-RWs. Also, because of their rewriting capabilities, CD-RWs cost more than CD-Rs.

Your best bet is to archive your photos to CD-R, but be sure to go with a reliable brand. Although you may be able to find dirt-cheap offerings, their quality can be suspect. Among the better brands of CD-Rs are Imation, TDK, and Sony.

Kodak created the Picture CD format to let consumers digitally archive their 35mm photos. Several retail outlets offer this option when you drop off your roll of film. Some image-management applications, such as Paint Shop Album, let you archive your digital photos to this format as well. The main difference between Picture CDs and CD-Rs or CD-RWs is that Picture CDs will save images in the JPEG format only. That's not a problem for camera phone images, which are saved in this format already. But if you plan on archiving images saved in other formats, such as TIFF, you'll have to go with CD-Rs or CD-RWs, which can store any format.

The advantage of the Picture CD format is that you can use images saved to the disk to order prints online from Kodak or use them to make prints from Kodak Picture Maker kiosks in retail outlets such as Walgreens, K-Mart, and Target.

Moving On

Now that you've got everything organized, it's time for a bit of sprucing up. In the next chapter, I'll show you how to use image-editing software to perform such tasks as cropping, straightening, and generally cleaning up your camera phone images. I'll also discuss file formats and explain the differences between three of the most popular image editors.

Chapter 5

Editing Your Photos

How to...

- Work with image-editing software
- Align a crooked picture
- Crop a photo
- Adjust brightness and contrast
- Sharpen an image
- Eliminate specks
- Change file formats

"We'll fix it in post" is a common phrase in Hollywood. That means whatever flaws are in the original footage will be edited in the post-production, or editing, process. The beauty of working with digital photographs is that you, too, can fix your pictures in post. Try using that phrase with your friends—see if they're impressed.

No matter how hard you try, it's tough to get the perfect shot every time. Given the spontaneous way most of us use our camera phones, it's easy to take pictures that are a bit crooked, are over- or underexposed, contain needless information in the frame, or need a bit of color correcting.

The image-management programs described in Chapter 4 contain basic editing functions. But if you want a more complete range of tools, you'll need to purchase an image-editing program. You may have heard of Adobe Photoshop, which is the most popular application of this type. But Photoshop is designed for professionals and has a price to match. Because most of us don't need this type of power (or expense), you can find plenty of low-cost image editors designed for a mass audience.

These programs typically cost $99 or less, and you can find them at the major consumer-electronics and computer stores. In this chapter, I'll present an overview of three of the top image-editors for Windows, then discuss editing techniques in detail.

Working with an Image Editor

Generally speaking, all image editors provide the same basic set of tools, allowing you to perform the following actions.

- Crop, rotate, and resize your images
- Control the brightness, contrast, and color composition
- Add text and special effects
- Sharpen images and clean up artifacts
- Combine multiple images into a single photo
- Save images to different file formats

So how do you determine which program is right for you? It depends on how much control you want over your images and how much time you're willing to spend learning certain procedures. The image editors detailed here are listed in order of most complex to least complex.

Adobe Photoshop Elements 2

Adobe wisely took some of the best parts of Photoshop and, without sacrificing too much power, packaged them in an easy-to-understand application designed for the average user. Basically, you have many of the same editing and retouching tools at your disposal that the professionals do, but you pay only $99 or so for the privilege. The only tools missing are those required for doing prepress work, which is something that you won't have to worry about anyway.

One of the better tools in Photoshop Elements is its batch processing feature, which allows you to make the same changes to several images simultaneously (see Figure 5-1). You can take all of the pictures in a given folder and convert them to a specific file type, change the image size, rename files based on date, serial number, or a name of your choosing, and move them to a different folder.

Another feature, Save for Web, optimizes pictures for posting to a website—a popular destination for camera phone images. The dialog box displays a side-by-side comparison of the original image and the altered file optimized for the Web (see Figure 5-2). You can set the file format and the quality and compression settings, and change the image size. The preview window also gives you the size of the new photo and the approximate time it will take for the image to download on a web page.

> **NOTE** *Because your camera phone images are already compressed, you'll want to change the compression setting to low or medium when using the Save for Web feature.*

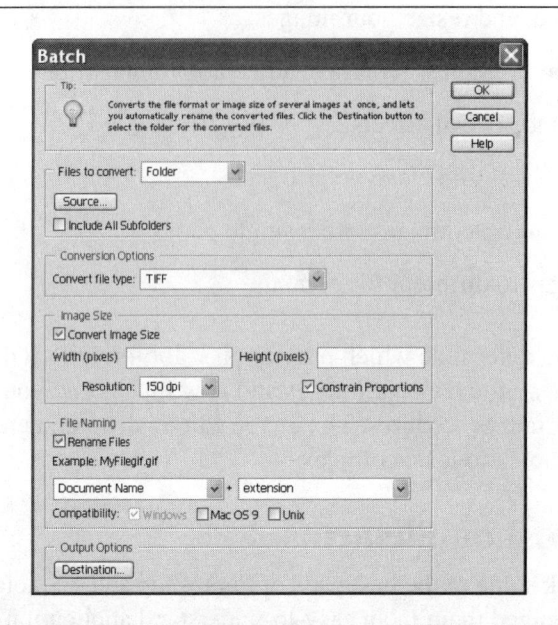

FIGURE 5-1 Photoshop Elements' Batch Processing tool lets you apply changes to file format, image size, and other parameters to an entire folder of pictures.

Photoshop Elements retails for $99 (or you can purchase it bundled with Photoshop Album for $129). With rebates or promotional offers, you can get Elements for about $70. If you'd like to try before you buy, Adobe offers a free 30-day download from www.adobe.com.

NOTE *Of the three image editors described here, only Photoshop Elements is compatible with the Macintosh platform.*

JASC Paint Shop Pro 8

Paint Shop Pro (PSP) was one of the first low-cost image editors designed for the average user, and its reputation as an easy-to-use program has only continued to improve over the years. Paint Shop's One Step Quick Fix feature, for example, adjusts color balance, contrast, clarity, saturation and sharpens and smoothes edges with a single click. If you don't like the results you get with the one-click fix, you can always manually control such changes yourself.

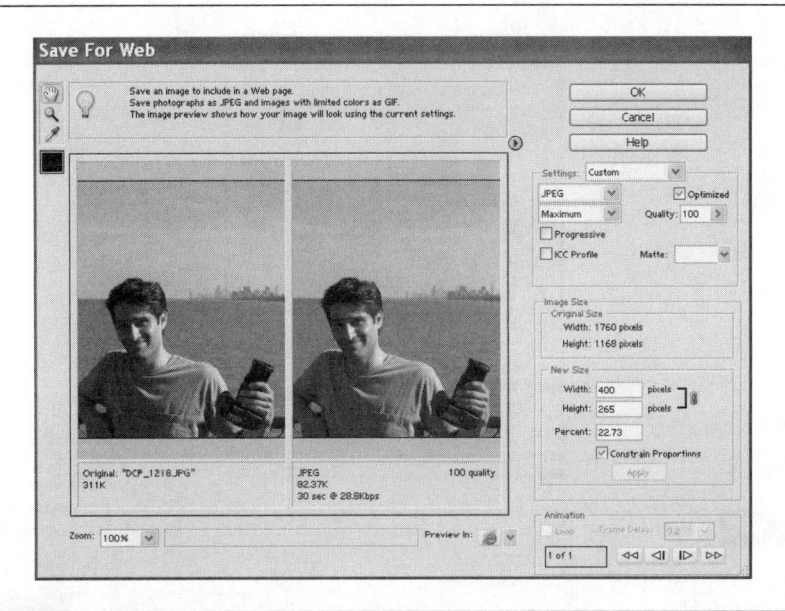

FIGURE 5-2 Photoshop Elements' Save for Web feature optimizes your photos for web publishing and displays the difference in a side-by-side comparison with the original image.

A JPEG Artifact Removal tool is especially handy for camera phone images, since the compression scheme can create image distortions—such as halos or checkerboard patterns on smooth backgrounds—that don't seem troublesome when viewing on a camera screen but are magnified when you print or post an image to the Web. When you click the JPEG Artifact Removal tool icon on the toolbar, a dialog box opens showing the original photo and a preview of the altered image.

TIP *Click the Zoom Out and Zoom In buttons to adjust the level of detail you wish to view in the compared images.*

You can set the adjustment's strength level (low, medium, high, maximum) and the desired crispness level (between 0 and 100) while viewing the changes in the preview window (see Figure 5-3).

PSP lists for $99; the Paint Shop Power Suite: Photo Edition, which includes PSP, Paint Shop Album, Paint Shop Xtras, and Animation Shop, costs $129. With rebates, you can get it for less. Like Adobe, JASC offers a free 30-day download from www.jasc.com.

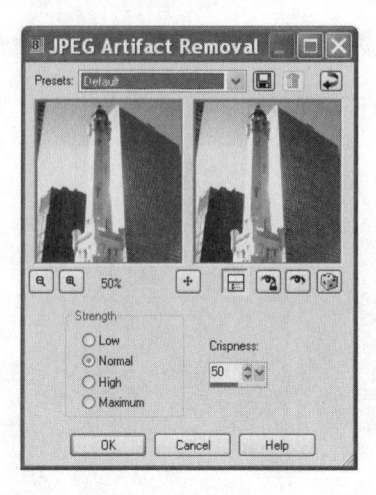

FIGURE 5-3 Paint Shop Pro's Artifact Removal tool comes in handy for low-resolution camera phone images.

Microsoft Digital Image Pro 9

Digital Image Pro's main asset is its interface. When you have multiple images open, for example, you can see thumbnails of all of them in the Files pane on the right side of the screen. The program displays the selected file in the main window, as shown in Figure 5-4. Clicking once on a thumbnail displays the image at full size.

Click the Common Tasks button on the toolbar and you're presented with a list of common touchup tasks, including Fix Red Eye, Brightness and Contrast, and Adjust Tint. The Common Tasks pane (see Figure 5-5) also includes drop-down menus for effects, formatting (including rotate and straighten), and an option eloquently titled Add Something (text, line, shape).

Digital Image Pro doesn't offer the wealth of fine controls found in either Photoshop Elements or Paint Shop Pro, but users unfamiliar with the ins and outs of image editors may find it easy to get up and running with this program. Digital Image Pro costs $99, or $129 as part of the Digital Image Suite, which also includes the Digital Image Library. As with the other image editors, you should be able to find rebates with Digital Image Suite.

Performing Common Editing Functions

As you become familiar with your image editor, you'll find just how many tools you have at your disposal for fixing, modifying, and transforming your camera phone images. However, the odds are that you'll usually want to perform only a few basic tasks to make your pictures look as good as possible before printing them or sharing

CHAPTER 5: Editing Your Photos 107

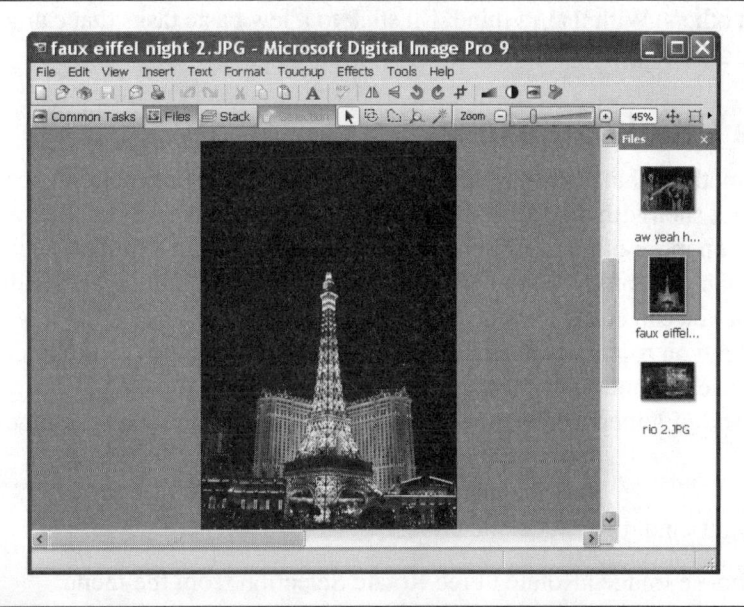

FIGURE 5-4 Digital Image Pro displays thumbnails of multiple images, allowing you to browse easily through all of your open files.

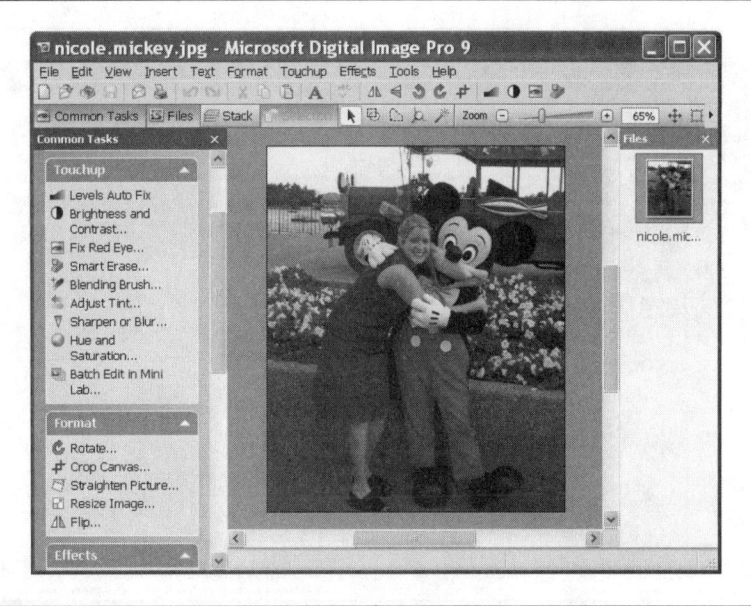

FIGURE 5-5 Digital Image Pro's Common Task pane provides easy access to common editing functions.

them with others. With that in mind, I'll stick to a few basic tasks that can go a long way toward shaping up your photos.

Align a Crooked Picture

This is something that's all too common, and because many of us aren't accustomed to framing a shot with an external screen instead of a viewfinder, taking a crooked photo is even more of a hazard when using a camera phone. Crooked pictures are particularly noticeable when the horizon or any type of straight line is visible in the image. But you can easily correct this problem using the rotate feature in your image editor. After you rotate an image, you'll also need to crop the picture to eliminate the white background in the corners, as you can see in Figure 5-6.

Photoshop Elements offers the most straightforward method for accomplishing this task:

1. Right-click the image and choose Select All.

2. Choose Image | Rotate | Free Rotate Selection from the menu.

3. Place the icon on one of the little boxes on a corner of the image. Click the left mouse key to grab it and use the mouse (or touchpad) to rotate the picture until it's straight.

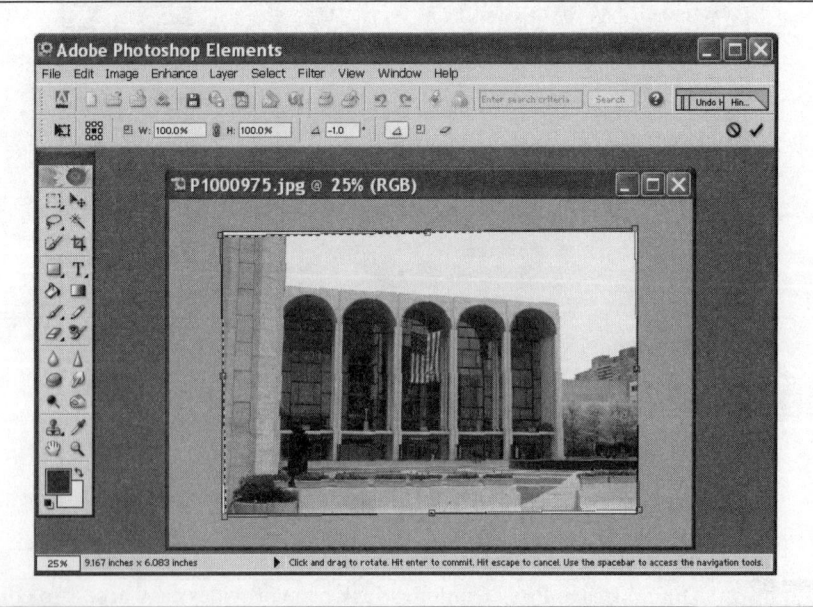

FIGURE 5-6   Photoshop Elements lets you freely rotate a selection of an image.

NOTE *Photoshop Elements also offers automated options called Straighten Image and Straighten and Crop Image, but these tools may not deliver the results you want.*

With Paint Shop Pro's Straighten tool, which you'll find on the toolbar, a straightening bar with end handles appears on the image. You click and drag each handle of the bar to align it with the part of the image that you want to be straight. Choose Make Vertical or Make Horizontal from the drop-down Tools Options menu, and select Crop Image. When you move the cursor over the straightening bar you'll see four arrows. Double-click the bar to make the change.

This method requires some practice and may not be as intuitive as the process Photoshop Elements employs, but it is highly effective.

CAUTION *Rotation causes degradation in JPEG images. If you don't like the results of a particular rotation, undo it completely and start from scratch. Multiple saved rotations can quickly ruin an image.*

Crop a Photo

Photography teachers will tell you that the best cropping takes place within the camera. That is, if you take extra care to frame the shot properly when taking the picture, you won't have to come back later to improve the composition. Well, that's fine

How to Do Everything with Your Camera Phone

when you have all the time in the world to set up the perfect shot, but most of us prefer to snap a shot quickly and hope for the best. Even when you think you've framed the shot perfectly, you'll often find that's not the case when you view your pictures on a computer. The most common mistake is standing too far away from your subject, which leaves a lot of unnecessary space above or on either side of the subject (see Figure 5-7). Even with a camera phone, which requires you to maintain a fairly close proximity to your subject, you may often discover that the composition is a little off.

The cropping process is the same in both Photoshop Elements and Paint Shop Pro:

1. Open an image and, using the Zoom tool, adjust the magnification level to where the entire image fills the screen.

2. Click the Crop tool.

FIGURE 5-7 Standing too far away from your subject can result in wasted space in your photo, as on the picture on the left; cropping the picture will help produce a more balanced composition.

CHAPTER 5:   Editing Your Photos   **111**

3. Click in the image and while pressing the left mouse button, drag the crop tool until you've drawn a rectangular outline around the portion of the image you want to keep. (In Photoshop Elements, the cropped selection will retain its natural lighting, while the portion you wish to discard will appear slightly dimmer.)

4. If you wish to change the size of the cropped selection, hold the pointer over one of the little squares on the borders of the selection. When you see a two-way arrow, click and drag to change the height or width of the box.

5. When you're satisfied with the area you wish to preserve, double-click inside the cropped area to complete the crop.

How to ... Create a Panoramic Image

Sometimes, those breathtaking scenes are simply impossible to capture in one image. An interesting feature of Paint Shop Photo Album is its ability to stitch several images together to create a panorama, which will come in handy for those pictures of the Grand Canyon or the Golden Gate Bridge.

1. Select two or more thumbnails from the album.
2. Click the Panorama icon on the toolbar at the top of the screen.
3. Choose a projection setting (use Perspective Projection for narrow-to-medium-width horizontal scenes or vertical images, and use Cylindrical Projection for wide field-of-view scenes).
4. Choose a blend setting (Smooth, for images that blend well but vary in brightness, or Sharp, for images that align poorly).
5. Choose an output size (small, medium, large, or very large).
6. Click Create.

TIP *To cancel a crop in Photoshop Elements, right-click and choose Cancel, or press the ESC key. In Paint Shop Pro, simply right-click anywhere in the image.*

Adjusting Brightness and Contrast

One of the most common problems with camera phone images is poor lighting. Whereas a digital camera will compensate for dark environments with a good flash, most camera phones don't provide this luxury. Your phone's screen, unfortunately, isn't the most accurate representation of what a picture actually looks like. Pictures often look darker on a computer monitor than they do on a camera phone display.

You have several options for adjusting the brightness of an image. The first and most obvious is using your image editor's Brightness control, which raises or lowers the entire image's luminance value. This is fine when the entire image is poorly lit, but that's not always the case. Sometimes it's only the subject or an object in the foreground or background that needs a lighting boost. When this is the case, it's best to use the Selection tool to select a portion of the image, then adjust the brightness level (see Figure 5-8).

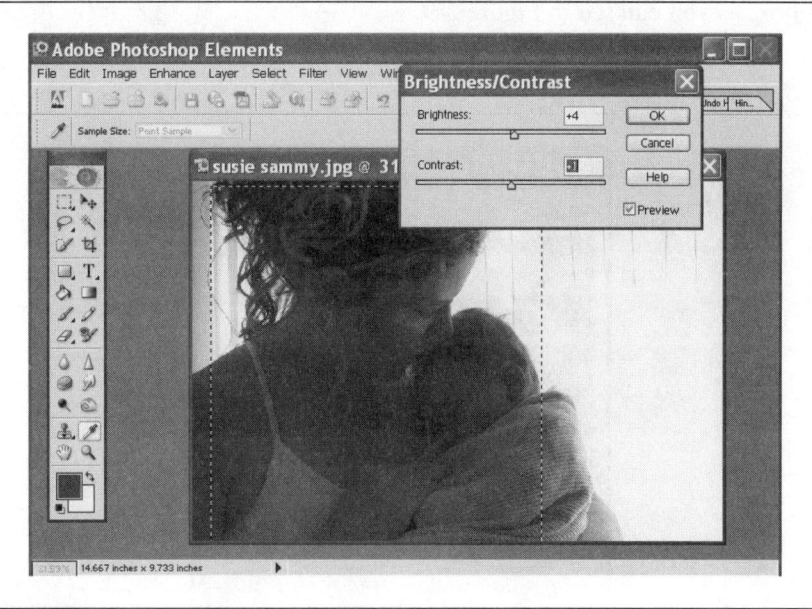

FIGURE 5-8 If the entire image doesn't need a lighting adjustment, select a portion of the image to make changes to a specific area.

You'll find the Brightness control in the Enhance or Adjust menu. You move a slider control in the dialog box to lighten or darken a photo or area. In Photoshop Elements, you can see the results as you make your changes before you save the image.

Paint Shop Pro, on the other hand, displays before and after thumbnails in the dialog box, as you can see in Figure 5-9.

FIGURE 5-9   Paint Shop Pro lets you compare brightness and contrast adjustments against the original image.

CHAPTER 5: Editing Your Photos   **115**

Camera phones, particularly those with sensors less than a megapixel, also have trouble capturing contrast levels, giving images a washed-out appearance. Besides, it's usually a good idea to tweak the contrast after making changes to the brightness level. That's why image editors group the Contrast and Brightness controls together.

Filling the Flash

Photoshop Elements includes another trick for lightening dark areas called the Fill Flash feature. When taking pictures in bright light, the shadows are often too dark to show any detail, like the building in Figure 5-10. The Fill Flash command will lighten those shadows.

Just as with the Brightness adjustment, you can apply Fill Flash to the entire image or just a selection:

1. Click Enhance | Adjust Lighting | Fill Flash.

2. Use the sliders to increase the lightness and color saturation to the desired levels.

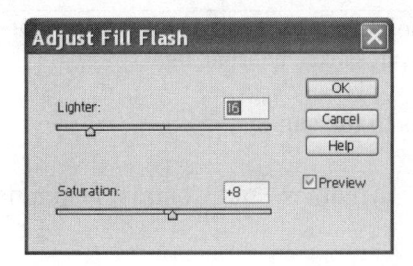

3. Click OK.

Gamma Corrections

Paint Shop Pro has its own trick for making fine adjustments to lighting with its Gamma Correction tool. The gamma curve has three components: the red, green, and blue of an image. The Gamma Correction command lets you adjust the color balance of these levels separately. What that means is instead of affecting the brightest and darkest parts of an image simultaneously, as the Brightness command does, Gamma Correction works on the midtones—the area of an image between the highlights and shadows.

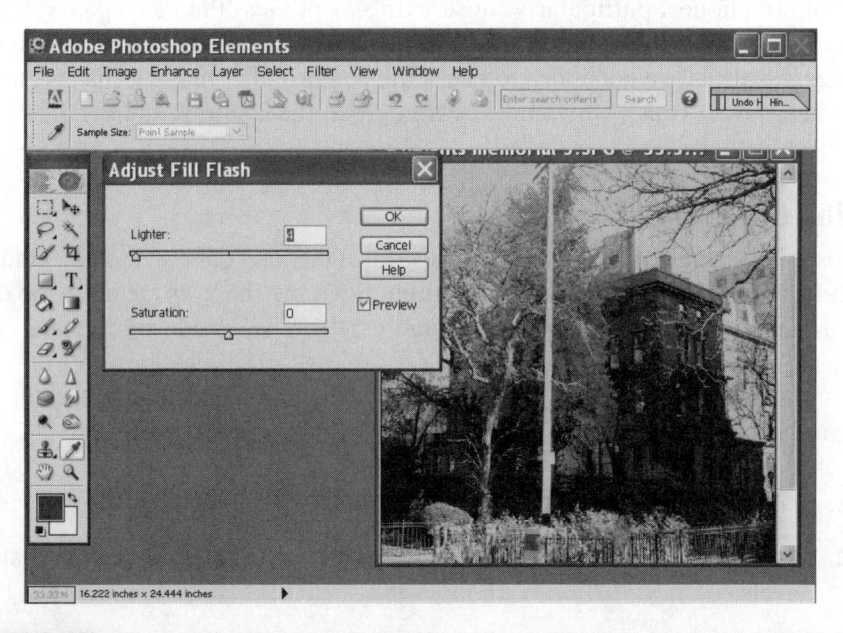

FIGURE 5-10 Photoshop Elements' Fill Flash tool highlights shadows that can result from pictures taken in bright light.

To make adjustments to the gamma:

1. Choose Adjust | Brightness and Contrast | Gamma Correction (see Figure 5-11).
2. If you wish to make adjustments to the red, green, and blue levels separately, deselect the Link button.
3. Move the sliders to make adjustments.
4. Click OK.

Sharpen Your Photos

The more pixels in a digital image, the sharper the picture will be. That's why photos from VGA camera phones in particular look grainy compared to pictures taken with a consumer-level 3-megapixel digital camera. An image editor can help sharpen your pictures, but before you get too excited, realize that it can only do so much.

CHAPTER 5: Editing Your Photos   **117**

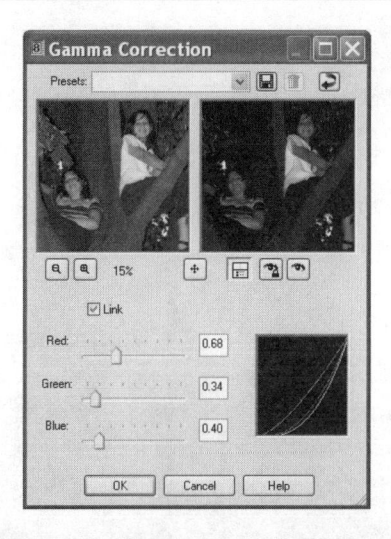

FIGURE 5-11   Paint Shop Pro's Gamma Correction tool makes adjustments to an image's midtones.

Image editors *can* help compensate for deficiencies, but they *can't* add information that wasn't there to start with. So if your photo is especially grainy because you took it in a poorly lit room, it will still look grainy. But if you're looking to print a decent-looking photo or post to a website that could use a little sprucing up, your image editor's Sharpen filter can help (Figure 5-12).

NOTE   *Most images taken with camera phones aren't suitable for printing. You can print smaller sizes, which is explained in Chapter 7.*

The Sharpen tool increases the contrast between pixels, which adds a little extra oomph to your image. Both Photoshop Elements and Paint Shop Pro offer three sharpening options:

- **Sharpen**   Affects all the pixels in your image.
- **Sharpen More**   The same as Sharpen but more intense.
- **Unsharp Mask**   Adjusts the contrasts between adjacent pixels to produce a lighter and darker line on each side of the edge. Most graphics experts recommend using the Unsharp Mask filter only, since it provides more detailed control.

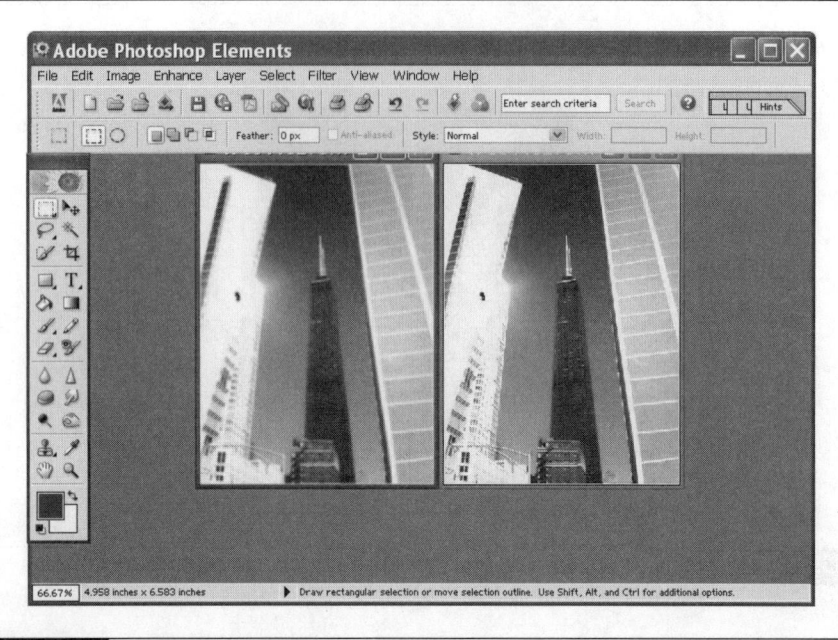

FIGURE 5-12 With the Sharpen filter applied to the image on the right, there's more discernible detail in the black building.

NOTE *Photoshop Elements also features a Sharpen Edges option, which works only on the edges of an image while preserving its overall smoothness.*

In Photoshop Elements, you'll find the Sharpen tools in the Filter menu. In Paint Shop Pro, the filters are in the Adjust menu.

You should resist the urge to apply too much sharpening to an image. The results can be disastrous, with lighter parts of the image becoming solid white (see Figure 5-13).

Eliminate Specks

With their low-resolution, camera phones often produce images with lots of specks, especially with photos taken in low light. Both Photoshop Elements and Paint Shop Pro include despeckle tools in their arsenals that remove single-pixel specks that are mostly white or black. The despeckler analyzes the brightness of each pixel and compares it to the surrounding pixels to determine if it should be removed.

For camera phone images, Despeckle is a good tool to use in conjunction with the Sharpen tool (see Figure 5-14). But again, don't go crazy with it or you'll lose even more detail in the image.

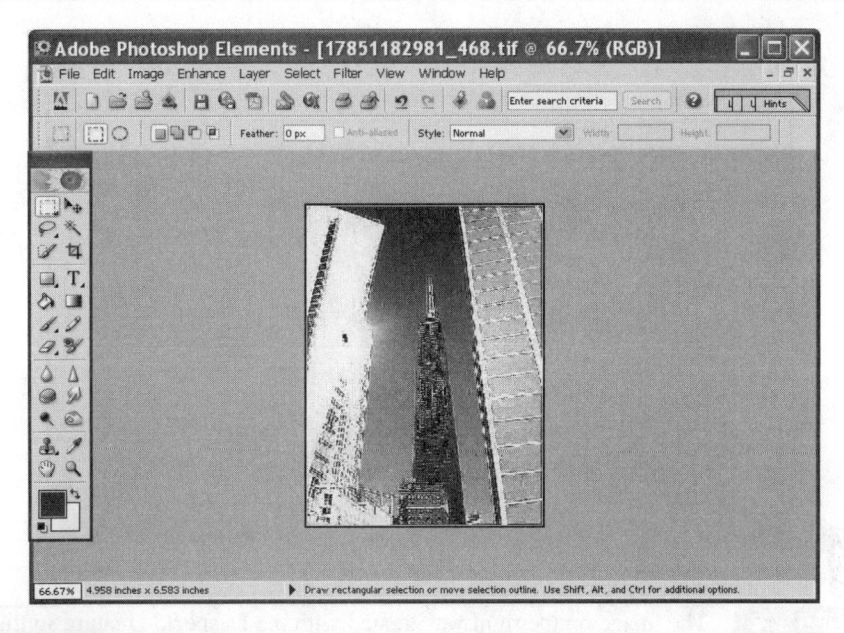

FIGURE 5-13 Overuse of the sharpen filter will produce disastrous results.

Change the Image Size

When it's time to print a typical 640 × 480 image from a VGA camera, you may be a bit disappointed with the size. However, an image editor will let you resize an image.

In Photoshop Elements, select Image | Resize | Image Size to open the Image Size dialog box:

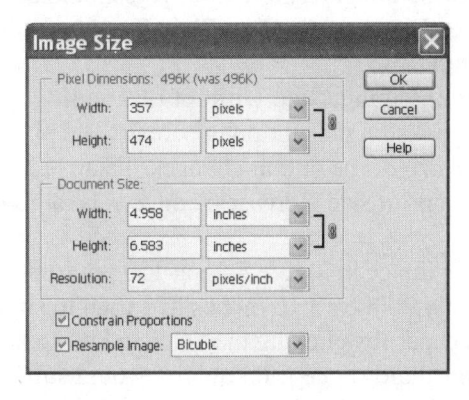

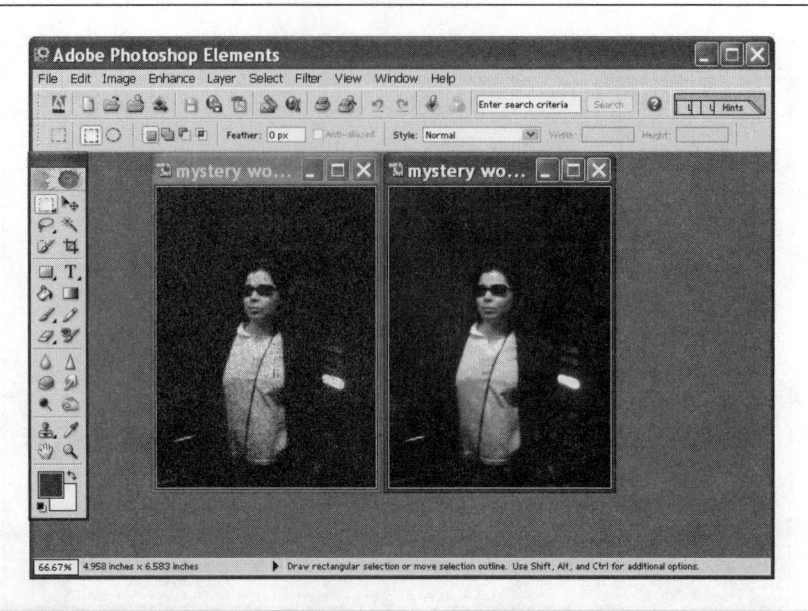

FIGURE 5-14 The image on the right was treated with the Despeckle feature so the tones appear smoother than the image on the left.

As you can see above, the box contains information regarding the image's pixel dimensions, the document size, and the dimensions of the photo at a given printer resolution (in this case, 72 pixels per inch, or ppi). The bottom of the box controls how resizing is performed.

Changing the Print Size

This is where it gets tricky. If you want to change the size without adding or removing pixels, which would cause image degradation, you should uncheck the Resample Image box in Photoshop Elements (in Paint Shop Pro, it's the Resample Using check box), as shown in Figure 5-15.

When you change the image size without resampling, you won't notice a difference in how it looks on the computer screen. The pixel dimensions remain fixed, but the physical size of the output changes. That is to say, when you lower the resolution (ppi), the print size increases; conversely, a higher resolution means a smaller print size.

If I were to print the image in Figure 5-16 at 150 ppi from Photoshop Elements, it would print out at only 2.38 by 3.16 inches. If I tried to stretch the image to fill a 4 × 6 sheet of photo paper (by clicking the Scale to Fit Media box in the Photoshop Elements Print Preview dialog), the print quality would suffer.

CHAPTER 5: Editing Your Photos **121**

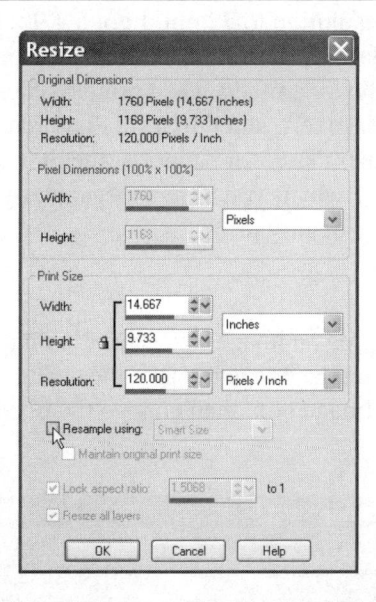

FIGURE 5-15 In Paint Shop Pro, you can resize a photo without changing its pixel dimensions by making sure the Resample box remains unchecked.

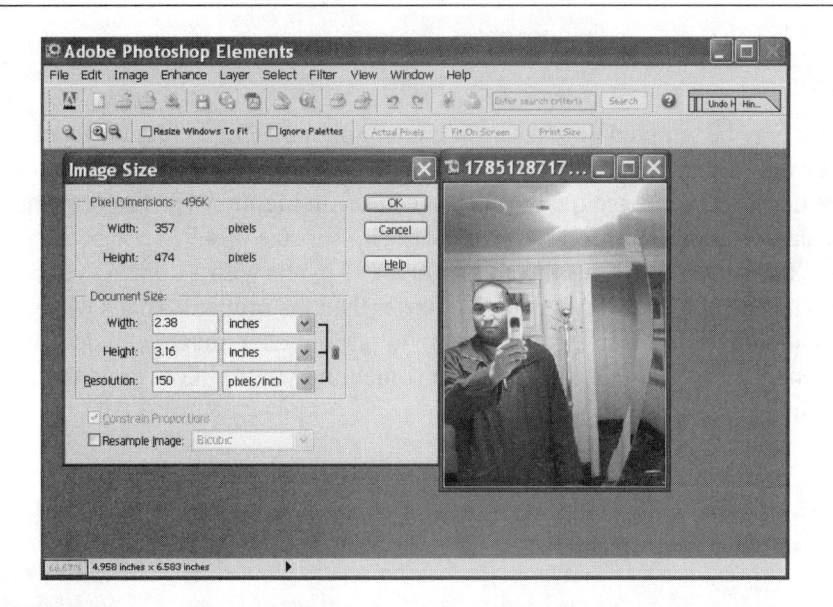

FIGURE 5-16 Changing the resolution without resampling an image results in a change in a photo's print area, but not in its pixel dimensions.

When I lowered the resolution to 72 ppi, I got a 4.9 × 6.6-inch printout (see Figure 5-17). I received a larger print with the lower resolution, but the 150 ppi image appears sharper and with fewer artifacts when printed on photo paper. That's because there's a greater density of pixels, albeit in a smaller area.

The more pixels a camera's sensor supports, the more pixel density you'll have in a larger print area. That's why if you have a megapixel-plus camera phone, you'll be able to get larger, better-quality prints.

Resampling

The other option for changing an image size is to resample it, in which the computer adds or removes pixels from the image to make the change. In Photoshop Elements, you check the Resample Image box, then change the pixel dimensions to your desired size.

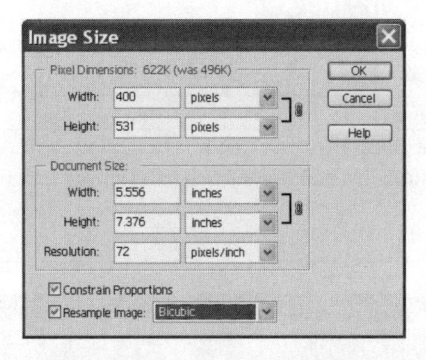

You may be tempted to make your camera phone pictures bigger, especially if you have a handset that only takes photos in low resolution. But resampling by nature degrades the image quality, as you can see in Figure 5-18. The original photo on the left measured 357 × 474 pixels, with a print size of 4.958 × 6.583 inches at 72 ppi. The same image, resampled to 600 × 797 pixels with a print area of 8.333 × 11.069 inches at 72 ppi, appears much fuzzier than the original. That's why graphics professionals recommend if you're going to resample an image, you decrease the size rather that increase it, but that's not something you're likely to do with camera phone images.

TIP *Before resizing a photo, be sure to make a master copy first. Also, never resize an image more than once. If you don't like the new size, undo the changes and start over.*

CHAPTER 5: Editing Your Photos   **123**

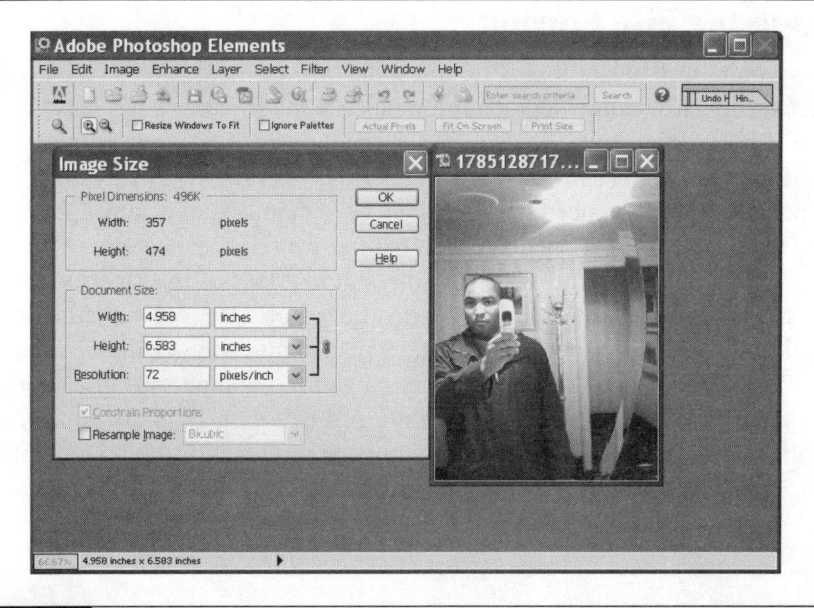

FIGURE 5-17   Lowering the resolution results in a larger print area, but the image quality suffers.

FIGURE 5-18   The picture at right, resampled to nearly twice it's original size, isn't nearly as sharp as the smaller original image.

Change the File Format

By now you're well aware that JPEG files, the type of images your camera phone produces, will suffer some degradation with each modification. It's reasonable to wonder if it's worth your while to save your pictures to a different format during the editing process. In case you were wondering, yes it is worthwhile.

When photographers need to make changes to their digital pictures, they usually change the format to TIFF, which doesn't suffer from the same compression issues as JPEG files. Basic changes that would result in a loss of information in JPEG files—such as rotating an image—have no effect on a TIFF file's quality. Because TIFF files retain so much information, they're also much larger in file size than JPEG files, which is one reason your camera phone—and many digital cameras—don't save files in that format to begin with. A 49KB camera phone image, for example, became a 506KB TIFF file in Photoshop Elements, taking up more than 10 times the disk space of the original image.

Did you know? Native File Formats

I've spoken a lot about JPEG and TIFF files, but I haven't mentioned formats specific to image-editing software programs. All image editors use their own proprietary, or native, formats. Adobe Photoshop uses the .PSD format, Paint Shop Pro uses .PSP, and Microsoft Digital Image Pro uses the .PNG format. Like TIFF files, these formats are designed to allow heavy editing without the loss of image quality. So why not use these formats for your camera phone pictures?

These native formats are designed for more advanced use, allowing users to edit specific layers while leaving the rest of the image intact. It's doubtful that you'll need such power at your disposal for cleaning up your camera phone images. Also, because these formats create layers, the file size is significantly larger than a JPEG. A 49KB JPEG file I changed in Photoshop Elements became a 505KB PSD file. Finally, because these are proprietary formats, they may not be recognized by other software programs—an important feature if you plan on sharing your pictures with others.

To save your images as TIFF files, use the following steps:

1. Open the image.
2. Choose File | Save As from the main menu.
3. In the Save As Type drop-down menu, scroll through the selections, then choose TIFF (see Figure 5-19).
4. Under Image Compression, select None.
5. Click OK.

Be aware, though, that when you save a photo to a new format, you'll now have two versions of the image with the same file name; only the file extensions (.JPG and .TIF) will be different. This can make it difficult to tell them apart when browsing through your collection in a software application. To avoid confusion, you might want to save the TIFF image with a slightly different file name. If, for example, the original JPEG photo you're working with is called Vacation, you may want to

FIGURE 5-19 Use the drop-down menu in your image editor's Save As dialog to change a photo's file format.

name the TIFF file Vacation Edit. That way, you'll know immediately that you've made changes to the image.

Moving On

Now that you've organized and spruced up your pictures, it's time to share them with the rest of the world—or your friends and family, at least. In the next chapter, you'll learn the various methods for sharing your photos, including online picture messaging sites and a fun and easy way to e-mail your images.

Part III
What to Do with Your Photos

Build Your Own Moblog

HOW TO DO EVERYTHING

Because I'm such a nice guy—and because my editors instructed me to include something special in the middle of the book—I decided to create a moblog just for you. Please, don't thank me now. You can show your appreciation by contributing your camera phone pictures to cameraphonebook.textamerica.com.

For those of you unfamiliar with the term, a *moblog* is a mobile web log. To backtrack a bit further, a web log, or *blog*, is a diary-type website. Blogs have become popular because they are easy to update and are usually presented chronologically. Similarly, moblogs have caught on in the camera phone community because users can easily send pictures directly from their phones to a website, which automatically arranges them like a scrapbook. Visitors to the site can comment on your pictures and, in most cases, you can create community sites on which others can contribute their pictures. Like standard blogs, moblogs are less time consuming to update than standard websites, and camera phone users love them because moblogs give them something to do with pictures that may be too small to print or too time consuming to share with several people at a time.

A moblog can be just about anything you want it to be, and it's appropriate for professional as well as personal use. Some popular uses for moblogs include online photo albums to share with friends and family; theme-centered sites such as photos from a particular city; and business-related sites like those used by real-estate brokers.

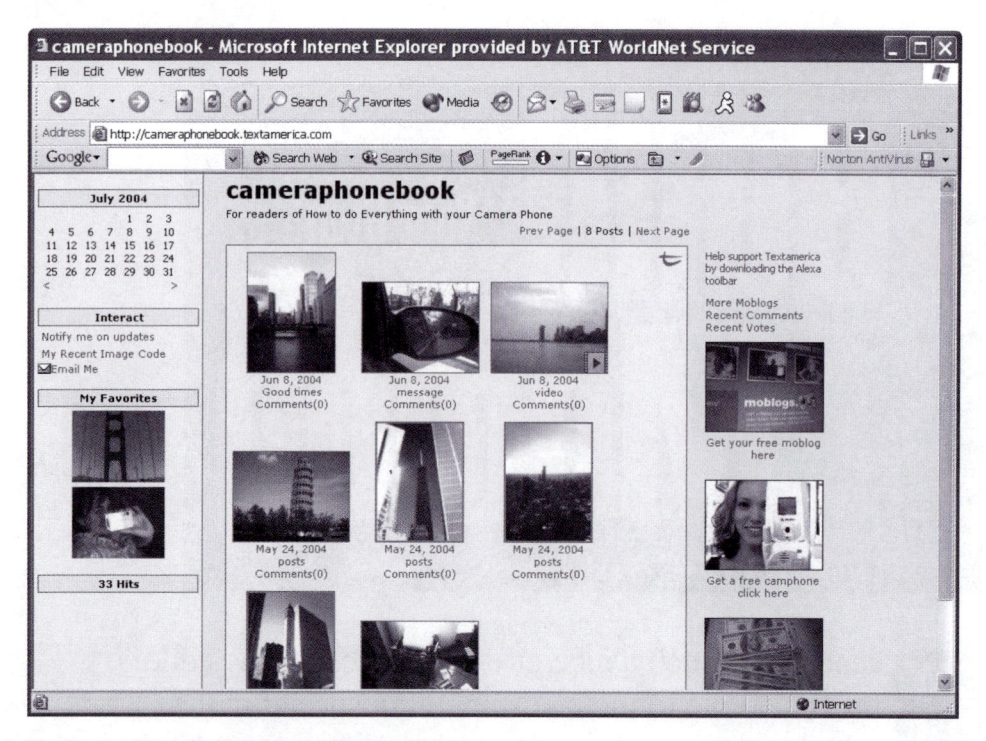

Figure 1. The Camera Phone Book moblog on Textamerica

I know some of you would love to create your own moblog, but you just don't have the time to maintain one; or perhaps you don't believe you have enough material to fill one on your own. With the blog shown in Figure 1, you can send pictures whenever you please.

Making the Moblog

There's no shortage of moblog sites, but Textamerica emerged as the best choice for this project. It features a selection of attractive templates, so I have more control over the way my site looks. Also, it supports camera phone video submissions, so it's more flexible than other moblogs. Furthermore, it draws a large, tech-savvy audience. My guess is that after you visit the site to check out your submission, you'll hang around and browse through other Textamerica sites.

Here's how I created the camera phone book site:

1. First, I clicked the Create Your Moblog link in the upper-right area of the main control panel (see Figure 2).

2. Next, I gave my site a title—cameraphonebook. Then I chose a domain name—cameraphonebook.textamerica.com (see Figure 3). For the Secret Word, which is the password you use to submit photos to the site, I went with Coltrane (one of my favorite jazz musicians).

Figure 2. Click the Create Your Moblog link to start building your Textamerica site.

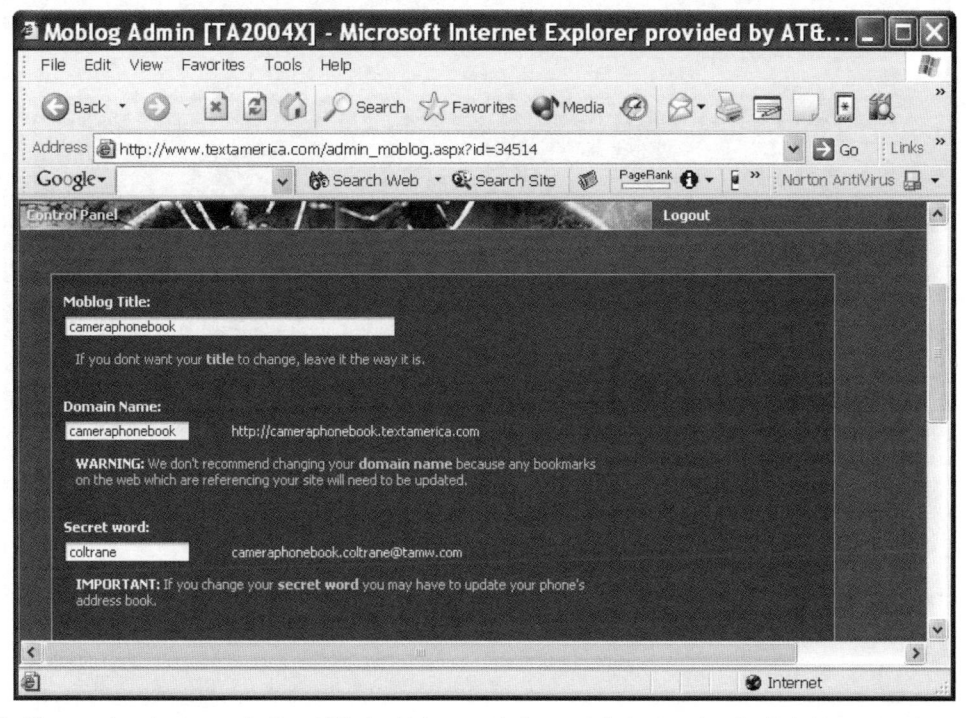

Figure 3. Choose a domain name and a Secret Word, which you and other contributors use to submit photos to your site.

3. Because I'll be accepting submissions from you, I selected Community Moblog from the choice of site types, as shown in Figure 4. For a brief description, which will appear as a subhead on the site, I wrote: "For the readers of How to Do Everything with Your Camera Phone."

4. Next, I was prompted to create my site. After clicking the Create button, my site was instantly generated. To find the site when surfing the web on your PC, just enter **cameraphonebook.textamerica.com**, the domain name I chose in Step 2. Alternatively, while on the Textamerica home page, you can enter **camera phone book** in the Moblog Search field at the top of the page.

Playing Favorites

Because this is a community moblog, I thought it would be a good idea to link to a few of my favorite Textamerica sites in the hopes that those sites will link back to me as well (a practice known as blogrolling). This is a good way to build an audience and gain acceptance as a Textamerica-approved community site. I added a link to Cat Schwartz's moblog, partly as a thank you for agreeing to write about moblogs for this book (see Chapter 8), but also because her site is a perfect example of someone using a moblog to connect with others on a regular basis.

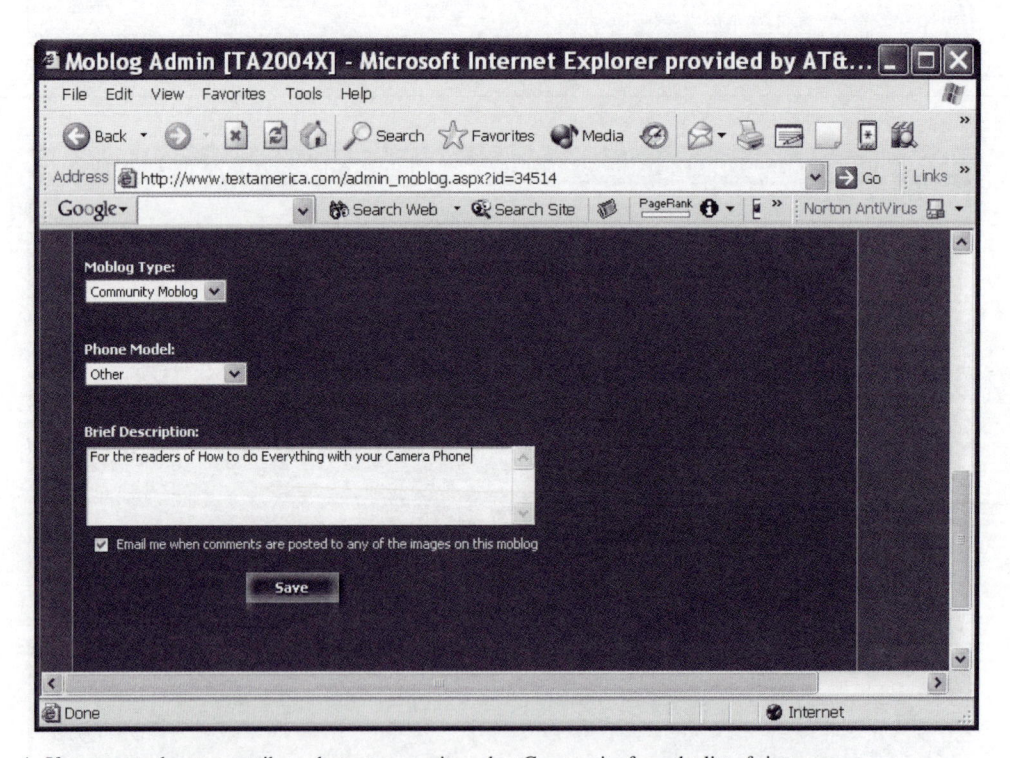

Figure 4. If you want others to contribute photos to your site, select Community from the list of site types.

> **NOTE**
>
> You can check to see who links to your moblog in the site's Control Panel.

To create my Favorites list I did the following:

1. In My Control Panel, I pointed to Favorites and clicked View My Favorites.
2. Under My Favorites, I clicked Create a New List.
3. In the Favorites List Name entry box, I typed the new name—Favorite Sites, as shown in Figure 5.
4. To add Cat Schwartz's site to the list, I typed the textamerica address (c4t.textamerica.com) in the Add A Favorite (domain) entry box, then clicked Add. I then saw a message notifying me that the site had been added successfully, along with a thumbnail image of the site (see Figure 6).

> **TIP**
>
> You can adjust the size of your thumbnails, but I suggest keeping them at the default dimensions (94 pixels high × 125 pixels wide).

Send Me Your Photos

Now that this site is "live," it's time to send me your pictures. In the true spirit of moblogging, I recommend that you send your pictures directly from your camera phone. At the very least, send pictures from your PC that originated from your camera phone.

The first thing you'll want to do is save the moblog's e-mail address on your phone, which will

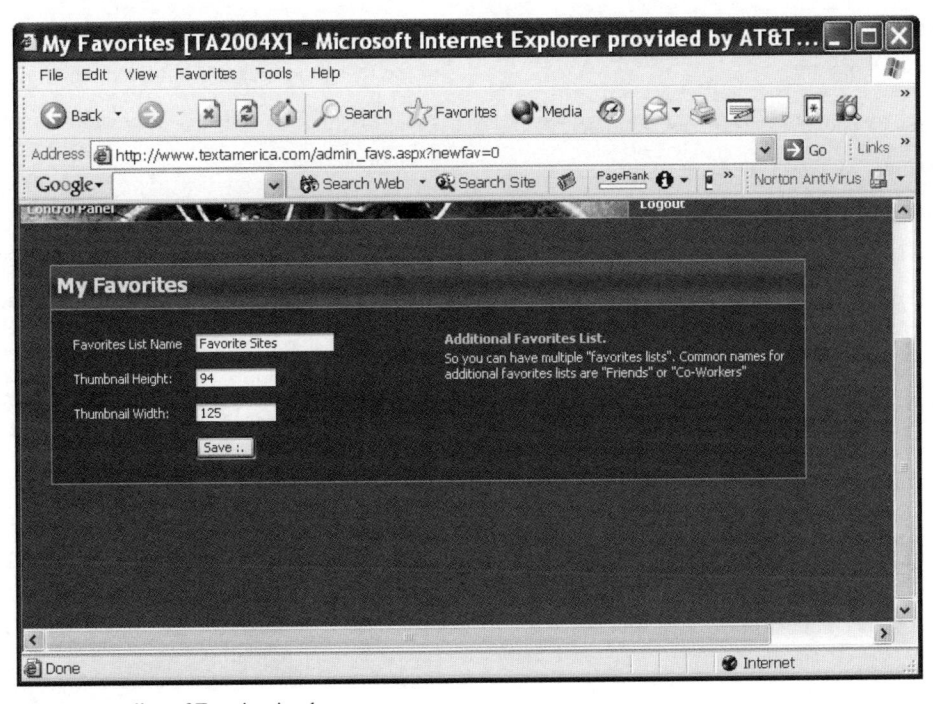

Figure 5. You can group lists of Favorite sites by name.

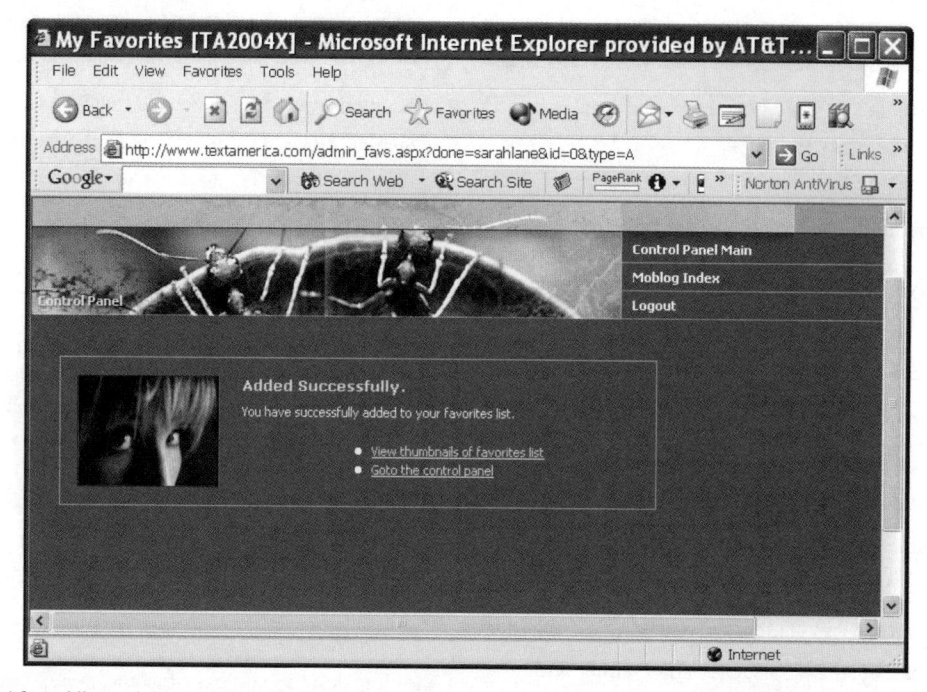

Figure 6. After adding a site to your Favorites list, Textamerica displays a message, complete with thumbnail, that the link has been successfully added.

prevent you from having to type it in every time you wish to send a picture.

1. Go to your phone's address book and select Add New Entry (or New Contact or something similar).
2. Enter a name for the contact (**Moblog** would be a good choice).
3. In the e-mail field, enter **cameraphonebook.coltranetamw.com**.
4. Click Save.

Now you're ready to fire off a picture to the site at a moment's notice. Let's say you are sightseeing in Chicago, and you come upon the Water Tower–one of the few structures that survived the city's Great Fire in 1871. You whip out your camera phone and get a good shot.

Immediately after taking the picture, you have the option to send a picture message. Choose Via E-mail, then select Moblog from your contact list. The subject line of your e-mail will appear as the

TIP

Remember, Textamerica only accepts photos that are 700KB or smaller.

NOTE

As the administrator of the moblog, I have final approval for choosing which pictures appear. That also means I can edit your titles and text descriptions. As long as you keep your text short and free of profanity or other offensive language, I'll keep my hands off your words.

title of the picture on the site. If you wish to include a description with your photo, type a short message in the Text Message field. Click Send.

> **CAUTION**
>
> Textamerica won't accept submissions with voice attachments, so do not include a voice memo with your picture messages.

A Few Tips

This is a good time to remind you of a few photography tips. Your pictures will be available for the world to see, so you'll want them to look as good as possible.

- **Keep subjects off-center**   Your picture's composition will be much more interesting when subjects aren't placed smack in the middle of the frame.
- **Use bright, natural light**   Your camera phone's CMOS lens is not especially sensitive to light, so dark areas tend to be filled with artifacts. An ample supply of natural light will also result in more vibrant colors and greater detail, as shown in Figure 7. Even phones that feature a built-in flash should be used in bright light, since the range of the flash is usually no more than about three feet.
- **Keep your subject close**   If you stand too far away from your subject, they'll appear small and distant. Standing within five feet of someone will help provide as much detail as possible, as shown in Figure 8.

Figure 7. Bright sunlight helps make colors more vivid in camera phone images.

Figure 8. Be sure to stand within five feet from people to capture as much detail as possible without image distortion.

Viewing the Site on Your Phone

One reason I chose Textamerica to house this site is because it's the only moblog that's optimized for viewing on cell phones and wireless-enabled PDAs, so you don't even need access to a PC to view the site. To avoid having to type in the site address each time, save the page as a Favorite or Bookmark. Each carrier handles Bookmarks in a slightly different manner, but the following example for creating Bookmarks on Sprint PCS should provide you with the basic principles involved:

1. Go to the web on your phone.
2. Choose Menu, then click Open Page.
3. Type in the site address (**tamw.com**).
4. When you're on the site, choose Menu with the right soft key, click the right navigation button until you reach the Navigation menu, then click Select.
5. Scroll down, then select Mark Page. The browser will confirm the site name and URL.
6. Click Save.

NOTE

Though you can view Textamerica on your camera phone, I should point out that you'll find yourself straining quite a bit unless you have a healthy screen size (at least 2 inches diagonally). Phones with larger screen sizes include the NEC 525HD and the Nokia 6600 and 7210 models. Even if your phone has a fairly large screen, however, it's a good idea to look away from the display every minute or so to avoid eye strain.

The Cost of Moblogging

As much as I want you to have fun and send as many pictures as possible to this moblog, I don't want you to go broke in the process. If you don't subscribe to some sort of data package that your carrier offers, your moblogging habit can get expensive.

If you're paying 25 cents per message, sending five pictures a month to a moblog adds another $1.25 (plus taxes and fees) to your bill. That doesn't sound like much, but if you're using your phone to browse the Textamerica site as well, you need to calculate how much data you're using while using the wireless web and, depending on your carrier, the minutes that are being deducted from your overall calling plan.

Some phones feature a data counter, which lets you know how many kilobytes of data you've consumed while surfing the wireless web. I used about 10KB browsing Textamerica on my cell phone for only a couple of minutes. The more you browse and the more pictures you view, the more data you'll be charged for. If you find yourself browsing the web nearly every day, those charges will quickly add up.

Check with your carrier about other pricing options, and remember to ask whether you're charged airtime minutes for surfing the wireless web. If so, those minutes will be deducted from your calling plan. Also keep in mind that carriers frequently change their pricing structures.

Keep Shooting

I hope you enjoy participating in this project. I certainly appreciate your contributions. Feel free to send suggestions for improving the site to cameraphonebook@hotmail.com.

Chapter 6

Sharing Your Photos

How to...

- Use MMS
- Send a picture message
- Work with carrier-operated picture messaging sites
- Use third-party photo storage and sharing sites
- Work with e-mail attachments
- Share pictures using Bluetooth and IrDA

I don't like to get all warm and fuzzy, but I have to admit that sharing is a wonderful concept. In practice, however, it helps to know your options. One of the key advantages of your camera phone, after all, is that it lets you send your wonderful pictures to friends and loved ones immediately after you take them. But understanding how this sharing thing works when it comes to picture messaging can be a bit confusing.

You may be scratching your head about why your friend can't view that photo you kindly sent to his cell phone, or why you received a message informing you that your message hasn't been transmitted.

In this chapter, I'll sort through the various methods for sharing your photos with others, including the carriers' online options.

Multimedia Messaging

Depending on your camera phone and wireless carrier, you may have noticed the phrase "MMS capable" on your phone's packaging. It's a great tool, but that doesn't always mean you'll be able to use it.

MMS (Multimedia Message Service) refers to phone-to-phone messaging of files that can include pictures, sound, text, and video. But you can send such messages only if the recipient also has an MMS-capable phone and uses the same carrier. That is, if your carrier is Cingular Wireless, you can't send an MMS message to a T-Mobile customer. That doesn't mean your friend will never see the picture, just that she won't be able to view it on her phone—at least not immediately (more on that later).

NOTE: *Carriers are working on cross-network MMS, but such developments are notoriously slow. Even when this does occur, your recipient's phone still needs to be MMS-ready.*

It's also worth noting that not all carriers use MMS for phone-to-phone messaging in the strict sense of the term. Both Sprint PCS and T-Mobile utilize their wireless web services, although the basic premise for sending multimedia messages between phones is the same as MMS.

Sending an MMS Message

One of the good things about MMS is that the process for sending a message is nearly identical regardless of the carrier. The menu options will vary from phone to phone, but the basics remain the same. If you know your recipient uses the same carrier and has an MMS-capable phone, use the following steps to send a picture message:

1. Take a picture or choose a photo from the gallery.

2. Select Options, then click Send (some phones will provide a list of options, such as Via Bluetooth and Via Infrared. Choose Via Multimedia to send an MMS message).

3. Select a contact from your address book, or enter a phone number (with some phones, such as the Nokia 3650, you must choose a contact previously stored in your address book).

4. Add a subject heading, text message, or sound clip (optional, if your phone supports this feature).

5. Click Send.

If the recipient uses a different carrier or doesn't have an MMS-capable phone, she'll receive a text message informing her of how to view the photo online, typically a website address where she can view the picture on her computer. And that leads us to the next topic.

CAUTION: *Recipients may not be able to listen to sound clips on their phones. If you're on a trip and plan to send lots of "talking postcards," send a few test messages before you leave.*

Picture Messaging Websites

If Sprint PCS, T-Mobile, or Verizon Wireless is your carrier, then you're in luck, because these carriers operate their own picture messaging sites. AT&T Wireless and Cingular Wireless, meanwhile, both have partnerships with third-party sites.

> **NOTE** *Cingular agreed to acquire AT&T Wireless in early 2004. As this book went to press, the companies expected to complete the deal by the end of 2004. It was unclear at the time how the merger would affect any picture messaging offerings.*

The carrier-operated picture messaging websites provide flexibility for sharing, managing, and presenting your camera phone pictures, but there are important differences among their offerings.

Sprint Picture Mail

With its Picture Mail site, Sprint PCS offers a complete picture messaging experience. To use the service, you must purchase the carrier's PCS Vision Pictures Pack for $15 a month (prices may vary based on promotions or company changes, and this is in addition to whatever you pay for your voice plan). Although that seems steep compared to the other carriers' MMS plans, the Pictures Pack does allow you to send and receive unlimited pictures messages, and it includes unlimited wireless web access and other web-based messaging tools. If you plan to send only a couple of pictures per month, you can forego the Pictures Pack plan and pay 1 cent per kilobyte, plus airtime, to send and receive picture messages. VGA-quality images are about 40KB to 50KB, so you can expect to pay between 40 and 50 cents for each message. If you choose this route, however, you won't get access to the Picture Mail site.

The site is a joy to use. If you're a PCS Vision customer, you'll be prompted to create a password when you first upload your pictures to the site from your phone. When you visit the site (pictures.sprintpcs.com) on your computer, you enter your cell phone number (no spaces or hyphens) and your Picture Mail password (see Figure 6-1). From there, you're taken to your uploaded images.

To upload your photos to Picture Mail:

1. Go to the phone's photo gallery.
2. Select the picture you wish to upload, then click Options.

FIGURE 6-1 Enter your Sprint PCS phone number and Picture Mail password to enter the Picture Mail site.

3. Click Upload, then Upload This to send the selected photo, or Upload All to send all the pictures in the gallery.

NOTE *The only way to upload photos to the site is through your Sprint PCS phone. You can't upload pictures from your PC, although you can download photos to your PC from the Picture Mail site.*

TIP *If you select the Remember Me option on the Picture Mail login page, you won't have to enter your information each time you go to the site. Simply click OK and you'll see your uploaded photos.*

Once you're in the site, you'll see thumbnails of your uploaded images. From here, you have several options for working with your photos, including sending picture messages. To send a picture message:

1. Click the Send Picture button next to the thumbnail image.

2. In the To field, type the Sprint PCS phone number or an e-mail address to which you wish to send the picture. Separate multiple recipients by a comma.

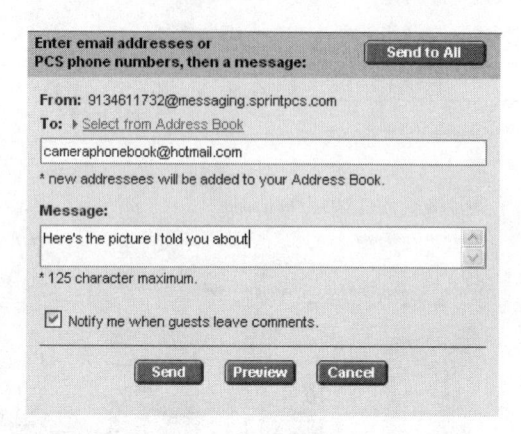

3. Enter a text message in the Message field.
4. Click Send.

> **TIP** *Picture Mail lets you maintain an online address book to simplify sending picture messages. Click the Address Book tab at the top of the screen, click the Create Address link, then enter the information. Whenever you're ready to send a message, click the Select from Address Book link to choose your contacts, or click the Send to All button to insert all stored contacts with a single click.*

If you wish to send more than one picture at a time, click the Send Multiple link in the Upload Options section, select the check boxes underneath the thumbnails of the pictures you want, click Send, then enter the contact information and send the message.

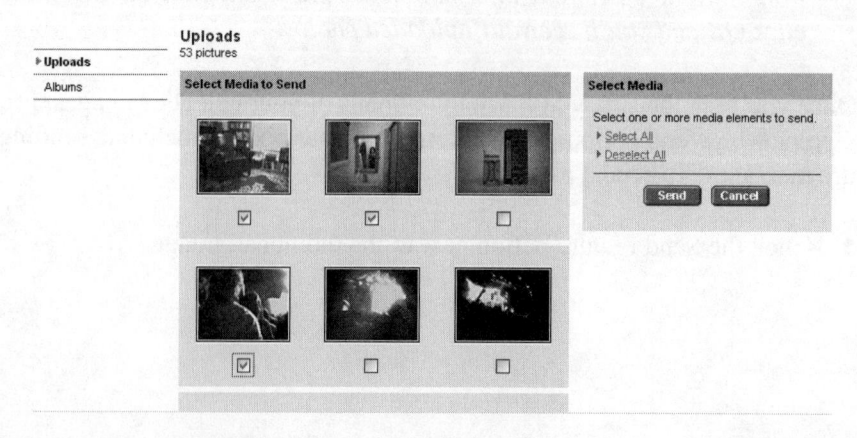

CHAPTER 6: Sharing Your Photos   **135**

Along with individual photos, Picture Mail lets you create and share photo albums, or groups of similarly themed pictures, by using the following steps:

1. Click the Move/Copy to Album link in the Upload Options section.

2. Select the pictures you want to move or copy. In the Move/Copy Pictures box, select whether you want to move the pictures, which deletes the pictures from your Uploads folder, or copy them, which retains the copy in Uploads.

3. From the drop-down menu, select New Album.

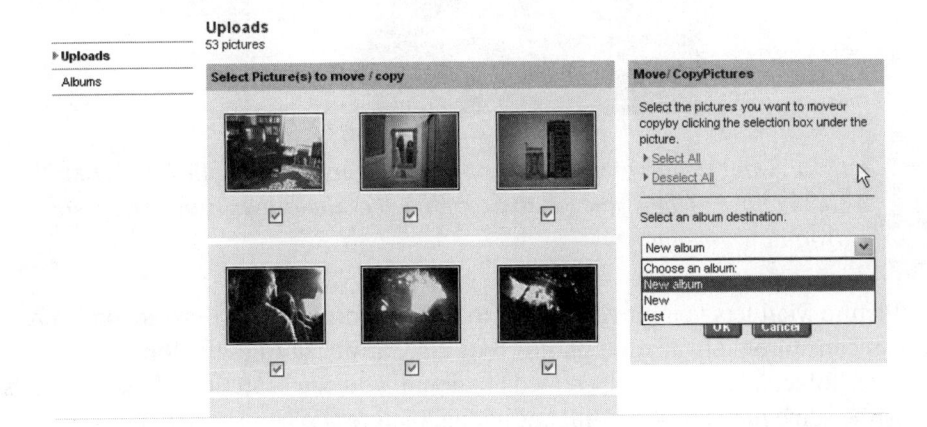

4. To give your new album a name, click the Albums link on the left side of the screen, then click the Edit link next to the album's thumbnail.

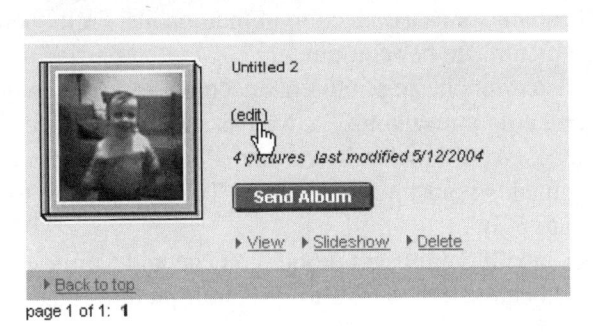

5. Type a name for the album in the Title field, then click OK.

> **TIP** *If you want to add pictures later to any album, simply follow the same steps above. When you get to Step 3, select the album name from the drop-down menu.*

Picture Mail lets you move pictures to as many different albums as you wish, so you can store that vacation photo from the Caribbean in both Holiday and Summer folders. Once you've created an album, you can share it with your friends using the same method as sending individual pictures. When in the albums folder, click Send Album, then choose your recipients (see Figure 6-2). If you send an album to an e-mail address, your recipient will receive a message with a thumbnail image and links to view the album as a slideshow, which displays all of the photos in the album sequentially, or as a collection of thumbnails. From there, the recipient can download the pictures to her computer.

Picture Mail also offers basic photo-enhancement tools, allowing you to rotate, lighten, darken, and crop your photos, as well as apply such effects as black and white and sepia tones. Additionally, if you're really into Bugs Bunny, you can add Fun Frames, which adds your favorite Looney Tunes character to the border of a picture (see Figure 6-3).

If you're in an equally whimsical mood, you can add Comic Bubbles, which can include up to 25 characters of text, to give your pictures that comic-strip feel (see Figure 6-4).

If you're the recipient of a picture or an album, you'll receive a text message on your phone informing you of a "Picture Share" or "Album Share." After selecting Go on your phone's menu, you can view the pictures individually, download the

CHAPTER 6: Sharing Your Photos 137

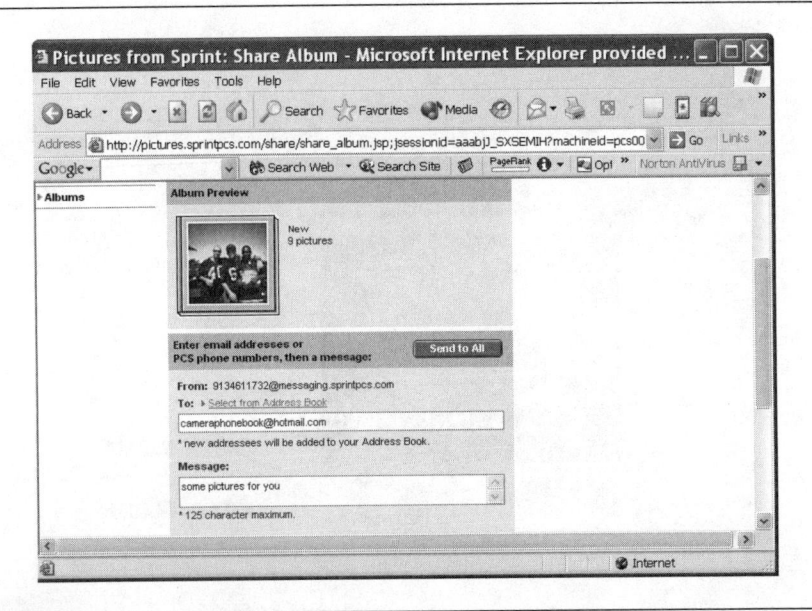

FIGURE 6-2   In Picture Mail, you can share entire photo albums with others.

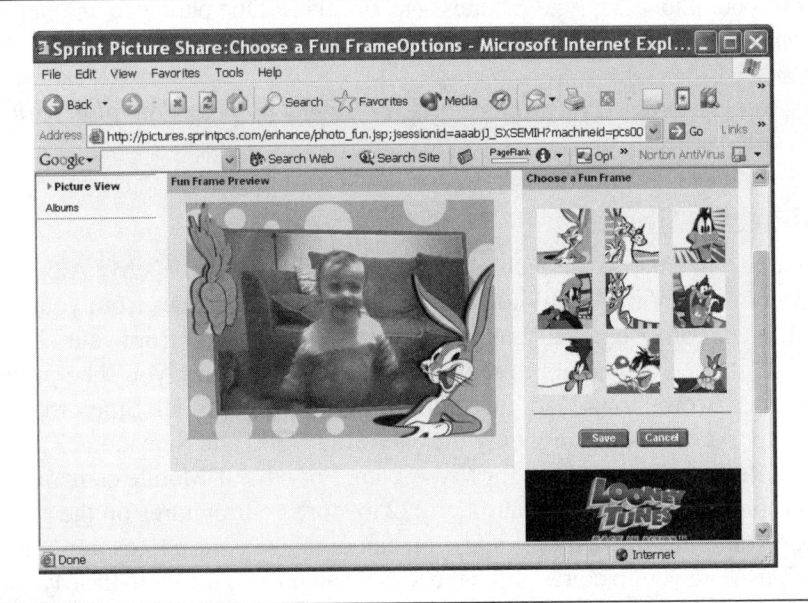

FIGURE 6-3   Picture Mail's Fun Frames adds a Looney Tunes twist to your pictures.

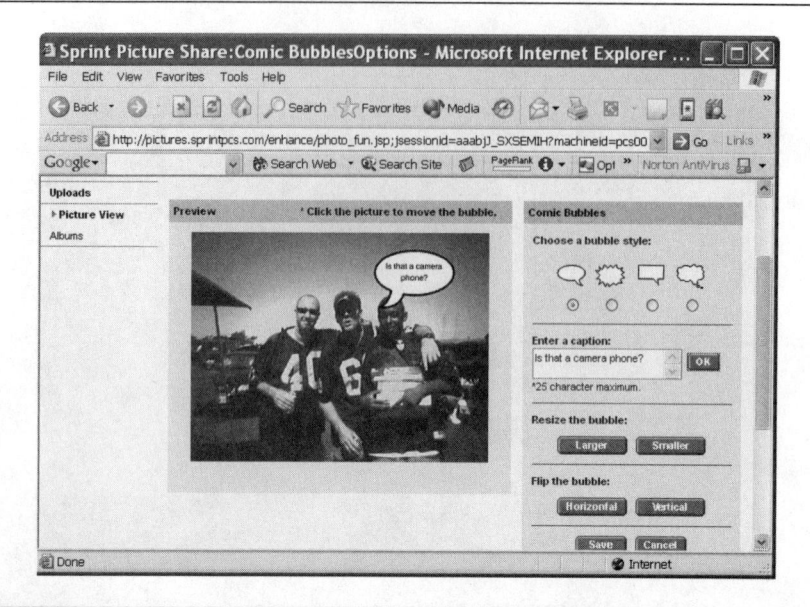

FIGURE 6-4 Give your pictures a comic-book feel with Picture Mail.

images to your phone, reply to the message, or forward the photos to another Sprint PCS number or e-mail address.

> **NOTE** *You can perform this task only if you signed up for a data plan with your cell phone.*

T-Mobile My Album

The most recent entry to the picture messaging field, T-Mobile's My Album (www.tmobile.com/myalbum) not only lets you upload pictures from your cell phone, but you can also upload any photo, audio, or video clip from your computer.

The first time you attempt to send a picture to My Album, you'll be prompted to enter a password. To upload your photos, take a picture, click Store, then select My Album. As of this writing, only the Motorola V300 and Samsung e715 camera phones featured built-in support for My Album. For other T-Mobile camera phones, you send pictures to the phone number 222 to store your pictures on the site.

Once your images are on the site, you can organize your photos into albums. If you wish to share your pictures with others, you can post your files to the My Journal online diary. From there, you can send out e-mail invitations to your friends and family. Your invitees will receive an e-mail with a link to visit your album, where they can view the pictures and post comments.

Verizon Pix Place

The third carrier-operated picture messaging site, Verizon Wireless Pix Place (www.vzwpix.com), is similar to Sprint PCS Picture Mail in its basic approach, but there are a few key differences. For starters, whereas you can store an unlimited amount of photos in Picture Mail, Pix Place provides only 1MB of storage. That means you'll have to frequently rotate the pictures you keep online.

Uploading pictures from your camera phone is essentially the same for Pix Place as it is for Picture Mail, except you select Online Album in the Options menu instead of Upload. The main difference is that you can't upload your entire gallery at once; you can only upload one photo at a time.

On the plus side, you can upload images to the site from your computer, which means you can keep any kind of photo on the site, not just pictures taken with your Verizon Wireless camera phone. Because of the site's space limitations, however, you may want to limit your uploads to camera phone images with their smaller file sizes. To upload pictures from your computer to Pix Place:

1. Click the Upload Files button.

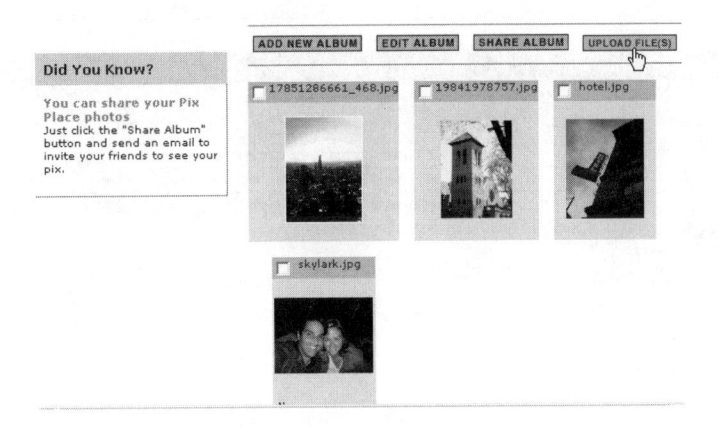

2. Click Browse to locate the folder and photo you wish to upload (you can upload up to three images at a time), then click Open (see Figure 6-5).

3. Click Upload Files.

NOTE *Individual picture uploads are limited to 100KB.*

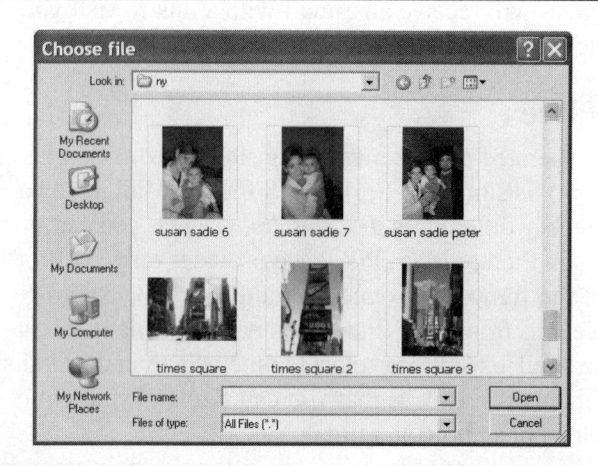

FIGURE 6-5 Upload up to three images at a time from your PC to Verizon Pix Place.

You log in to the site the same way you access Picture Mail—enter your phone number (no spaces or dashes) and password, and the next screen you'll see will be a list of your albums (see Figure 6-6).

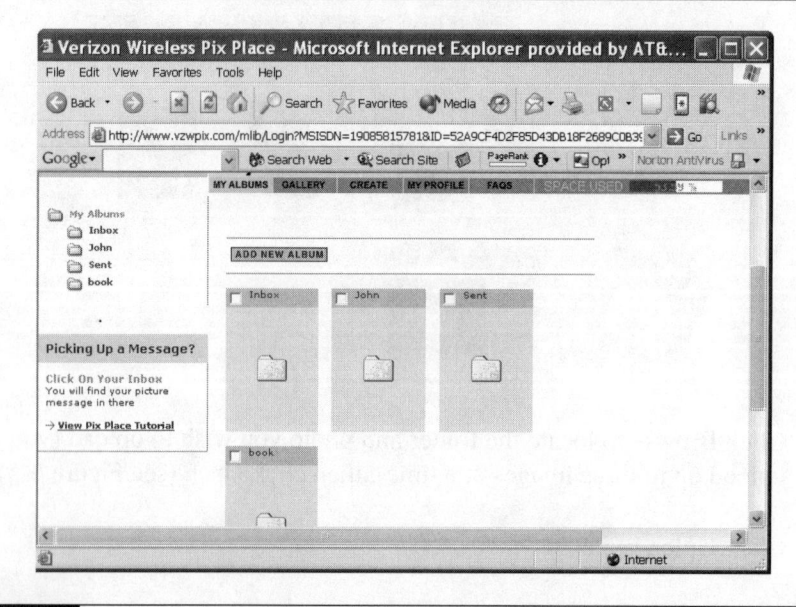

FIGURE 6-6 Pix Place's opening screen provides you with a list of your saved albums.

CAUTION *You may not be able to log in to Pix Place if your computer is operating behind an Internet firewall. I had to shut off Norton Internet Security in order to log in to the site, leaving my system vulnerable to hackers.*

You'll find images uploaded from your phone in the Inbox folder. From there, you'll see thumbnails of each picture. Clicking the photo will present a full-size image.

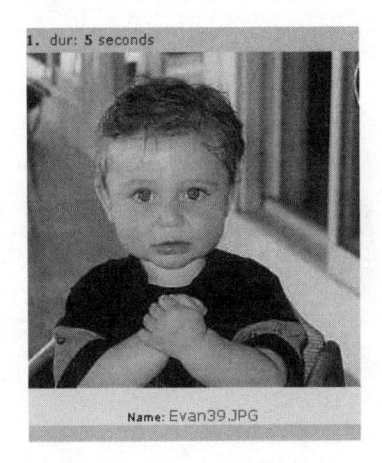

If you want to send a picture, click the check box above the thumbnail, then click Send. Next, you'll see fields to enter recipient information—either the phone number of another Verizon Wireless subscriber or an e-mail address (you can enter up to 10 numbers or e-mail addresses, separated by commas)—and a subject heading (see Figure 6-7).

If you have an audio clip stored on your computer that you wish to add to a message, click the musical notation icon, then click Browse to locate the folder and file you wish to attach to the message.

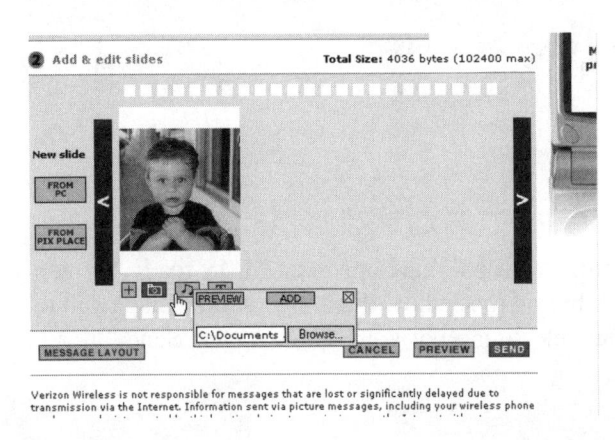

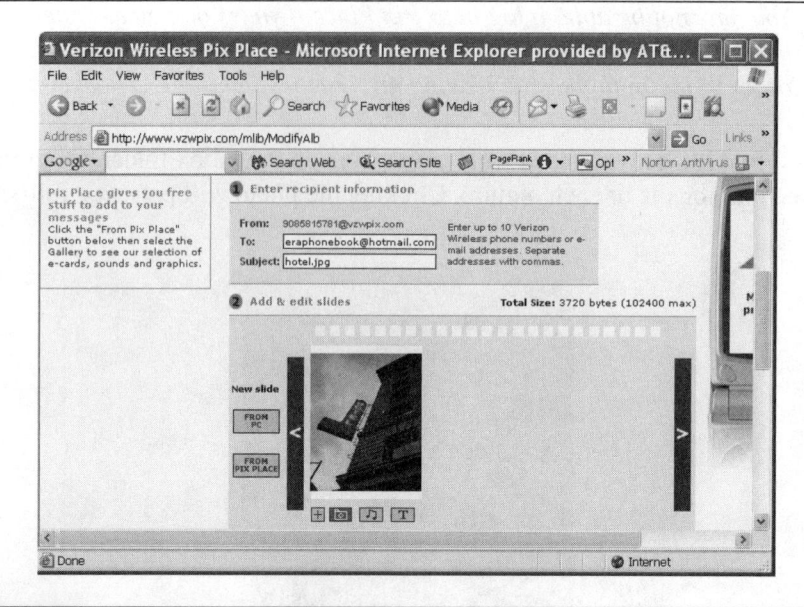

FIGURE 6-7 The Send Picture dialog in Verizon Wireless' Pix Place.

You can also insert additional images, text, or audio by clicking the appropriate button under New Slide in the preview window. For files stored on your computer, choose From PC; if you already uploaded the files to the site, select From Pix Place.

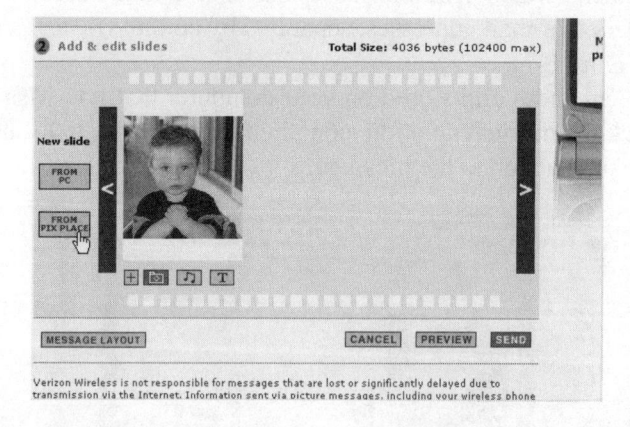

If you're sending an MMS message to an MMS-ready Verizon Wireless phone, click the Preview button to see how the image will be displayed on the screen (see Figure 6-8). After selecting all of your options, click Send.

CHAPTER 6: Sharing Your Photos 143

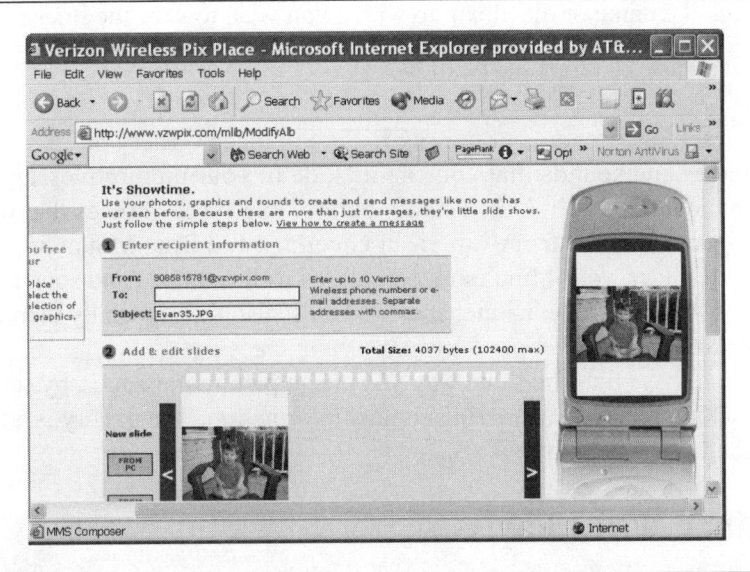

FIGURE 6-8 When sending an MMS to a Verizon Wireless customer, Pix Place displays a preview of how the photo will look on the phone.

NOTE *Pix Place limits picture messages to 100KB.*

Like Picture Mail, Pix Place lets you create multiple albums, and you can save a picture in more than one album. Click the Add New Album button, type a name for the new album, then click Add Album. To add images to the album:

1. Go to Inbox (or a previously created album).

2. Click in the check box above the thumbnails of the images you wish to select, then click Copy.

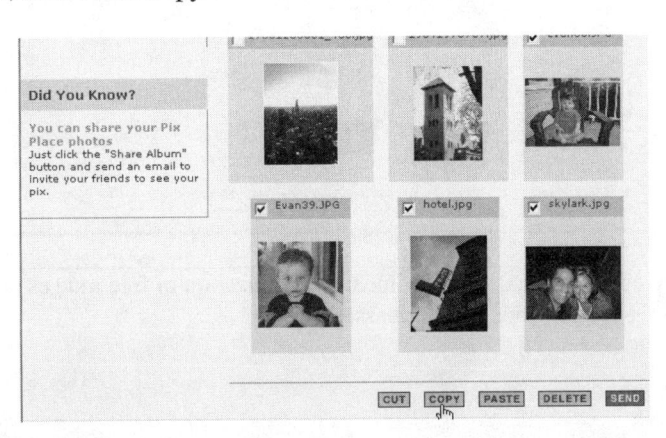

3. Click the name of the album to which you wish to save the images.

4. Click Paste to insert the pictures.

If you want to spice up your messages, the Pix Place Gallery offers a collection of free images and sounds that you can include in your picture messages (see Figure 6-9). When you click the Gallery button, you'll see choices that include electronic greeting cards from American Greetings and Blue Mountain. In the Stuff to Send folder, you'll find more e-cards, as well as music and sound clips and thematic illustrations (love, nature, sports). You'll also find specially themed files, such as photos from *Lord of the Rings: Return of the King*.

You insert these files the same way you create picture messages, by selecting the file, clicking Send, then entering contact information. The gallery is a fun way to add a song clip to a picture message.

How Much Will I Pay?

I know I've been going on about how much fun it is to use these services, but before you get carried away, you should know that none of these services are free. Regardless

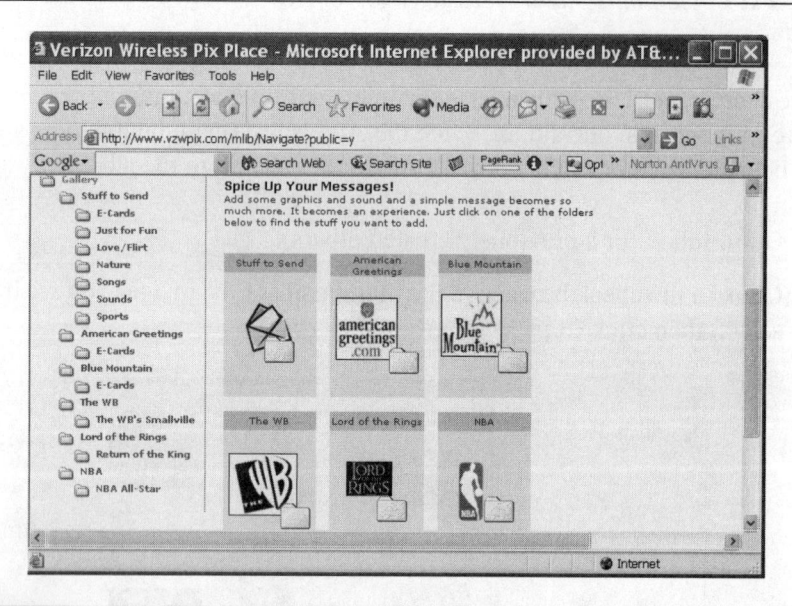

FIGURE 6-9   The Pix Place Gallery includes a collection of free images and sounds to spice up your picture messages.

Voices from the Community: Helping the Bride

I wasn't interested in buying a camera phone at first. I just figured it would be a feature I'd never use. Then my sister bought one and she showed me how easy it was to e-mail a picture directly from the phone. I went out and bought one a few weeks later.

It really came in handy when my sister was planning her wedding. She lives in New Jersey, so I couldn't be there to help her with a lot of the details. But when she went shopping for her bridesmaids' dresses, she took a few pictures and sent them to my phone while she was still at the shop, so I was able to give her my input right away.

I use the Sanyo 8100, the same one my sister has. I still use a regular digital camera, but it's nice to have the camera phone with me when I'm out shopping. I've taken pictures of furniture and showed them to my husband—it's better than trying to explain what something looks like. Right now it's more of a convenience, but if the quality of the pictures gets better I'll probably take even more pictures with it.

—Nancy Garcia
Evanston, IL

of how much or how little you use your carrier's picture messaging options, you'll have to pay, as Table 6-1 makes perfectly clear. If you're an occasional user, you

Carrier	Monthly MMS/Picture Messaging Subscription	Pay As You Go Price
AT&T Wireless	$2.99 for 10 outgoing multimedia messages	40 cents per outgoing message (50KB maximum); incoming messages free from other AT&T Wireless customers
Cingular Wireless	$2.99 (up to 20 messages)	25 cents per message sent or received
Sprint PCS	$15 for PCS Vision Pictures Pack (unlimited picture messages)	1 cent per KB for each message
T-Mobile	$2.99 (up to 20 messages)	25 cents per message sent or received
Verizon Wireless	$4.99 (unlimited picture messages)	25 cents per message sent or received

TABLE 6-1 Wireless Carriers' Picture Messaging Services Prices

can get away with paying for each message as you go. But if you plan to make a habit of sending picture messages, you should go with a monthly plan.

The prices vary and are always subject to change, but as I explained earlier, so do the services. Also keep in mind that some carriers may offer bonuses, such as a month of unlimited messaging, when you sign up for service.

Third-Party Online Services

If you're not a Sprint PCS or Verizon Wireless customer, don't fret: you too have online options at your disposal with which you can store and share your camera phone pictures.

Ofoto

Now owned by Kodak, this site lets you create, edit, and share online albums for free (see Figure 6-10). You can also order prints and frames for your favorite shots (more on this in Chapter 7).

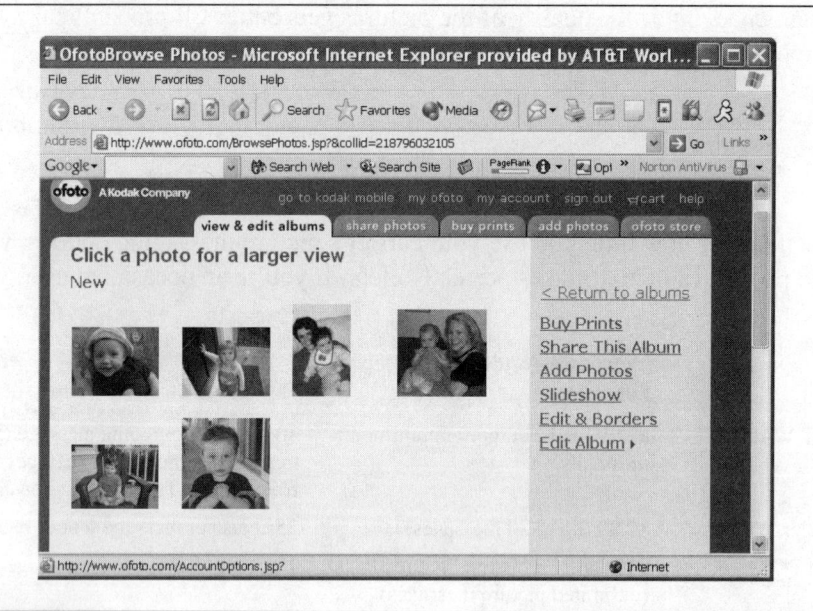

FIGURE 6-10   Create, edit, and share your camera phone pictures with Ofoto.

CHAPTER 6: Sharing Your Photos   **147**

With Ofoto, you share albums or individual photos by e-mail using the following steps:

1. Click the Share Photos tab.

2. Click the album you wish to share.

3. Enter one or more e-mail addresses separated by commas or semicolons.

4. Add a message (optional).

5. Click Send (see Figure 6-11).

If you check the box requiring your friends to sign in to Ofoto, they will be able to save the pictures and order prints. Also, you'll be able to see who viewed your pictures in the guestbook.

At the bottom of the screen, you'll notice a link to Free Upload Software. You'll want to install this on your computer, as it allows you to move pictures from your hard drive to the Ofoto site. After downloading the software, which takes just a couple of seconds with a high-speed Internet connection:

1. Click the Add Photos tab at the top of the screen, then choose a name for your album.

2. Click the Choose Photos button.

3. Select the folder containing the pictures you wish to upload, select multiple photos by holding the CTRL button while clicking the filename, then press Add.

4. Click Start Upload.

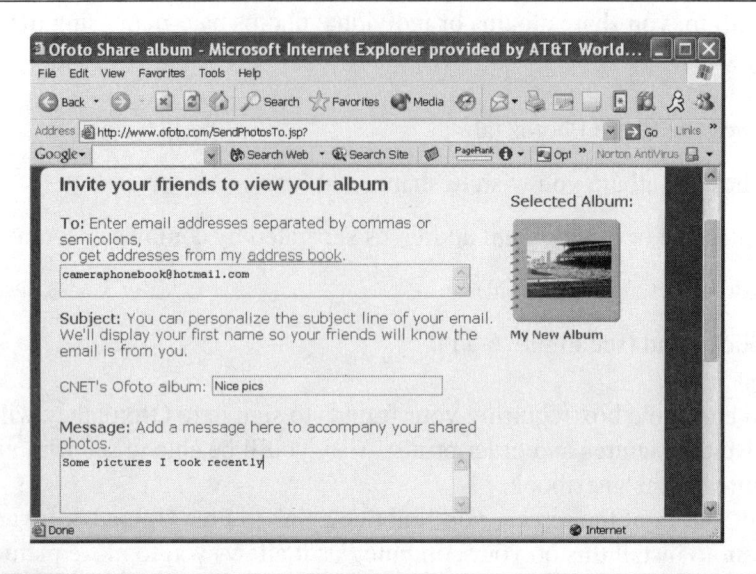

FIGURE 6-11   Send invitations to your friends to view your albums on Ofoto.

Ofoto provides basic image-editing tools, such as cropping, red-eye removal, rotation, and an Instant Fix option that automatically corrects color and contrast settings. Effects settings let you add different color tints or artistic filters to your photos, while a collection of borders lets you add a decorative frame to your shots (see Figure 6-12).

A Print@Home feature lets you make prints directly from the site (click the link to install the free Print@Home software).

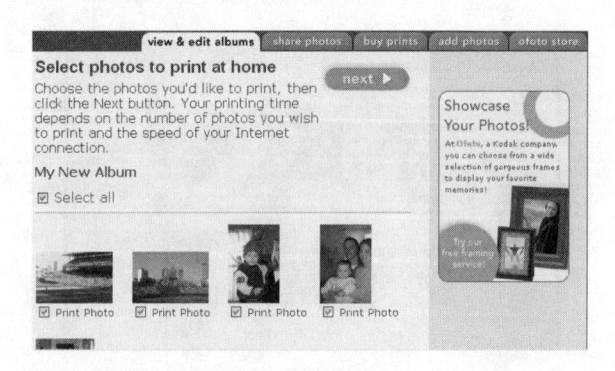

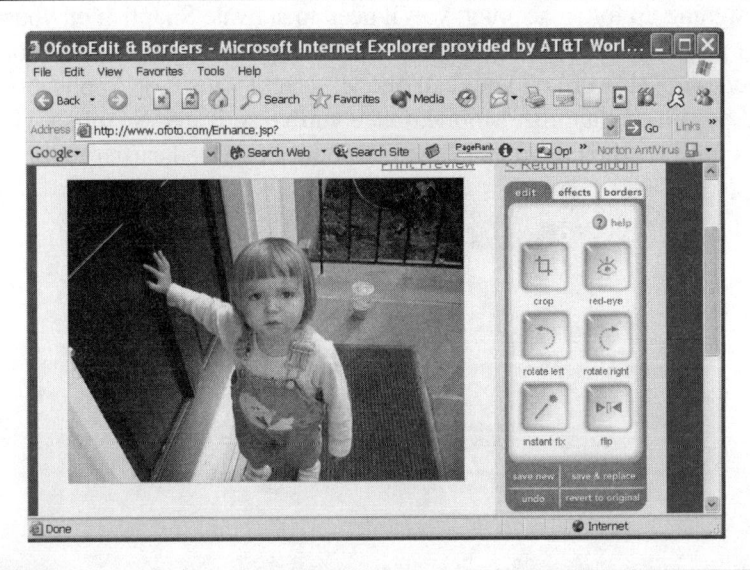

FIGURE 6-12 Ofoto offers a decent selection of photo editing and enhancement tools.

With the Ofoto Store, you can use your photos to create greeting cards, calendars, or physical albums. You can also purchase frames and order an archive CD.

Snapfish Mobile

This site (www.snapfish.com/mobile) is available to customers of AT&T Wireless, Cingular Wireless, and Verizon Wireless (check the site to make sure your phone is compatible with the service). You can try the site for free for one month. After the introductory period, pricing depends on your carrier.

After signing up for an account, you'll need to activate Snapfish on your phone. This exact process depends on your carrier, but essentially you need to connect to the Internet (wireless web) on your cell phone, select Pictures or Applications, then select and download Snapfish Mobile. Once you've activated Snapfish, you use the basic steps for uploading pictures from your phone described earlier in this chapter.

Fujifilm.net

Fuji Film's Get the Picture Mobile Service is affiliated with AT&T Wireless, although the company says it is expanding to other carriers. For $2.99 a month, you can upload pictures to the site, download pictures to your phone, and send photos via e-mail or MMS to other AT&T Wireless customers.

E-mail Your Pictures

If paying a monthly fee for an online service isn't your cup of tea, there's always e-mail, either from your phone or from your computer. For sending pictures to friends who don't subscribe to your carrier, don't have cell phones capable of accepting images, or—the horror—don't have a cell phone, e-mail is your only sharing option.

The details will vary from phone to phone, but the basic concept is the same. To e-mail directly from your cell phone:

1. Go to the picture gallery, then select a picture to send.

2. Click options, then Send.

3. If you previously saved the contact information, select the address from the phone book. Be sure to select the e-mail address from the contact information, not the phone number. Otherwise, you'll need to enter the e-mail address manually.

4. Insert a text message or audio clip (optional).

5. Click Send.

If you've already stored photos from your camera phone on your computer, you can send a picture as an e-mail attachment. The advantage here is that you can send more than one picture at a time, although some e-mail systems limit the amount of information you can send in an attachment. Free web-based e-mail programs, such as Hotmail and Yahoo! Mail, typically limit attachments to 1MB. Given the small size of camera phone images, however, this shouldn't be an issue.

The following steps apply specifically to Microsoft Outlook, although the process is similar across e-mail applications.

1. Click the New button in the Outlook toolbar to create a new mail message.

2. Enter the appropriate e-mail address in the To box. Separate multiple addresses with a semicolon.

3. Enter a subject name in the Subject box.

4. Enter a message in the text box.

Here are the pictures we discussed earlier

5. To add an attachment, click the paperclip icon in the Outlook toolbar, which accesses the Insert File dialog box. Navigate through your system's folders to find the picture(s) you wish to send. If you want to add multiple pictures from the same folder, hold the CTRL key while clicking the filenames.

6. Click the Insert button to close the dialog box and insert the images in the message.

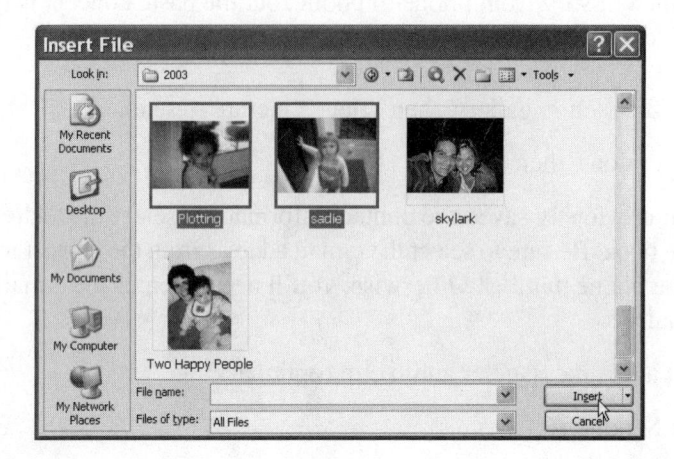

7. Click Send.

Receiving Attachments

Yes, it's better to give than receive, but not *much* better. If you're lucky enough to have received a picture message as an e-mail attachment, you can open or save it in a couple of simple steps:

1. Double-click the attachment name in the message to access the Opening Mail Attachment dialog.

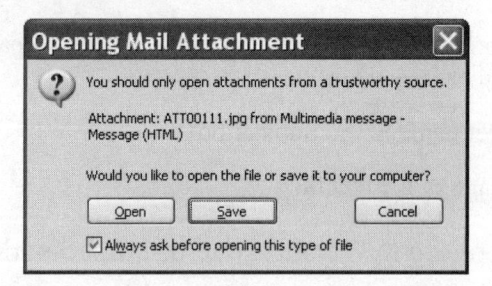

2. To view the file without saving it, click Open. The image will appear in your computer's default image viewer (for Windows XP, it's the Windows Picture and Fax Viewer).

3. To save the image, click Save to open the Save As dialog box. Navigate to the folder you wish to store the picture, then click Save.

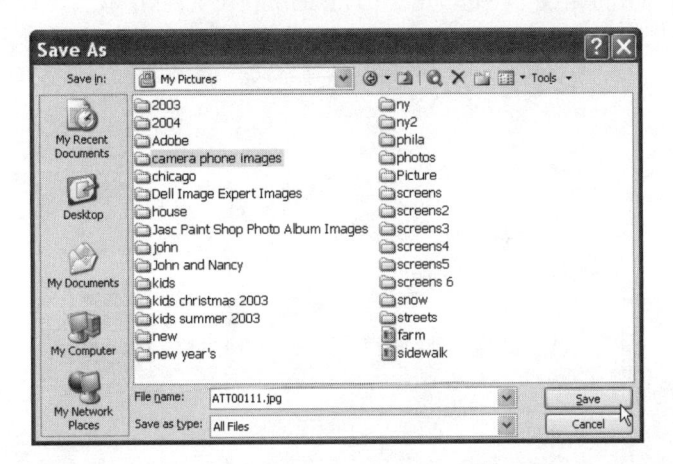

> **NOTE** When sending via IrDA, make sure the phone's IrDA port lines up with the port on the other device and that the devices are no more than three feet apart.

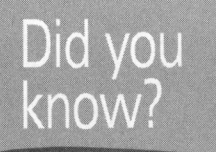

Did you know?

SendPhotos Gold

Some people have trouble working with e-mail attachments. If that's the case with you, there is an alternative. Novatix Corp. offers a program called SendPhotos Gold, which embeds photos directly into the body of an e-mail message. It also provides options for displaying your pictures creatively with a collection of decorative frames and layout options.

When you first launch SendPhotos and choose E-mail Pictures from the opening screen, you'll see your My Pictures folder and subfolders. Find the picture or pictures you want, click the check box next to the thumbnail image, then click the Next button at the top of the screen (you can click the Back button at any time to make changes to an earlier process).

Next, you select a piece of "stationery," a collection of more than 100 designs that frame your picture. If you click the Layout button, you can change the size of the photo, the frame, background, and text colors, add a drop shadow, and change the layout of the text message and caption.

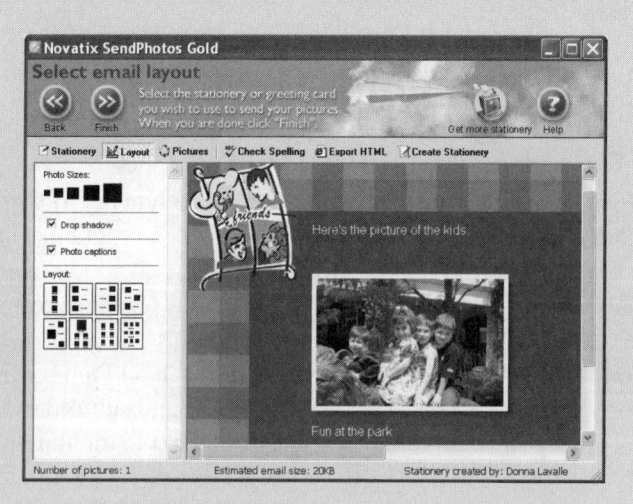

Clicking the image opens an editing window where you can make basic brightness and contrast adjustments, crop the image, and remove red-eye (though this usually isn't a problem with camera phone pictures).

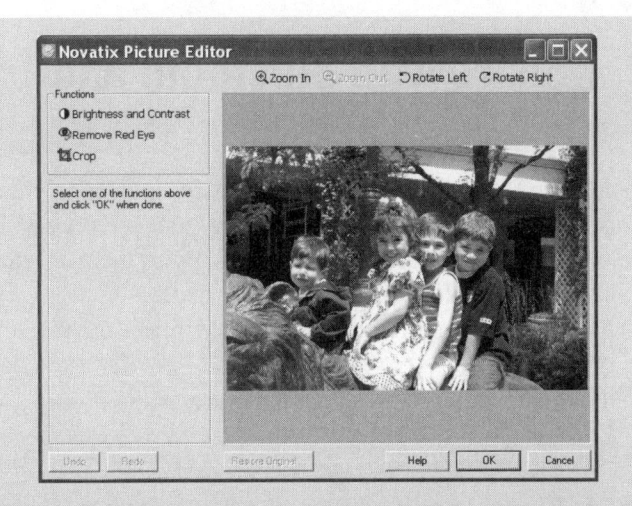

The first time you click Finish to send a message, SendPhotos sets up your e-mail preferences, with options for Microsoft Outlook 2000/XP, Outlook Express, and one for other programs, such as AOL Mail, Hotmail, and Eudora. (For Outlook, you may need to insert the application's installation CD to access a configuration file necessary to allow the program to work with SendPhotos.) Once your settings are complete, you'll see the picture embedded in your e-mail application. The only step left is to enter the appropriate contact information, type a subject heading, and click Send.

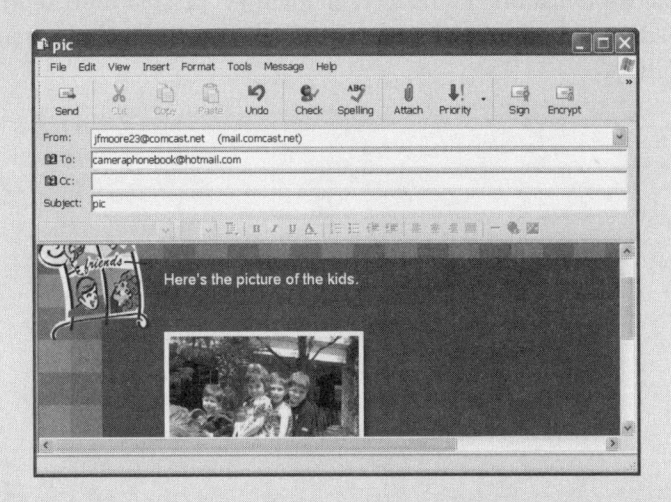

SendPhotos Gold costs $19.95. You can download a free trial of SendPhotos from www.novatix.com. After you send six messages, however, the program will insert watermarks over your photos.

How to ... Share with Bluetooth and IrDA

Not only can you use Bluetooth and IrDA to transfer images to your PC, but you can also use these wireless protocols to share your pictures with other cell phones or personal digital assistants (PDAs) that support them. It's much quicker and less of a hassle than dealing with MMS or e-mail.

To share a picture with another cell phone or wireless device:

1. Go to the image gallery and select a picture.
2. Click Options, then Send.
3. Select Via Bluetooth or Via Infrared. After your phone detects the other device, click Select or Add. Your phone will display a message notifying you that the file has been sent.

Moving On

You've been so kind to share your pictures with others, but now it's time to move on to more hands-on matters. In the next chapter, I'll discuss how to print your pictures, including a cool, convenient way to do it at your local pharmacy and other retail outlets.

Chapter 7
Printing Your Photos

How to...

- Choose a printer
- Print with Bluetooth and IrDA
- Size your pictures for printing
- Work with online printing services
- Operate retail printing kiosks

Many of us prefer to have physical evidence of certain things. It's much more impressive to show your friends a print of the picture of the elk that wandered into your backyard than it is to say, "Wait, let me get my cell phone so I can show you the picture. Everyone, gather around the tiny screen!"

Printing pictures from a camera phone is similar to printing pictures from a digital camera: for the most part, you have to get the photos onto your computer first. But, as with digital cameras, more options have arrived or are on the way to making the printing experience more convenient.

In this chapter, I'll discuss how to get the best output possible from your camera phone, especially those handsets with sensors less than a megapixel. I'll also provide an overview of some online printing services and examine some of the newer technologies at your disposal.

> **CAUTION** *This chapter is for those with camera phones that support a resolution of at least 640 × 480. Unless you like the feel of crushing disappointment, I don't recommend printing pictures if your handset's resolution doesn't meet this standard. Feel free, however, to read on for future reference.*

Choosing a Printer

Let's get the debate out of the way right now: don't use a laser printer to print your cell phone pictures. Yes, the cost of color lasers has come down to well below $1,000, but the output is more suited for documents with color elements, such as presentations with lots of graphs and charts, not for pictures printed on photo paper.

That leaves you with inkjet printers. You'll find lots of models marketed as "photo printers" from the top manufacturers—Canon, Epson, and Hewlett-Packard—as well as offerings from Olympus and Sony. These are inkjets designed to work seamlessly, or close to it, with digital cameras and, more and more, camera phones.

So how do you figure out what you need? A couple of options can make printing pictures from your camera phones a bit easier. Both eliminate the need to save pictures to your computer first. Nevertheless, as you'll find out later when I explain the virtues of adjusting the image size, saving the pictures to your PC first does have its advantages.

Memory Cards

Although some handsets are beginning to include mini USB ports, the overwhelming majority of models on the market don't offer a direct method for connecting your camera phone to a printer. That's yet another reason why the memory card is an important tool for storing camera phone images. The better photo printers accept several formats of memory cards, including CompactFlash, Secure Digital, SmartMedia, and Multimedia Card. This comes in handy if your camera phone supports external memory cards (although most phones don't feature memory options, this will likely change as storage demands rise with multi-megapixel camera phones). Epson's PictureMate (see Figure 7-1), which the company promotes as a "personal photo lab," accepts CompactFlash, Secure Digital, MMC, SmartMedia, and Sony MemoryStick memory cards, among others.

FIGURE 7-1 Camera phone users will appreciate Epson PictureMate's slots for several memory card formats, as well as its Bluetooth and infrared support.

NOTE *It's worth seeking out a printer that features a preview screen. That way, you simply plug the card into the appropriate slot and view your pictures in the display before printing them.*

NOTE *A new memory card, the SanDisk TransFlash, began appearing in select Motorola camera phones in 2004. The TransFlash's small size makes it ideal for camera phones.*

Bluetooth and IrDA

Several manufacturers have come out with mobile printers. Hewlett-Packard offers the HP-450wbt Mobile Printer, which includes integrated Bluetooth support (see Figure 7-2). You can connect your Bluetooth-enabled camera phone wirelessly with the printer the same way you would with a PDA or PC.

If your phone supports Bluetooth but your printer doesn't, you can find Bluetooth printer adapters from such companies as Belkin (www.belkin.com) and MPI Tech (www.mpitech.com). You simply connect the adapter to your printer's USB or

FIGURE 7-2 The HP-450wbt Mobile Printer's compact design and Bluetooth support make it an attractive choice for camera phone users.

Voices from the Community: Printing Developments

By 2008, we estimate that there will be about 312 billion captured, saved, and shared images from digital still cameras, scanners, and camera phones. About 82 billion of those will be printed, and camera phone users are expected to print about 37 billion of those images. Groups such as the MIPC (Mobile Imaging and Printing Consortium) are trying to make it so that more images will be printed.

The goal of MIPC is not to create new standards, but leverage off of existing standards. Bluetooth is one of those standards, as well as the various memory cards. Our goal is to get both printer and handset manufacturers to adopt these technologies so that an MIPC-compliant phone will have compatibility with MIPC-compliant printers. That way, my user experience of when I use my phone to print, and your experience when you use a different brand of phone and printer, will be the same.

You're going to see more printers that have wireless capabilities, either through local area networks or Bluetooth. Also, just as you see with the wireless hot spots, you'll see printing devices populated outside the home, in places like your local Starbucks or Borders.

—Ramon Garrido
Chairman, MIPC
Consumer Imaging and Printing Program Director, Hewlett-Packard

parallel port (depending on the model), then follow the same steps for linking your camera phone to the printer as you would any other Bluetooth-enabled device.

If your camera phone and printer both support infrared connections, you can print wirelessly by syncing your camera phone and printer's IrDA ports. Epson's PictureMate is Bluetooth- and IrDA-compatible, and both wireless technologies are opening up retail printing opportunities, such as the Kodak Picture Station kiosks, which I'll discuss later in this chapter.

Other Features

When examining your photo-printer options, keep in mind exactly how you plan to use the product. You can spend up to $700 and get such niceties as an automatic paper cutter (the Epson Stylus Photo 2200) or the ability to make poster-size prints (the Canon i9900), but if you don't need these features, why pay for them? On the other hand, $99 can get you a basic model that will deliver quality prints, but you probably won't get a preview monitor or slots for printing directly from media storage cards. As you can see in Table 7-1, most photo printer manufacturers offer several options. Check out their websites to determine which model is right for you, then go to a local retailer to get a look at the printer. While you're there, ask a sales representative to make a test print from the printers you're considering.

Making the Print

When the first digital cameras hit the market, many people complained that the print quality wasn't on par with what you get with film. That gap has long since been bridged, and the same will eventually happen with camera phones. If you try printing a 4 × 6 picture taken with a VGA-quality camera, you'll notice the results aren't as sharp as you get with your 3-megapixel digital camera. But that doesn't mean you can't get decent-looking results at all.

Adjust the Size

Less really is more when it comes to printing photos from your camera phone. That is, you'll get a better-looking print from a smaller printout than a larger one, especially if you're using a sub-megapixel camera. As I said in Chapter 5, when you lower an image's resolution, or pixels per inch (ppi), the print size increases, while increasing the resolution decreases the print size. A higher resolution produces a sharper-looking printout, however, leaving you with the dilemma of choosing quality over size.

Manufacturer	Available Models	Price Range
Canon (www.canon.com)	CP-200, CP-220, CP-300, CP-330, i560, i860, i900D, i960, i9100, i9900	$99–$499
Epson (www.epson.com)	Stylus Photo R200, Stylus Photo R300M, Stylus Photo 1280, Stylus Photo R800, Stylus Photo 2200, PictureMate	$99–$699
Hewlett-Packard (www.hp.com)	Photosmart 7260, Photosmart 7660, Photosmart 145, Photosmart 245, Photosmart 7760, Photosmart 7960	$99–$299
Olympus (www.olympus.com)	P-10, P-400, P-440	$199–$499
Sony (www.sony.com)	DPP-EX50	$179

TABLE 7-1 Photo Printer Manufacturers and Available Models

For pictures taken with a VGA-quality camera phone (0.3 megapixels), your best results will come from pictures printed out at about 2 × 3 inches, which is certainly good enough for displaying pictures of children on your refrigerator door.

I find it's best to print pictures directly from an image editor, such as Photoshop Elements. The first step is to change the image size. Under Image | Resize, uncheck the Resample Image box to maintain the image's pixel dimensions, then change the width to 3 inches. The height of the picture will automatically adjust to maintain the original proportions and the resolution will automatically increase (see Figure 7-3).

Now that the image has been resized for printing, you're ready to create a print.

1. Click File | Print Preview.

2. Click the Page Setup button, then click the Printer button. If you have more than one printer installed, choose the appropriate one from the drop-down menu, then click Properties.

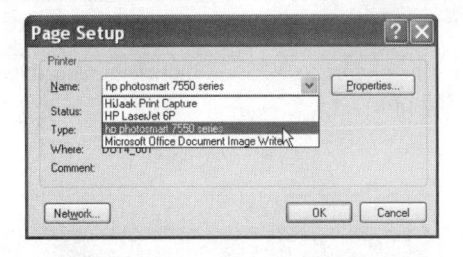

3. Click the Layout tab, then choose a paper size from the drop-down menu, as shown in Figure 7-4.

4. Click OK in each dialog box until you return to the Print Preview dialog.

Now you can see exactly how the image will look when printed. In Figure 7-5, it's a 2.25 × 3-inch image printed on a 4 × 6 sheet of photo paper. When you're all set, click the Print button.

When I attempted to print the same picture at its original size (4.958 × 6.583 inches), I noticed more white dots in the blue of the sky and jagged edges in the details of the buildings. That's because at full size, the resolution was only 72 ppi, so there weren't enough pixels to fill in certain spaces. With the smaller print size, the resolution was 178.5 ppi, and the increased pixel density resulted in a sharper image.

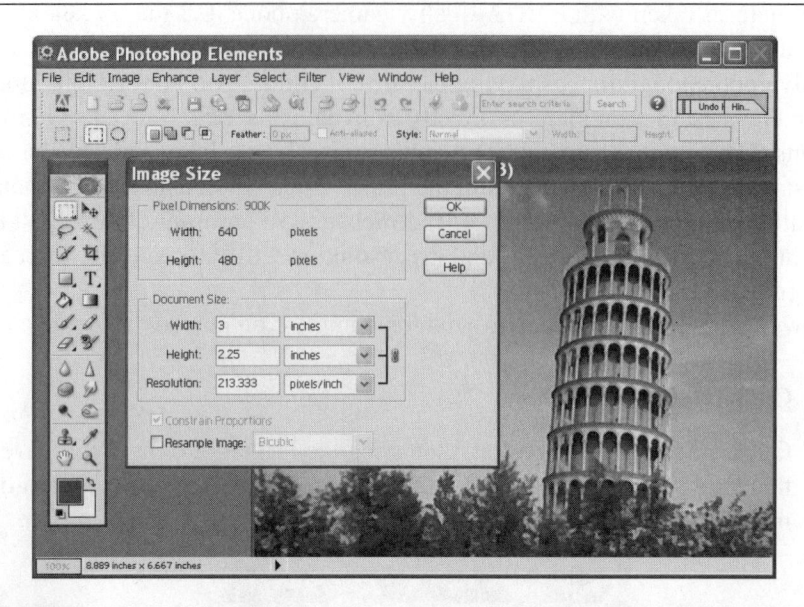

FIGURE 7-3 Resizing this picture to 2.25 × 3 inches increased the resolution from 72 ppi to 213.333 ppi.

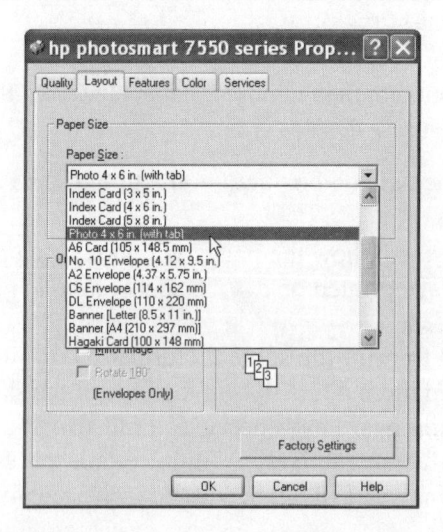

FIGURE 7-4 Choose the correct paper size from Photoshop Elements' Page Setup option.

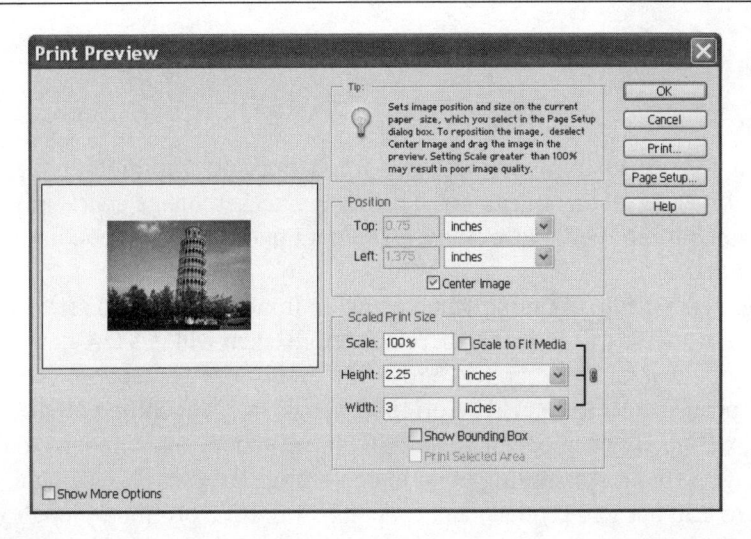

FIGURE 7-5 An image editor's Print Preview feature displays how your image will look after resizing.

I took that picture with a VGA camera (the Toshiba VM4050). If you have a camera phone with an image sensor of 1 megapixel or more, you should be able to make decent 4 × 6 prints.

TIP *You'll get better results from pictures taken in daylight than in dark environments, which are more prone to graininess and other anomalies.*

Beware of Running Costs

One thing you'll notice about inkjet photo printers is the attractive purchase price. You can get a feature-rich, name-brand model for less than $300 from your local consumer electronics retailer. But the cost of maintaining an inkjet can get pricey.

It's preferable to purchase an inkjet that uses separate cartridges for black, color, and photo ink, since you can replace them as needed if one color runs out before the other (unless you also use your photo printer for lots of text documents or black-and-white photos, the black cartridge tends to last longer). But the lifespan of inkjet cartridges is much shorter than laser printer toner.

The HP Photosmart 7000 series of photo printers uses separate black, photo, and color cartridges, with an average yield of 450, 400, and 125 pages, respectively. It costs about $80 to replace all three cartridges.

How to ... Determine the Print Size

It's easy to experiment with print sizes when working with high-quality photos from a 4 megapixel digital camera. The more pixels an image contains, the more room you have to work with. But with camera phone images, you have to know your limits.

The general rule of thumb when using an inkjet printer is to set the image's print size between 150 and 300 ppi. For a picture taken with a VGA-quality camera phone (one that takes pictures at 640 × 480 pixels, or 0.3 megapixels), say you set the print size to 150 ppi. The original image size, depending on the camera phone, will likely be between 72 and 96 ppi, which means you need to resize the image without resampling in an image-editing program. Resizing a VGA image to 150 ppi will produce an acceptable 4.3 × 3.2 printout, though you'll still notice that colors and textures appear flat on close inspection. For better results, resizing the photo to 200 ppi will produce a better-looking but smaller 3.2 × 2.4 printout.

If you're working with pictures from a camera phone with a sensor that supports 1 megapixel or slightly better, you can safely resize an image to 200 ppi and produce a decent 4 × 6 printout.

Then there's the issue of paper. You'll be printing your pictures on photo paper, which is more expensive than standard inkjet paper (I do recommend that you print drafts on standard inkjet paper, however). Expect to pay between $30 and $35 for a 100-pack of 4 × 6 photo paper (see Chapter 9 for printing your pictures on specialty paper).

You can see why it's important to make sure your images are edited and sized properly before printing.

> **NOTE** *Printer manufacturers fine-tune their photo paper to work well with their printer inks, so you may achieve the best results by using the same brand of paper as your printer.*

Online Print Services

If you don't have a color inkjet printer and you don't think you'll be printing enough pictures to justify the expense of buying and maintaining one, you can order professionally made prints just as you do with film. In fact, the two biggest film companies, Kodak and Fujifilm, offer online printing services specifically for camera phone users. Not only will you save yourself trouble, but you'll get a better-quality print than you would with a consumer-level inkjet printer.

Kodak Mobile/Ofoto

This service is available to Kodak Mobile and Ofoto members. After signing up, you upload pictures with your AT&T Wireless camera phone. To upload pictures already stored on your computer, click the Add Photos link, then the Choose Photos button, browse your hard drive for the pictures you want, click Add, then click Upload.

When you're ready to make an order, click the Buy Prints tab on the top of the screen, select the album containing the pictures you wish to print, click the Buy Prints check box next to the appropriate thumbnails, then press Next. When you select a photo for prints, a green plus sign indicates that it's the recommended size for the image, while a red minus sign means the resolution of the image may not produce a quality print in the specified size (see Figure 7-6).

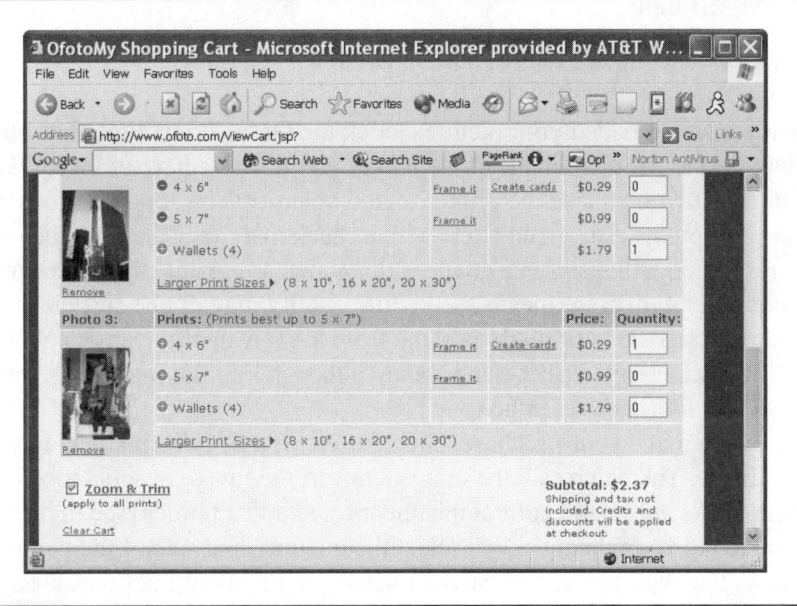

FIGURE 7-6   Ofoto's print ordering site lets you know if a photo's resolution is insufficient for a particular print size.

Ofoto includes a Zoom & Trim feature to help your photos fit the specified paper size. You can choose to skip this feature by unchecking the Zoom & Trim check box on the print order page. If you took a picture with a megapixel-plus camera phone and would like to receive a 4 × 6 print, you can order a frame to come with your picture (prices range from $10 to $28).

Fujifilm.net

You can join and upload pictures to Fujifilm.net for free. It's a good deal when you want to make prints, but if you're looking for long-term storage, this site becomes rather pricey. Your free uploaded pictures remain on the site for 30 days. If you wish to keep them longer, you'll have to purchase Album Space. The first 100 spaces cost $20 for one year. Every 25 spaces after that costs $1.25 per three-month period. You can store up to 100 new uploads at once.

After clicking the Upload Pictures button:

1. Click Select Files, then browse through the folders on your hard drive to find the pictures you want. Individual files cannot be larger than 6MB (this isn't an issue with camera phone images), while multiple uploads carry a 90MB limit.

2. Click the Upload Pictures button, as shown in Figure 7-7.

Once you've uploaded your pictures, click the Order Prints link, then click the check box next to the thumbnails of the photos you'd like to have printed, then click Continue. Next, you choose the print size and quantity. You'll notice icons next to the print size options. The green circle with a check mark indicates that the selected photo's resolution will result in a quality print at that size, while the yellow triangle with the exclamation point means the picture quality may not be sufficient at the specified print size. If your pictures came from a VGA-quality camera phone, your best bet is the set of eight wallet-sized photos, although Fujifilm may say the resolution isn't sufficient for that size, either.

Before you make your purchase, click the Preview & Edit link next to the print size you desire. You can rotate the image, convert the image to sepia tone or black and white, make automatic color adjustments, and add a border (see Figure 7-8).

After saving your changes, you select the quantity and size of the pictures you want, then click Add to Cart. Then you choose your shipping options, enter your address and billing information, and wait for your pictures to be delivered.

CHAPTER 7: Printing Your Photos   **169**

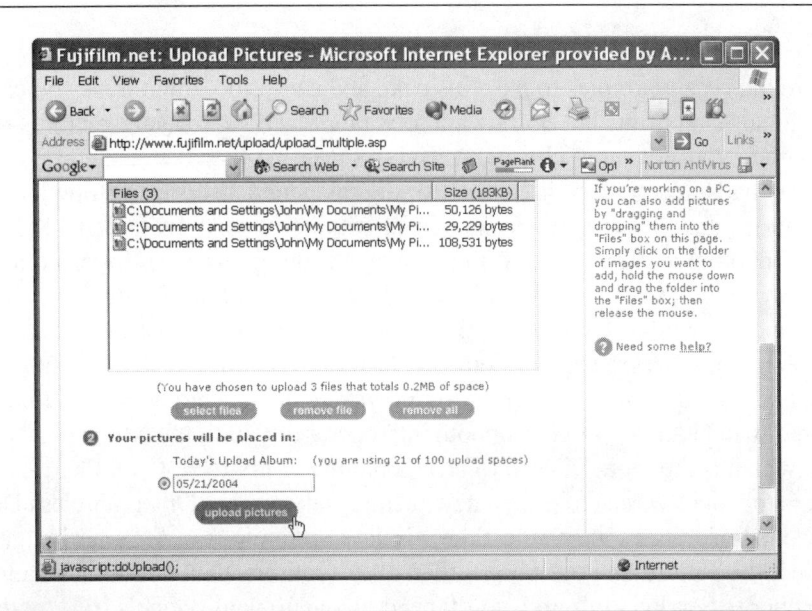

FIGURE 7-7 Upload pictures from your PC to Fujifilm.net, where you can store them free for 30 days.

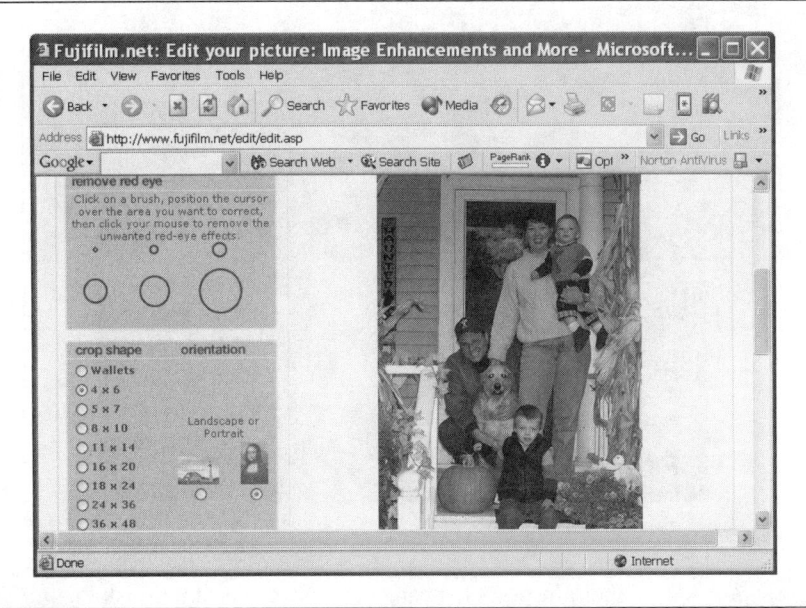

FIGURE 7-8 Fujifilm's photo site lets you make last-minute adjustments to your pictures before placing an order.

Using In-Store Kiosks

If you're the type who likes to have his cake and eat it, too—that is, if you crave professional-level prints but don't want to wait a few days for your pictures to arrive—then you'll want to check out Kodak's printing kiosks.

Kodak had already made life easier for digital camera users by putting its Picture Maker do-it-yourself printing kiosks in such retail outlets as Walgreens, K-Mart, and local photography stores. Now the company is doing the same for camera phone users with a mobile version of its Picture Maker, as shown in Figure 7-9.

The mobile Kodak Picture Maker accepts all varieties of memory cards—Multimedia Card, Secure Digital, CompactFlash, and Memory Stick—but the coolest feature is its ability to transfer photos to the system via infrared or Bluetooth. Kodak partnered with Nokia to provide smooth interoperability with the Nokia 3650 camera phone, which is the model I used to print a picture at my local CVS Pharmacy.

Press the touch screen to print a new picture, select From Other Wireless Device from the list of sources, then select the wireless option to transfer your images.

Select the picture on your phone, then click Options, then Send via Bluetooth (if you choose Send via Infrared, you'll need to line up your phone's IrDA port with the Picture Station's port, located on the right side of the device).

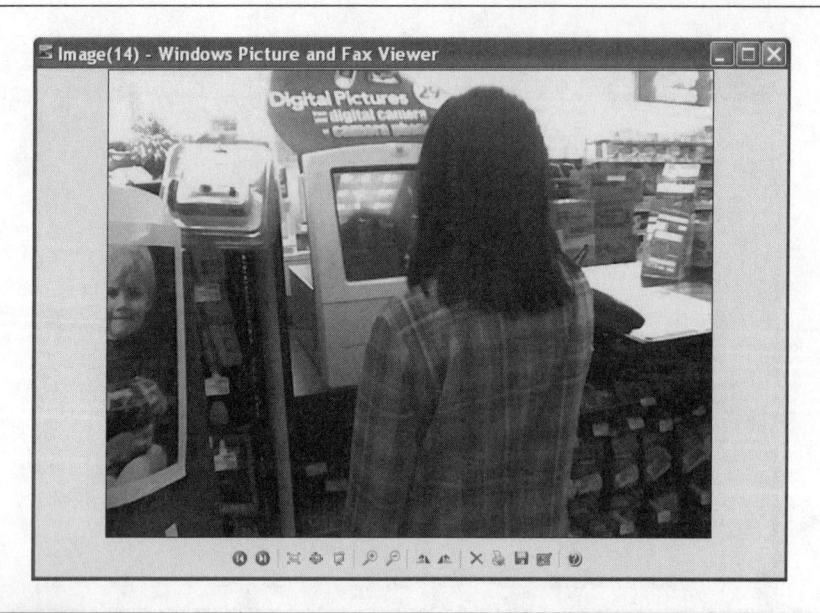

FIGURE 7-9   A customer processes her camera phone prints at a Kodak Picture Maker kiosk.

After your phone recognizes the Picture Station, click Select to link the device.

In about three seconds, the picture you selected will appear on the Picture Station. From there you can perform basic editing chores, such as crop, rotate, and lighten or darken. After saving the changes, select the print size you want and the quantity. The picture station will inform you whether the picture resolution matches the print size you request. After informing me that a 4 × 6 print of the picture I selected wouldn't provide the desired results, I chose a 3.5 × 5-inch print, which was the smallest size available (some kiosks offer 2 × 3-inch prints).

To complete the order, the Picture Station asks for your last name and phone number, then a password (a CVS employee had to enter this). Once your order is complete, that's a good time to shop around and stock up on dental floss and allergy medicine, because it takes between five and ten minutes to process the picture. The result was decent. When viewing the picture up close, I could see all the flaws, such as color distortions and pixelization, but with a casual look the print was perfectly acceptable for display. Each print costs 29 cents.

Not to be outdone, Fujifilm has added camera phone capabilities to its Aladdin Digital Photo Center kiosks (see Figure 7-10), which are located in more than 10,000 retail outlets across the U.S. The new Aladdin kiosks feature integrated Bluetooth support.

FIGURE 7-10 Fujifilm now offers Bluetooth connectivity for camera phone users in its Aladdin Digital Photo Center kiosks.

Did you know?

New and Emerging Printing Technologies

You don't need Nostradamus-like powers to figure out that camera phones are rapidly becoming the next ubiquitous consumer device. Computer printer makers are certainly aware of the untapped potential of that market. With the image quality from camera phones improving, demand for printing pictures are expected to increase substantially.

Market research firm InfoTrends expects camera phone users to print more than 5 billion images in 2004, and it expects that number to reach 37.2 billion by 2008. Depending on whom you ask, forecasts call for 55 percent to 85 percent of all handsets to feature an integrated camera by 2008.

With that in mind, computer printer giants Canon, Epson, and Hewlett-Packard formed the Mobile Imaging and Printing Consortium (MIPC) to promote standards for printing images taken with camera phones. Leading cell phone makers Nokia, Samsung, and Siemens are members, as well. Among the technologies that will constitute the connectivity platforms are Bluetooth and PictBridge, a standard created by the Camera & Imaging Products Association that enables direct connections between digital cameras and printers. Camera phones that support PictBridge will be able to work seamlessly with such printers, as well. The group plans to make guidelines available by the end of 2004.

Also, HP developed a Mobile Printing Application for the Nokia 3650, 6600, and 7650 camera phones. With the software installed on the phone, you can print directly to HP's Deskjet 450 mobile printer. After selecting Print from the phone's menu, select an image from the gallery, click Print, choose a layout and size, then click Print. The phone connects wirelessly with the printer via Bluetooth. For more information, visit www.hp.com. To download the application, visit www.nokia.com.

Moving On

Printing your pictures gives you that sense of long-lasting gratification, the knowledge that your pictures actually *exist* in the real world. But that's hardly the final step in working with camera phone photos. Not by a long shot. The next chapter details the hottest trend among camera phone users—the moblog.

Chapter 8

Creating a Moblog

How to...

- Send pictures to a moblog
- Create a moblog
- Control community commentary

It's time to get a little more adventurous. Why limit the sharing of your pictures to family and friends when you can show off your skills to the entire world? This chapter delves into the latest online trend, the moblog, which was designed with camera phone users in mind.

What's a Moblog?

Moblog. It sounds like a creature from *Land of the Lost*, or something much worse. In fact, it's a combination of *mobile* and *blog*. Web logs, or blogs, are diary-type websites that have become popular in the journalism and political realms (political journalist Andrew Sullivan's blog, www.andrewsullivan.com, is a perfect example). Blog software requires little or no technical expertise on the user's part, which is why blogs are usually updated daily and presented in chronological order, beginning with the most recent addition. The mobile twist comes in when you add camera phone pictures to the mix.

Moblogs allow people to take pictures anywhere, anytime, and have them appear on a website within minutes. Visitors to the site can (and usually will) comment on the pictures. Some moblogs, like Mobog.com, will only accept pictures that come from a cell phone e-mail address. Others, such as Textamerica.com (see Figure 8-1), aren't restricted to camera phone images. To be involved in the true spirit of moblogging, however, you should submit only pictures taken with a camera phone, even if they've already been downloaded to your PC.

Generally speaking, you have to work within the format of the moblog site, which means your options for customizing the look of your particular moblog site are limited. Textamerica provides a variety of themes and layouts (see Figure 8-2) but warns that any additional customization "should not be attempted if you aren't highly skilled at writing your own website source [code]."

Individual vs. Community

Generally speaking, there are two types of moblogs: individual and community. Individual moblogs are sites on which one person posts their own images. These

CHAPTER 8: Creating a Moblog 175

FIGURE 8-1　Sites such as Textamerica create virtual communities for camera phone users.

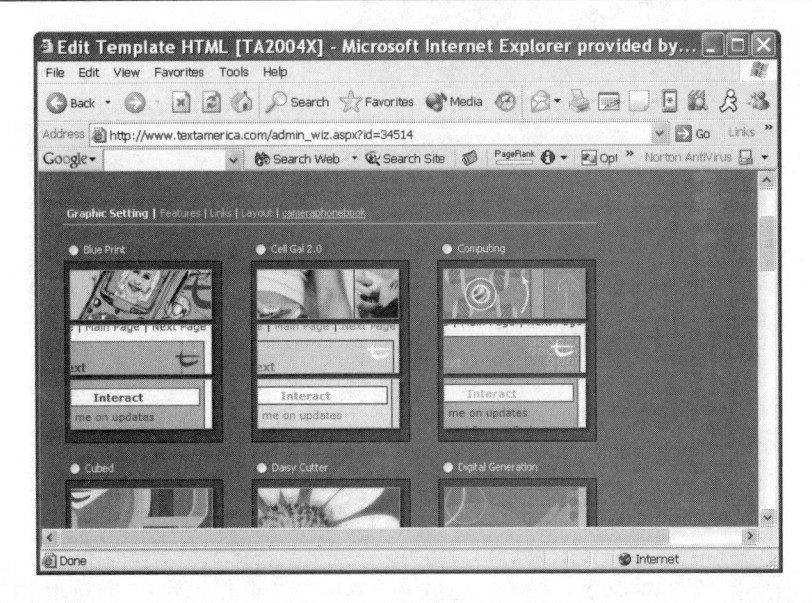

FIGURE 8-2　Textamerica provides a variety of templates for creating your moblog.

sites are password protected, so only the registered, authorized user has access to uploading images.

Community moblogs, on the other hand, are sites in which anyone can post a picture. Community sites typically involve a theme, such as Los Angeles, cute couples, or celebrities (see Figure 8-3). It's the community moblog that turns camera phone aficionados from voyeurs to participants, or at least participant-voyeurs.

Next, I'll take a look at three of the top moblog sites, each of which delivers its own twist on the moblogging concept.

NOTE *Although these sites cater to camera phone users, only Textamerica is optimized for viewing on your phone's web browser. Otherwise, these moblogs are best enjoyed on a PC.*

Buzznet.com

Buzznet allows users to post up to 10 images per day and up to 200 images per month. Users can contribute to theme-oriented communities, such as pictures of New York City, pets, and, of course, hot girls and hot guys.

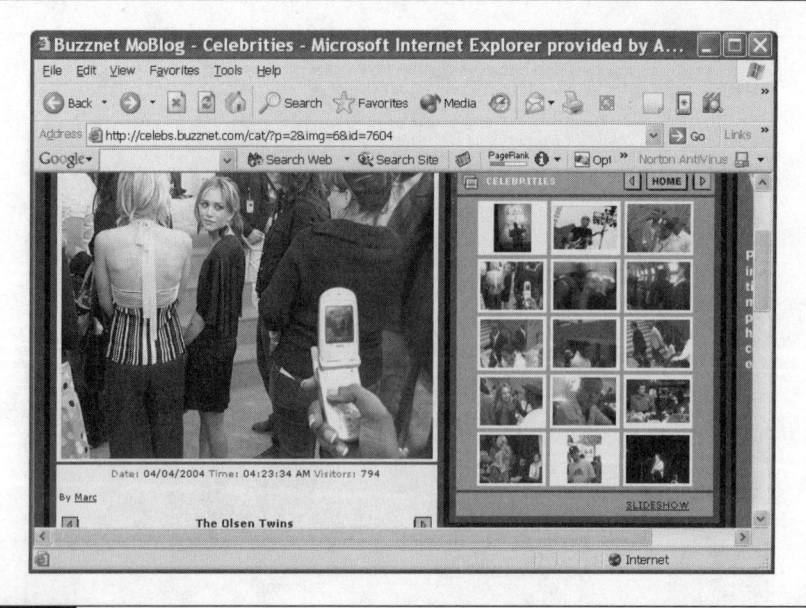

FIGURE 8-3 Community sites allow you to submit pictures based on a common theme, such as Buzznet's celebrity moblog.

CHAPTER 8: Creating a Moblog 177

> **NOTE** *At press time, Buzznet was developing premium services. Although the company planned to maintain some free services, it was unclear how many posts would be allowed without charge.*

With Buzznet, you click a thumbnail to view the picture in the larger window on the left. You can also choose to view all of the images in a particular page as a slideshow (see Figure 8-4).

Below the main image window is a box where Buzznet members can send a comment based on the selected picture. You enter your name, e-mail address, then type your message (maximum 1,000 characters). You also have the option to send a private message that only the moblog owner will be able to view.

> **NOTE** *If you've created your own moblog, you have the option of turning off the messaging feature.*

When submitting a picture, be sure it's saved as a JPEG file and that the filename includes the .JPG extension. Buzznet resizes all photos to a maximum of 400 × 400 pixels, so those 640 × 480 camera phone images will be smaller, but they'll also

FIGURE 8-4 Buzznet features a slideshow view for all of its moblogs.

look a little better on a computer screen. Any text included in the subject heading or body of an e-mail message sent from a PC, or any text included in a message sent from a camera phone, will appear as the caption of the photo on Buzznet. The site doesn't specify a character limit for these captions, but it's best to keep your messages as short as possible.

> **TIP** *If your picture is smaller than 400 × 400, you can tell Buzznet not to resize the image to the larger size. In the Preferences screen of your account, under Resize Images, select No.*

> **CAUTION** *Buzznet does not support audio tags, so if you send a picture directly from a camera phone that includes a voice memo, you won't be able to listen to it on the site.*

To create your own site on Buzznet, you need to register (click the Sign-Up button at the top of the screen). The username you select will become the name of your site. If you choose the user name "cameraphone," for example, your site will be cameraphone.buzznet.com. The keyword you select will become part of the e-mail address you send pictures to post to the site. So if the keyword is "book," you would send images via e-mail to cameraphone.book@buzznet.com, either from a computer or a camera phone.

> **TIP** *If you plan on sending images directly from your camera phone, try to keep the name of your moblog as short as possible. Typing long addresses on numeric keypads becomes tedious in a hurry.*

> **TIP** *Store your new Buzznet address as a contact in your phone book before you start snapping and sending pictures.*

As the owner of the site, you can also post images via the online form. Click the Browse button to find the picture you wish to post from your computer's hard drive. Include a title and body text if you wish, then click Save (see Figure 8-5). The image is immediately posted to your site.

Buzznet allows you to organize your photos into separate galleries. You can, for example, create a Vacation gallery, and those pictures will be just a click away from your main page. You can post to a specific gallery from your camera phone by using the following e-mail format: username.keyword.gallery name@buzznet.com. Be sure not to include any spaces when addressing your e-mail. To e-mail pictures

FIGURE 8-5 Buzznet lets site owners post images stored on a computer.

to the Vacation gallery of the hypothetical camera phone site, for example, the address would be cameraphone.book.vacation@buzznet.com.

> **NOTE** *When you place pictures in a gallery, they no longer appear on your main page's thumbnail index. When you delete a gallery, however, Buzznet returns the pictures to your main index page.*

If you want to allow friends or family to contribute photos to your moblog, you can create a Public Keyword for your gallery. On your site's home page, click the Edit link next to My Galleries, then enter a public keyword (see Figure 8-6). When you give others the public keyword, they can upload pictures by e-mailing them to username.public keyword.gallery name@buzznet.com. Conversely, you can make your gallery as private as you wish. After you type in a password, users attempting to view that page will need to enter the password.

Buzznet's User Buzz page, which you access by clicking the tab at the top of the screen, displays the day's most commented post, the most recent photos, and links to the three most popular sites of the month (see Figure 8-7). You can search for a particular site by username, country, city, state, or by most active.

Mobog.com

Unlike the other sites discussed in this chapter, Mobog.com is a pure camera phone site. Mobog will not accept photos e-mailed from a standard e-mail account.

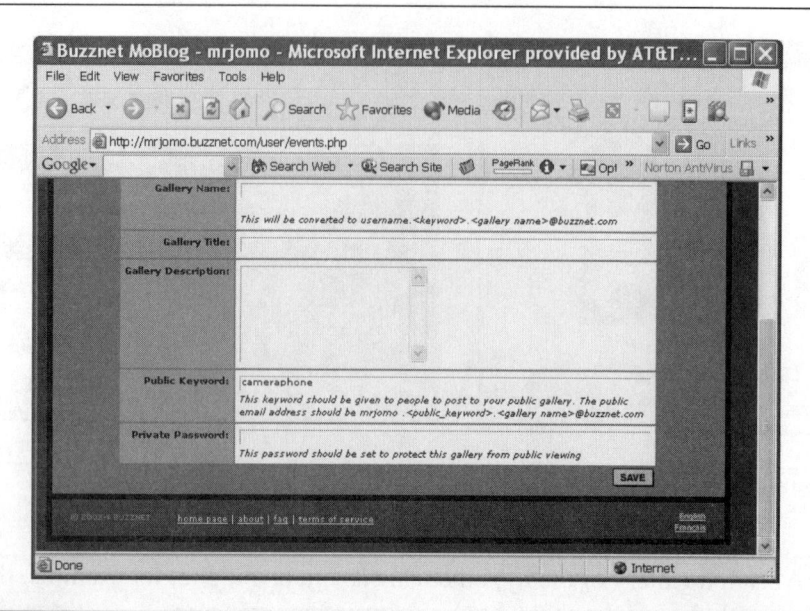

FIGURE 8-6 Create a public keyword on Buzznet to give your friends uploading privileges to your moblog.

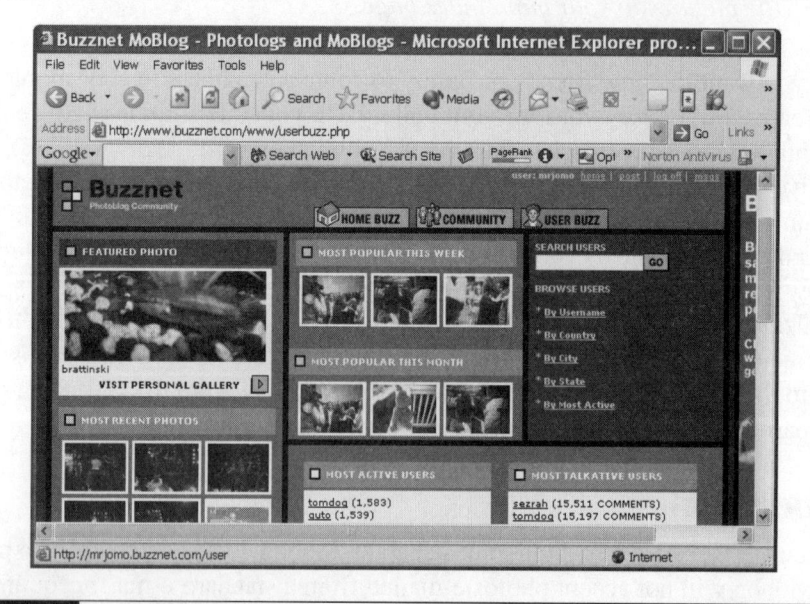

FIGURE 8-7 Buzznet's community features include links to the month's most popular sites on the User Buzz page.

> **TIP** *If you send a picture from your phone and it doesn't show up on the site within a few minutes, it may be because the site doesn't yet support your carrier. Send the photo to test@mobog.com and the site will add the carrier to its supported list.*

When you send a picture, the text you include in the subject line appears as the caption on Mobog. You can send pictures anonymously or register with a site as a member, and membership does have its privileges. When you register with Mobog, the site immediately delivers visitor comments to your cell phone. You can then reply to those messages from your cell phone.

> **NOTE** *Most phones carry a 128-character limit to text messages.*

> **CAUTION** *Sending and receiving several text messages can get very expensive. Unless you have a great data plan or deep pockets, you may not want to use this feature. Remember, you can always respond to comments from your PC.*

You send pictures to Mobog directly from your camera phone by sending the file as an e-mail message to pics@mobog.com. The first time you send a picture, you'll receive an activation password on your phone. When you visit the site on your PC, click Login, then enter the password to create your own moblog. With your personal page, you'll have the ability to rotate and delete pictures, as well as delete comments posted to your page. However, you don't have to accept the password to continue uploading pictures to the site. If you choose not to accept the password, your photos will appear on the site as submitted from Unknown.

> **TIP** *If you see your picture on the site but don't receive your password, click the Login/Register link at the top of the page, then click the link below the Activation password box that reads "Posted a pic but never received your activation password." From there, you enter your picture's web address and your phone's e-mail address. You'll automatically receive the activation password on the screen.*

If you decide to create your own page, you can make it password protected so that only users with the password can view your moblog. You can also turn off the commenting feature in the Preferences menu.

Unlike Buzznet, Mobog doesn't divide sites into themes or create individual blogs. Rather, each picture is added to the main page as it comes in (see Figure 8-8). When you click a photo submitted by a member, you'll see a page with a larger version of the picture, as well as thumbnails of the member's most recent pictures. You can click the View All link to see all of that member's submissions.

The site includes a link to the day's most frequently updated moblogs. Mobog features censored and uncensored viewing modes. The censored mode prevents pictures containing "adult content" (to say the least) from appearing on the site, although some less-than-family-friendly images occasionally slip through the cracks.

Textamerica.com

Textamerica is perhaps the most popular moblog site. Like Buzznet, Textamerica lets you create community and individual sites (see Figure 8-9). You can upload pictures from a PC as well as from your camera phone, although the site limits individual images to 700KB or less. You can create as many sites as you like with

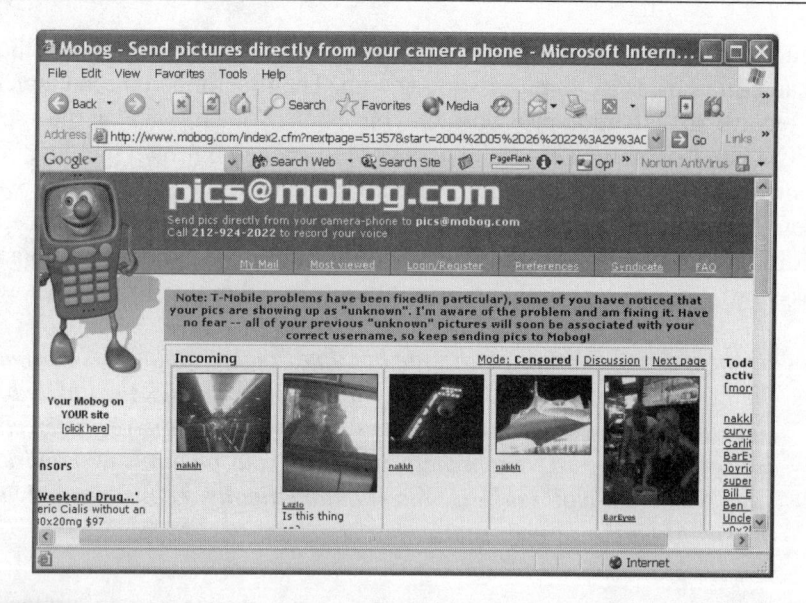

FIGURE 8-8 Instead of organizing sites into themes or offering individual blogs, Mobog displays pictures submitted to the site chronologically.

CHAPTER 8: Creating a Moblog 183

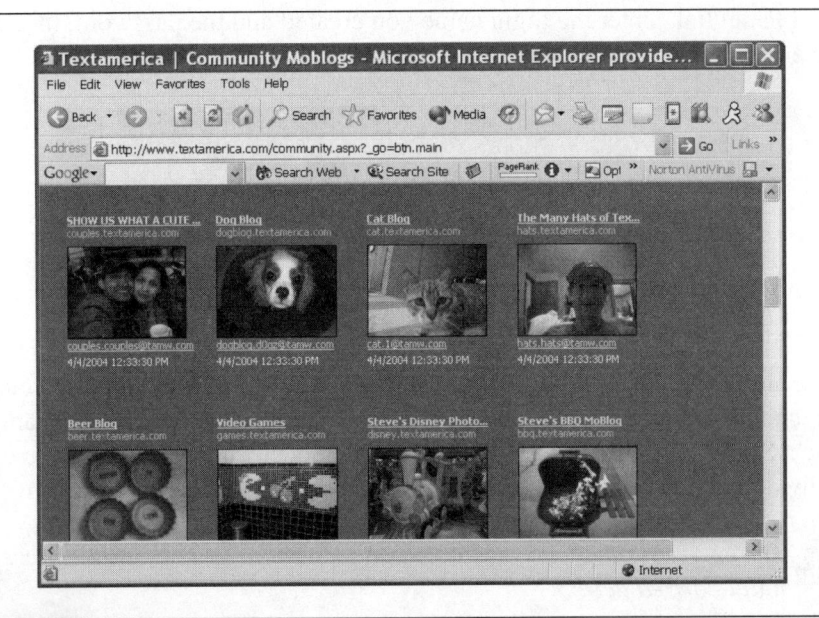

FIGURE 8-9 With Textamerica's network of community sites, you submit pictures by clicking the e-mail link below the thumbnail.

as many images as you wish on each site. Unlike Mobog, Textamerica doesn't accept pornographic images or pictures of any kind of nudity (although some contributions are a bit risqué, as a stroll through cleavage.textamerica.com makes clear).

CAUTION *If you send a picture to Textamerica with a voice memo attached, the site will not receive the picture. Worse, you won't get a notification on your cell phone to tell you that the message hasn't been received. This is unlike Buzznet, which will post the picture without the audio clip.*

NOTE *Textamerica also accepts video clips created on camcorder phones. You submit video files the same way you send pictures. I'll explain this feature in more detail in Chapter 11.*

When you register at Textamerica, you'll get a temporary password, which you should immediately change after you log in for the first time. To log in, click the

184 How to Do Everything with Your Camera Phone

Control Panel link, enter the login name you created and the password, then click Change Password from the My Account menu.

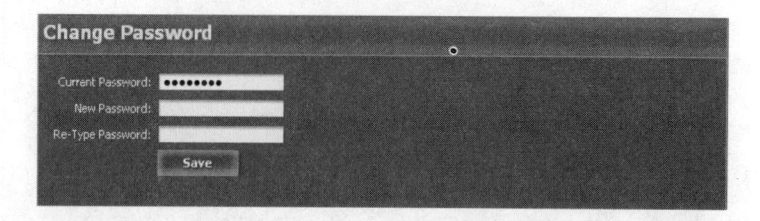

Once that's taken care of, click the Create Moblog icon in the upper right area of the main control panel to begin building your site. From there, you give your site a title, choose a domain name (cameraphonebook.textamerica.com, for example), choose a Secret Word, select your camera phone model, choose a standard to create an individual site, then enter a brief description of your site (see Figure 8-10).

> **NOTE**
> *The Secret Word allows you to upload pictures to your site while preventing unauthorized access.*

Next, click the Create button and your site is instantly generated, as shown in Figure 8-11.

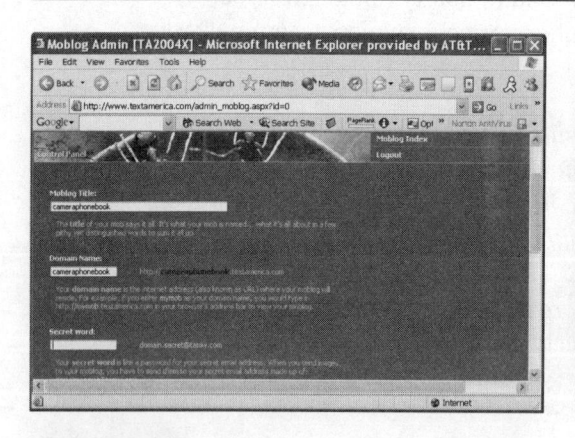

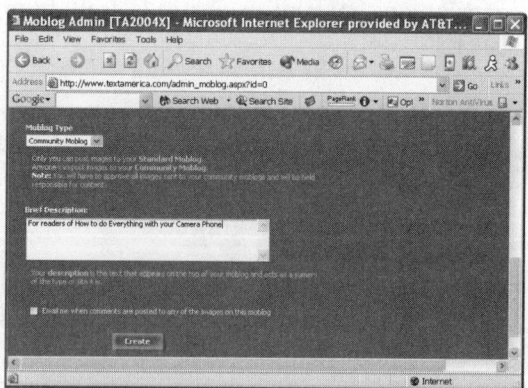

FIGURE 8-10 Enter your moblog name, domain, and description in Textamerica's Control Panel.

CHAPTER 8: Creating a Moblog 185

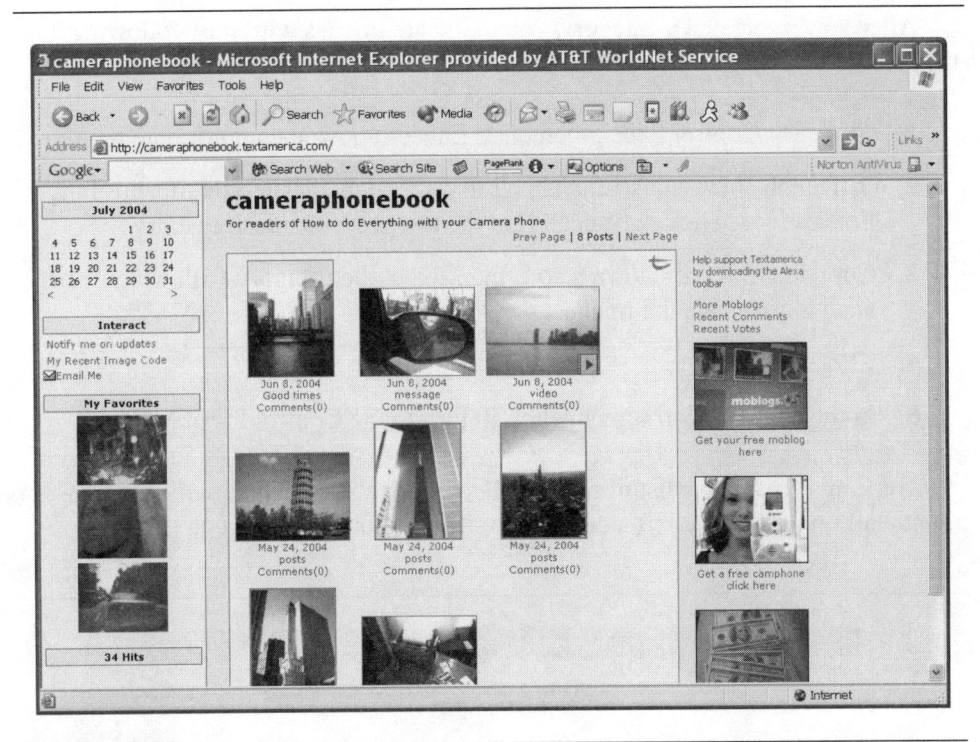

FIGURE 8-11 After clicking the Create button, Textamerica immediately posts your site to the web.

Textamerica lets you place similarly themed pictures into categories. Pictures of all your friends can go in the Friends category, for example. To create a category:

1. Click My Control Panel, then click Categories above the associated moblog.

2. In the Create a Category text box, type the category name, then click Create.

TIP *Although you can create as many categories as you want, it's best to keep them to a manageable number, since they take up space on your site's home page.*

After you've created a category, you associate images with it by following these steps:

1. Click My Control Panel, then click Entries above the appropriate moblog.
2. In Thumb View, click Edit This Entry above the desired thumbnail. In List Entries view, click Advanced Edit next to get to the desired entry.
3. Click the Category down arrow, then select the category with which you wish to associate the image.
4. Click Update.
5. In the confirmation screen, click Return to the Control Panel Main.

You can also create a list of favorite Textamerica sites, which will appear as thumbnail images on the left side of your site, as shown in Figure 8-12.

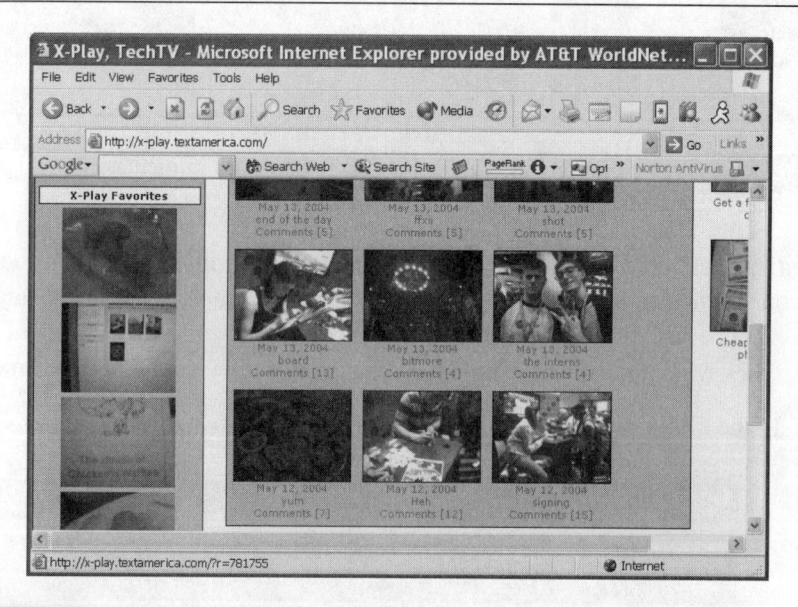

FIGURE 8-12 Your favorite sites appear as thumbnail images on the left side of your moblog.

CHAPTER 8: Creating a Moblog 187

To create a Favorites list:

1. In My Control Panel, point to Favorites, then click View My Favorites.
2. Under My Favorites, click Create a New List.
3. In Favorites List Name, type the new name.
4. In the Add a Favorite field, enter the website address of the site you wish to display. This must be a Textamerica site (see Figure 8-13).
5. To adjust the thumbnail dimensions, type the new values in the Thumbnail Height and Thumbnail Width boxes.
6. Click Save.
7. Choose View Moblogs on this list to add the moblog to the list of Favorites.

If you're wondering whether your site is attracting an audience, Textamerica lets you check how many visitors your site has received. In your Control Panel, click the Web Traffic link and you'll see a summary of your moblog visitors (see Figure 8-14). Not only will you see the total number of visitors, but you'll also get

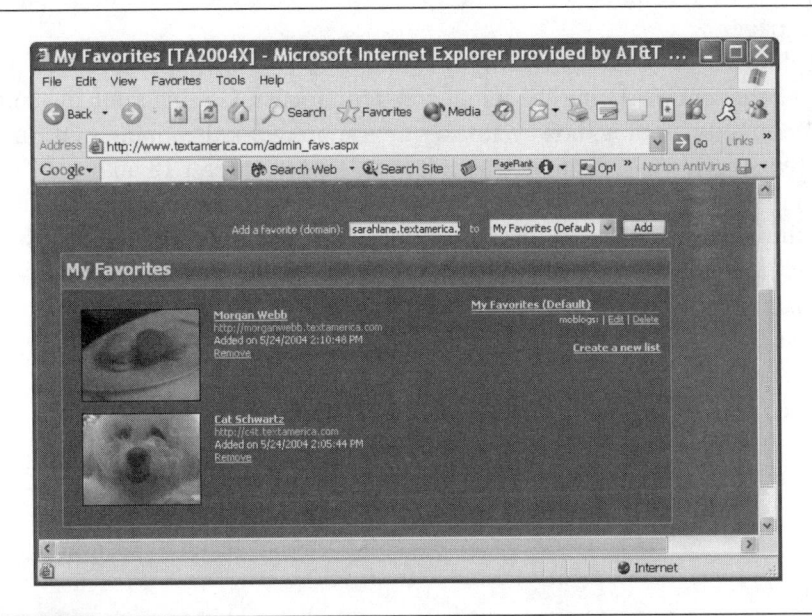

FIGURE 8-13   Add your favorite Textamerica sites to your moblog.

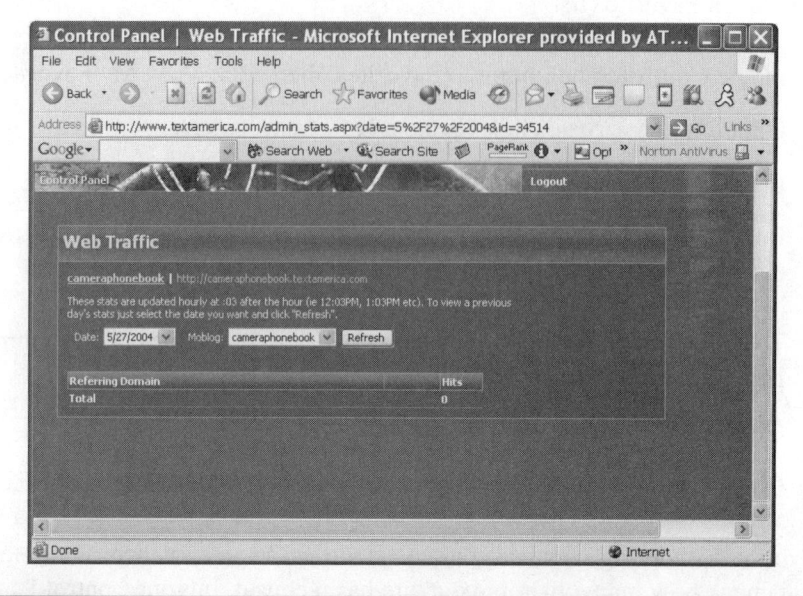

FIGURE 8-14 Check how much traffic your site is receiving on the Textamerica Control Panel. This site, unfortunately, isn't doing too well.

a tally of the referring domains—that is, which site the user is coming from to link to your page.

Technically speaking, creating a community site is simply a matter of selecting that option during the initial creation process. Getting your site certified as a community moblog, however, takes a bit more work than it does on Buzznet. With Textamerica, after you pick a topic, you'll need at least 18 authentic images related to the topic already posted. You'll also have to create community support by getting other members to link to your page on their sites and getting a sufficient number of people to send photos. After an editorial review, the site will be included in Textamerica's directory if deemed appropriate.

To suggest a community moblog:

1. Click the Community Moblogs link on the home page.
2. Click the Suggest a Community Mob link.
3. Type a suggested URL, as shown in Figure 8-15.

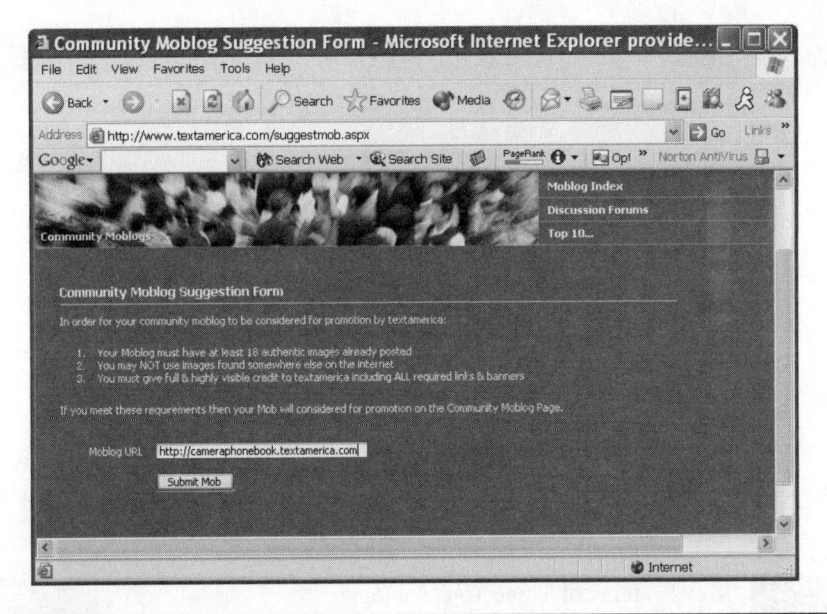

FIGURE 8-15 After meeting certain criteria, you can apply your site for Textamerica community status.

If you simply want to send a picture to a community site, e-mail the file to the address given on the site's page. To send a picture to the Show Your iPod moblog (ipods.textamerica.com), send an e-mail with the picture attachment to ipods.apple@tamw.com.

Textamerica features Editor's Pick sites. You'll want to keep your pictures centered around a particular theme and include titles and descriptions with the photos. Textamerica says Editor's Picks, which are featured on the site's home page, can get more than 10 times the normal exposure they normally would in the site index, a huge list of every registered Textamerica site.

Moblogs at a Glance

As you've undoubtedly figured out by now, each of these moblogs bring their own unique spin to the concept. Table 8-1 summarizes the differences among the site discussed. Of course, there's nothing stopping you from creating your own moblog on each site.

Site	URL	Maximum Image Size	Upload Limit	Upload From PC	Member Directory	Upload Video Clips	Special Features
Buzznet	www.buzznet.com	400 × 400 pixels	10 per day/ 200 per month	Yes	Yes	No	Public Keyword allows others to upload pictures to your site
Mobog	www.mobog.com	None specified, but only accepts camera phone images	None	No	No	No	Accepts anonymous posts to main site
Textamerica	www.textamerica.com	700KB (1MB for video clips)	None	Yes	Yes	Yes	Can view site traffic statistics

TABLE 8-1 Key Features of Three Top Moblogs

Upload to Community Moblogs

You see all of the great moblogs out there and you want to be part of the action. So how do you go about joining the community? Sending your pictures to a moblog is simply a matter of e-mailing your pictures, either from your camera phone or your PC (if the site allows you to do so).

Voices from the Community — For Her Fans

I first saw moblogging in action when (G4techTV anchor) Leo Laporte created one on the show. I knew the technology existed, but once I actually saw the concept executed I was impressed. The fact that it was free made me know I had to have one immediately (c4t.textamerica.com).

I have a website (www.catschwartz.com) that I don't update frequently, and moblogging is an easy way to add new content. I think it's fun for the fans to check out what's going on with me and get to know my personality outside of just being on TV. It's voyeurism at its finest. It's voyeuristic, but I have control over it, so I don't have to let them see everything, as shown here:

CHAPTER 8: Creating a Moblog

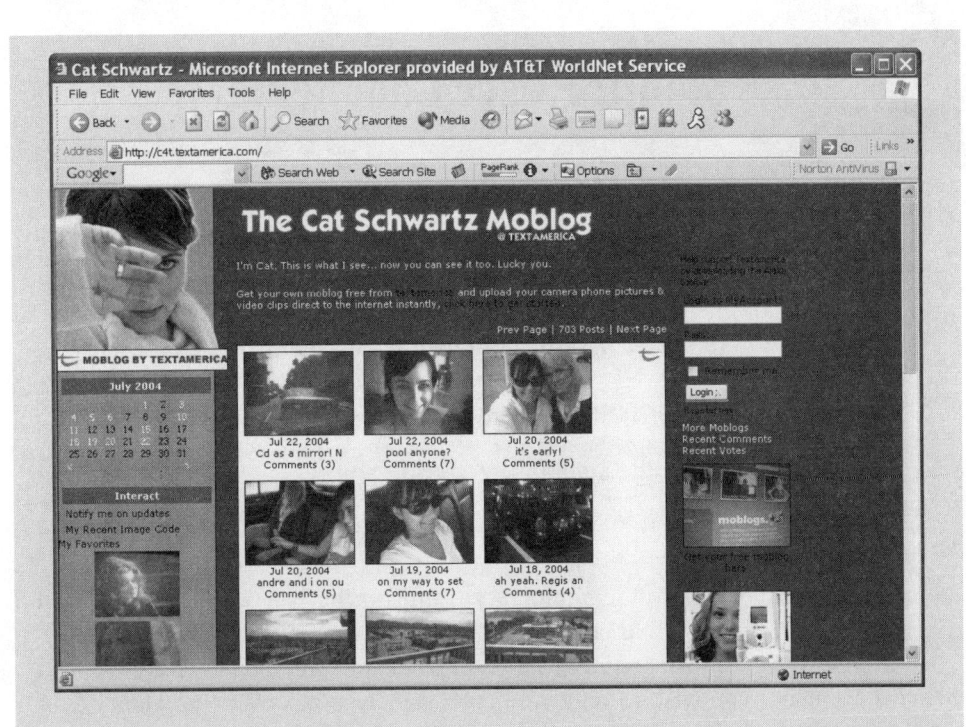

Most people who visit the site are nice, but some people are really rude and obnoxious. Anytime you're putting yourself out in the public eye, you're going to get all kinds of reactions, and you have to be ready for it. Anyone that creates a moblog is going to get a mixture of opinions. It's a forum where you have to let people express their views.

I use a Nokia 3650. In good light situations, it takes pictures that I can post on my website that are pretty decent. I'm waiting for a smaller candy bar–type phone to come out from Nokia.

One concept that I think is going to grow as moblogging becomes more popular is the ability to capture news as it happens, turning moblogging into a news source. The ability to get real-time information from anywhere in the world as long as anyone is participating with their camera phone is going to be unique.

—Cat Schwartz
Columnist Stuff magazine, Former anchor
G4techTV

How to ... Monitor User Commentary

The great thing about being part of a community is that it gives everyone a voice. The downside of being part of a large community is that some people just don't have anything nice to say. All three sites mentioned earlier give you the ability to block user commentary or to remove specific comments.

If you want to remove a specific comment in Buzznet:

1. Click the thumbnail of the appropriate photo.
2. Click Edit under the main image.
3. Click the X next to the entry you wish to remove.

If you'd rather block all commentary from Buzznet, click Edit Profile, then under Profile Info, click No next to Allow Comments.

To remove a comment from Mobog, select the picture, then click Delete next to the comment you wish to remove. If you want to block all commentary from your site, click Preferences at the top of the page, then uncheck the Comments box.

To remove a comment from Textamerica:

1. Go to your Control Panel, then click the Entries tab.
2. Click the Edit Comments link to view the offending entry.

If you wish to exclude all comments from your site, go to your Control Panel, then click Change Site Settings. Under the Image Comments drop-down menu, select Do Not Allow Users to Comment on Images.

When you find the moblog to which you wish to contribute, simply click the e-mail address link (or type it in your e-mail program), include a subject heading and body text, which—depending on the site—will appear as text for your blog post, attach the photo, then send it off. The same rules apply for pictures sent directly from your phone. Your pictures will have to be approved by the moblog owner to be posted.

CHAPTER 8: Creating a Moblog   **193**

Did you know?

Nokia Lifeblog

With moblogs becoming such a popular tool for camera phone users, Nokia decided to give its customers a leg up by creating its own multimedia diary site. Called Nokia Lifeblog, the site automatically organizes photos, videos, text messages, and multimedia messages in a timeline, as shown here:

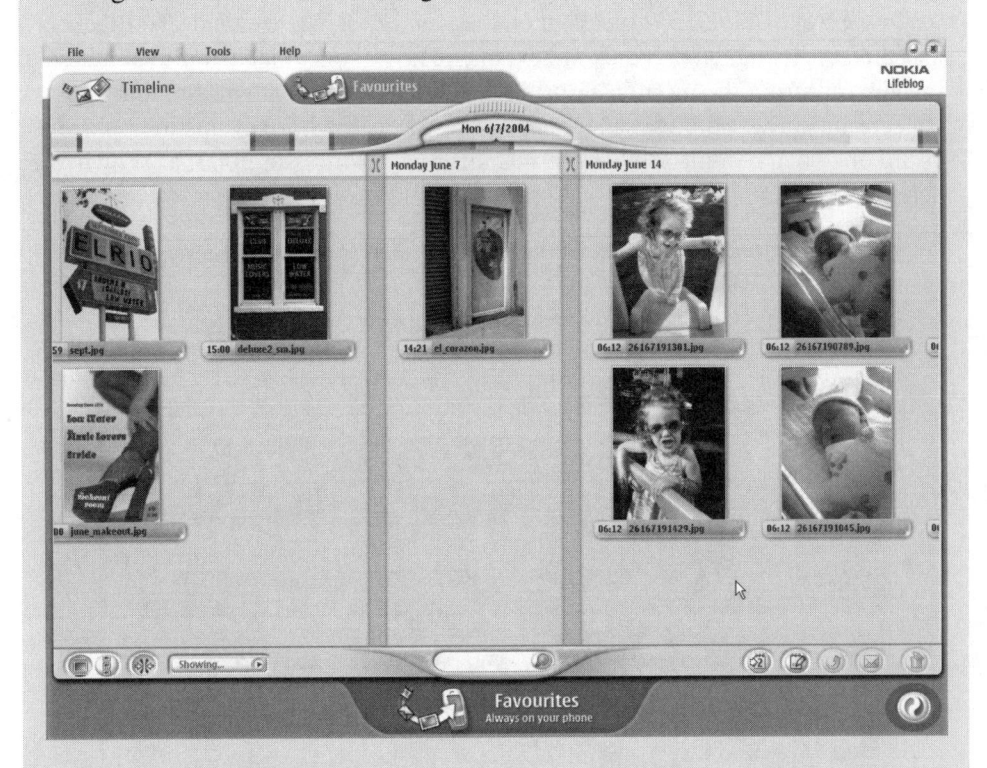

The Nokia 7610, Nokia's first megapixel camera phone, is the first phone to support Lifeblog. You can upload images to your own moblogs directly from the handset, and you can view files in the timeline on both the phone and a Windows PC. You can also share Lifeblog images via e-mail from your PC. Nokia will include Lifeblog support in its other smart phones that run on the Symbian operating platform.

Did you know?

The Next Wave of Moblogs

Although moblogging is currently considered a fun little hobby for camera phone enthusiasts, the expectations for the medium in the near future are high. Technology continues to blur the line between professionals and amateurs, especially when it comes to documenting events.

In the wake of the 2003 blackout on the East Coast, a site called The Blackout appeared on Textamerica (blackout.textamerica.com) on which people submitted images capturing the moments during the power outage. Several moblogs concerning antiwar protests also popped up soon after those events took place, as did one documenting the Southern California wildfires of 2003, as shown here:

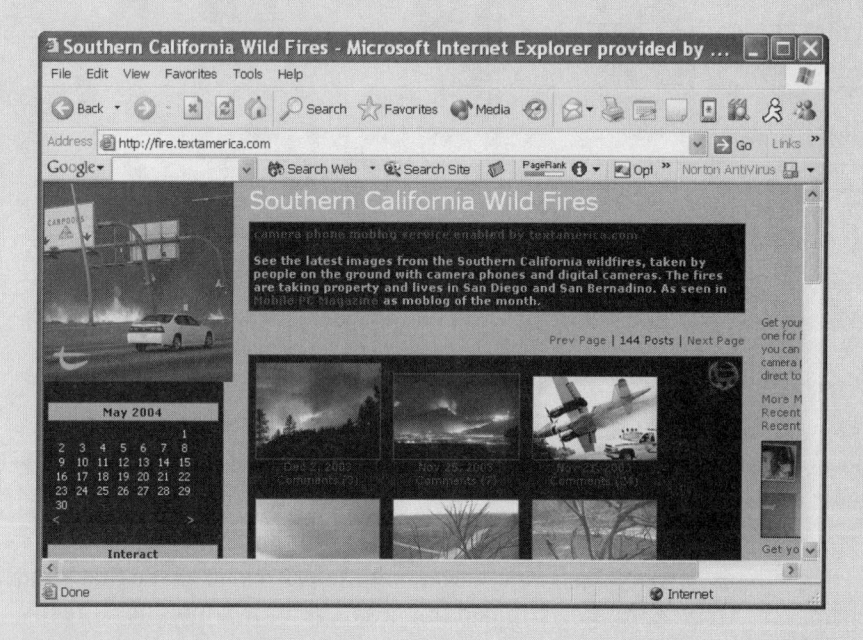

Such sites are often able to document the human element of news events in a faster, more immediate way than news agencies can. With that in mind, not only did the British Broadcasting Company (BBC) set up moblogs in 2003 to document the antiwar rallies—essentially turning ordinary citizens into de facto journalists—the network gave 40 of its reporters and producers Nokia 3650 phones with camera and video capabilities to document news events. Because of a camera phone–carrying producer, the BBC had the first images of a deadly bus crash in Wales in early 2004. Philips Software provided enhanced software for the BBC's phones, enabling the handsets to capture up to 15 minutes of video at a time, instead of the usual 15-second clip.

> **TIP** *If you plan to contribute to a couple of moblogs on a regular basis, it's a good idea to add those e-mail addresses to your phone's contact list. That way, you won't have to type it in every time you want to upload a picture.*

Moving On

Go ahead, admit it. You like moblogs, and you really like moblogging. You can even say moblog without feeling weird. It's hard to believe that there could be anything as fun as moblogging, but there is. In the next chapter, I'll take a look at some of the other fun things you can do with your camera phone images, including displaying your photos in a virtual frame.

Chapter 9

Other Fun Stuff for Your Photos

How to...

- Set up picture caller ID
- Create photo albums
- Make a slide show
- Make a virtual movie
- Create greeting cards
- Use digital frames

Not that everything we've discussed to this point hasn't been fun, but there are even more cool and creative things you can do with your camera phone images. The fact that camera phone pictures are digital and designed for instantaneous communication means you have a wealth of options at your disposal for composing and sharing some of your more unique creations.

In this chapter, I'll discuss a few other fun things you can do with your camera phone pictures, such as creating greeting cards and assembling virtual movies.

Set Up Photo Caller ID

One of the most common uses for pictures on your camera phone is photo caller ID, whereby you associate a picture with a contact stored in your phone's address book. It's just one of the ways we use technology to create virtual intimacy—seeing your husband's picture appear on the screen as he's calling you can make you feel he's really there with you. Okay, maybe not, but it's a nice feature, nevertheless.

Linking a picture with a contact takes only a few steps, although the language used in the menu choices will vary from phone to phone. Also keep in mind that some earlier camera phones don't support this feature. The following steps represent the typical way to establish photo caller ID:

1. Go to the photo gallery.
2. Highlight a picture.

CHAPTER 9: Other Fun Stuff for Your Photos   199

3. Select Options.

4. Select Assign or Set As from the menu listing.

5. Select Contacts or Phone Book.

6. Scroll through your contact list and select a name.

7. Click Save.

The next time that person calls, the picture you associated with the contact will appear on the screen as part of caller ID. Some flip phones, however, don't provide enough pixels or color density on their external screens to display the picture. If you want to see the caller ID photo, you'll need to flip open the phone. In this case, it's best to change your settings so that the phone doesn't automatically answer calls when you open the cover.

CAUTION *If you receive a call from someone who has blocked caller ID information from their phone, you won't see a picture on your screen, despite the fact that their name is listed in your phonebook.*

Photo Creations

And you thought we were finished working with the photo organizing software. Oh no, not at all. In fact, one of the best features of Adobe Photoshop Album is the ability to make Creations.

Create a Photo Album

A photo album doesn't have to be something you dig out of a trunk and dust off before boring your friends to tears. You can bore them just as easily with digital photo albums, complete with style templates and layout options (see Figure 9-1). The best part, of course, is that you can share these albums with others via e-mail or save them to a CD.

Adobe Photoshop Album offers the richest set of tools for working with virtual albums:

1. Click the Create button, choose Album from the list of templates, then click Next, shown in the following illustration:

FIGURE 9-1 Adobe Photoshop Album's Creations Wizard offers a variety of templates for creating virtual photo albums.

CHAPTER 9: Other Fun Stuff for Your Photos

2. Choose an Album style.

3. Enter a title for your album and select how many pictures you want to display on each page. Also, choose whether you want to include captions for each picture and display page numbers. Click Next.

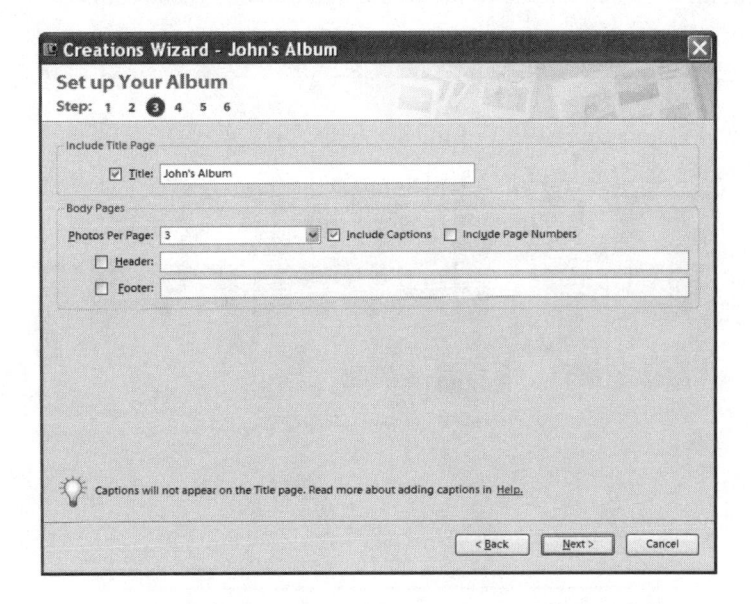

4. Select the photos you want to add to the album by clicking the check boxes next to the thumbnails. Click Add to Creation when you're done, then click OK.

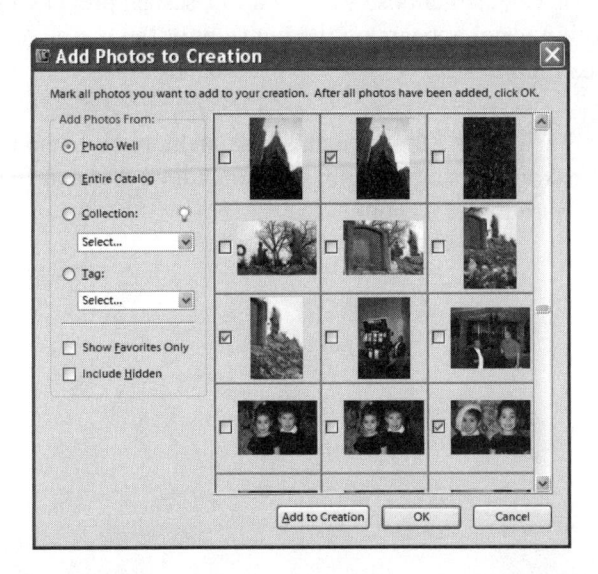

5. On the Pick Your Photos page, you can change the order of the pictures by clicking and dragging a thumbnail to the desired spot. You can also delete a picture from the album by clicking Clear or duplicate a picture to include it more than once. Because the first picture appears on the title page of the album, you may decide to include it again inside the album.

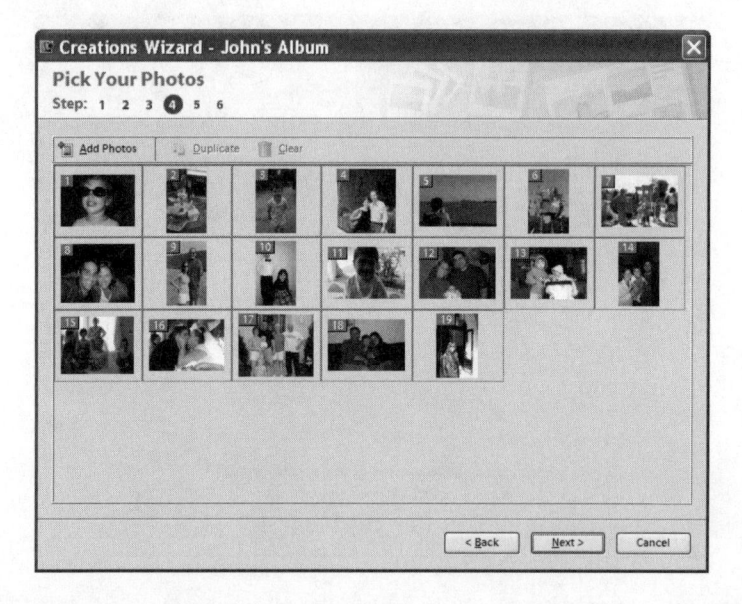

6. On the Customize Your Album page, click the thumbnail to resize or reposition the image on the page. If you wish to undo a change, click Reset Photos. You can also choose to view a full-screen preview of your album. A navigation panel appears on the top right of the screen to flip through the pages (see Figure 9-2).

7. On the Publish Your Album page, shown next, click Done to save it to your hard drive. You can save the album as an Adobe Acrobat PDF file or print, e-mail, or burn it to a CD or DVD.

CHAPTER 9: Other Fun Stuff for Your Photos 203

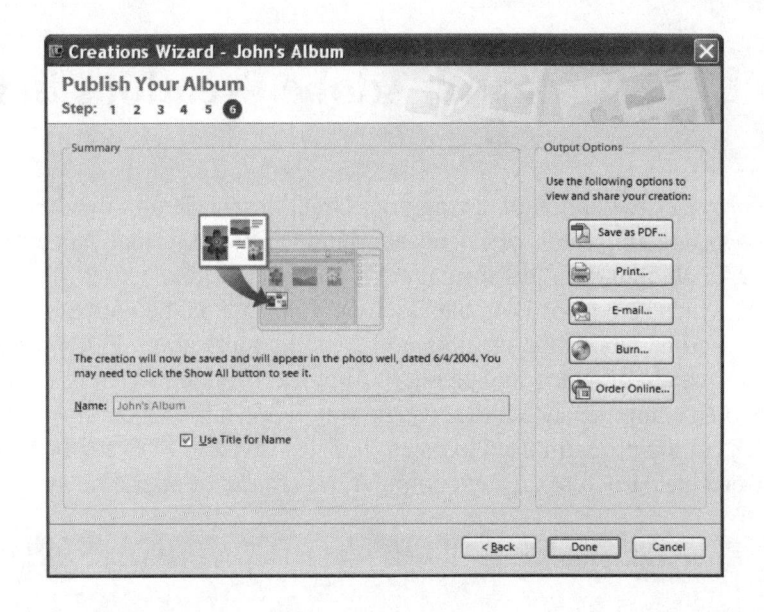

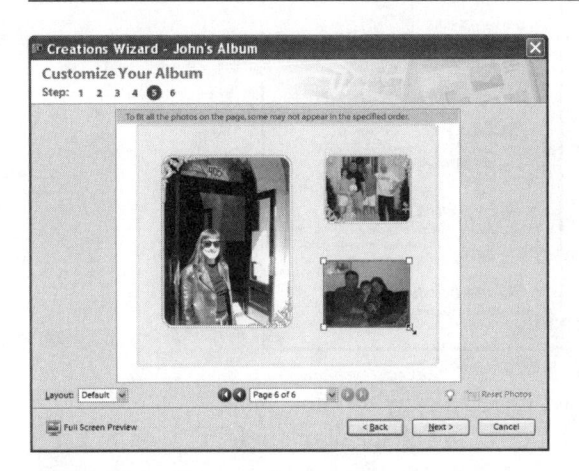

FIGURE 9-2 You can resize and reposition pictures and preview your results before finishing your photo album.

How to ... Work with Adobe Creations in PDF

Adobe provides the option of saving your Creations—whether they're albums, slide shows, greeting cards, or calendars—in the PDF file format. Not everyone, however, is familiar with this format or its purpose.

PDF, which stands for Portable Document Format, is the native format of Adobe's Acrobat document creation and viewing application. PDF preserves the fonts, images, graphics, and layout of a source document. That is, a document appears on a computer screen exactly the way it appeared when first created, regardless of the program used to create it. Files saved in PDF can be viewed in their original structure on any computer, regardless of operating system.

If you e-mail a Creation, your recipient will need a copy of Photoshop Album on their computer to view the files properly. Saving an album in PDF ensures that your recipient views the files in the correct sequence, at the proper size, and with the formatting options you selected. Your recipient will need to have a copy of the Adobe Reader software installed on their computer, which is available as a free download from www.adobe.com.

> When viewing an Photoshop Album Creation in the Adobe Reader, not only can you view the slide show with all of the original elements intact, you can also manage the photos through the Reader's Picture Tasks option. After clicking the Picture Tasks button, which is located in the toolbar near the top of the screen, you're presented with options to export (or save) the pictures to your PC, edit the photos in Photoshop or Photoshop Elements, print the images on your home printer, or order prints online. For each of these options, you can select individual photos from the Creation or all of the files. If the Creation is a slide show that includes a music soundtrack, however, you won't be able to save or otherwise work with the associated audio file.

Once you've saved the album, double-click the album name in the Photo Well to add or remove pictures or print, e-mail, or archive it.

Create a Slide Show

There's nothing that will kill a party faster than bringing out the projector and showing your friends a slide show of your latest vacation. That's because sitting down to watch a slide show is forced fun, emphasis on *forced*. With a digital slide show, on the other hand, your friends can watch at their convenience on their own computers. What's more, you can add multimedia touches such as audio captions and background music.

In Photoshop Album, creating and sharing a slide show involves the same steps as creating an album, except you choose Slide Show from the template options. Paint Shop Photo Album also offers a slide show feature. Creating one with Paint Shop is simply a matter of selecting pictures from the album window:

1. Go to the album or file folder containing the pictures you wish to include. To select several noncontinuous images, hold the CTRL key while clicking the thumbnail.

2. Click the down arrow next to the Slide Show button on the toolbar to open the drop-down menu, then click Settings.

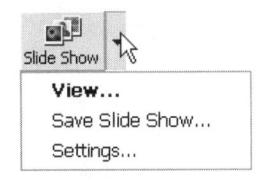

3. Select whether you want the pictures to display at actual size or be resized to fit the screen. Also select the duration of displayed images, the transition effects, and the audio options. Click OK.

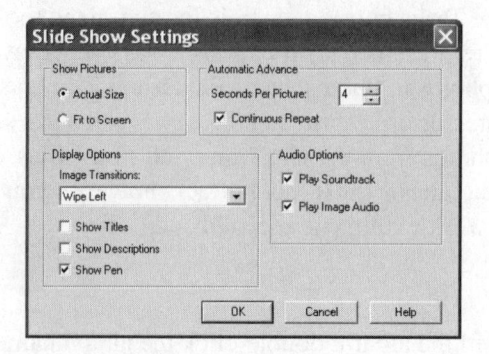

4. In the Slide Show drop-down menu, click Save Slide Show. Choose a name, select the folder to which you wish to save the file, and click OK.

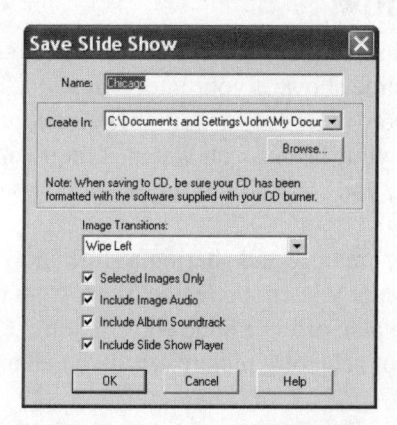

5. To view the slide show, click the Slide Show button. The Slide Show will automatically begin playing. You can use the toolbar at the top of the screen, shown in the following illustration, to stop the show, navigate the images in the slide show, and even rotate pictures.

CHAPTER 9: Other Fun Stuff for Your Photos 207

TIP *To add a soundtrack to your Paint Shop slide show, go to Audio | Album Soundtrack | Choose, then browse your computer's folders to find the audio file you wish to associate with the selected album. When you create a slide show, make sure there's a check mark next to the Play Soundtrack option.*

If you want to share your slide show, Paint Shop Photo Album lets you save the file with the Slide Show Player. When you e-mail the slide show, recipients can view the file even if they don't have Paint Shop Photo Album installed on their computers.

NOTE *The Slide Show Player is available to Windows users only. If your recipient uses a Mac, they won't be able to play a slide show created in Paint Shop Photo Album. In this regard, Photoshop Album's platform-neutral PDF export feature is the better option.*

Both Photoshop Album and Paint Shop Photo Album let you save slide shows to a video compact disc (VCD), which will let you play a show on a television set or on any computer with a CD-ROM drive. You can play VCDs on any DVD player that can read the VCD format and CD-R/CD-RW media. Check to make sure your DVD player supports these media.

Make a Movie

If your camera phone has the ability to take pictures in multishot or burst mode (taking between 2 and 15 shots at a time), depending on the model, Paint Shop Photo Album offers a movie-making option that can turn those images into simulated short films. This is especially useful if your phone's multishot mode takes six or more pictures simultaneously.

To make a movie in Paint Shop Photo Album:

1. Select the images you wish to include.

2. Choose Tools | Make Movie to open the Make Movie dialog.

3. Click Browse to choose the folder to which you wish to save the file.

4. Enter the number of seconds per frame at which you want the movie to play. The lower the number, the faster the movie will play. A speed of 0.5 seconds/frame, for example, will give the appearance of a flip-book.

5. Enter the width and height (in pixels) for the movie; 640 × 480 is a good size.

6. Mark the Preserve Aspect Ratio check box. If you uncheck this box, your movie will appear stretched either vertically or horizontally.

7. Click OK.

Paint Shop Photo Album saves movies as Apple QuickTime .MOV files. The QuickTime player is available for free download from www.apple.com. However, if you want to share a movie and you're unsure whether your recipient has the QuickTime player, you can export movies to different file formats. Double-click the thumbnail of the movie file, then select File | Export to open the Save Exported File As dialog. In the Export drop-down menu, you'll see lots of file format choices. To be safe, save your movie as an AVI or MPEG-4 file, which are common formats that most computers will support.

CAUTION *If your movie contains any video effects, you can save it only as a QuickTime MOV file.*

CHAPTER 9: Other Fun Stuff for Your Photos 209

> **TIP** *If your phone supports an external media card, you can save the video file on the storage medium and view it on your phone. Once it's on your phone, you can send video messages to other phones that support MPEG-4 files.*

Create Greeting Cards

With their small file sizes and the fact that they're suitable for viewing on a computer screen, camera phone images are ideal for virtual greeting cards. Your pictures can spice up an invitation to a kid's birthday party or add a personal touch to a Valentine's Day greeting.

Photoshop Elements provides a selection of greeting card templates (see Figure 9-3) in its Creations Wizard, including party invitations, birth announcements, and thank-you notes, which you can save as PDF files and e-mail.

If you prefer to exploit your recipients' camera phone capabilities and you happen to be a Verizon Wireless customer, Verizon Wireless' Pix Place lets you send greeting cards directly to an MMS-capable Verizon Wireless cell phone. You can also send cards via MMS or e-mail from Pix Place (see Figure 9-4). The best

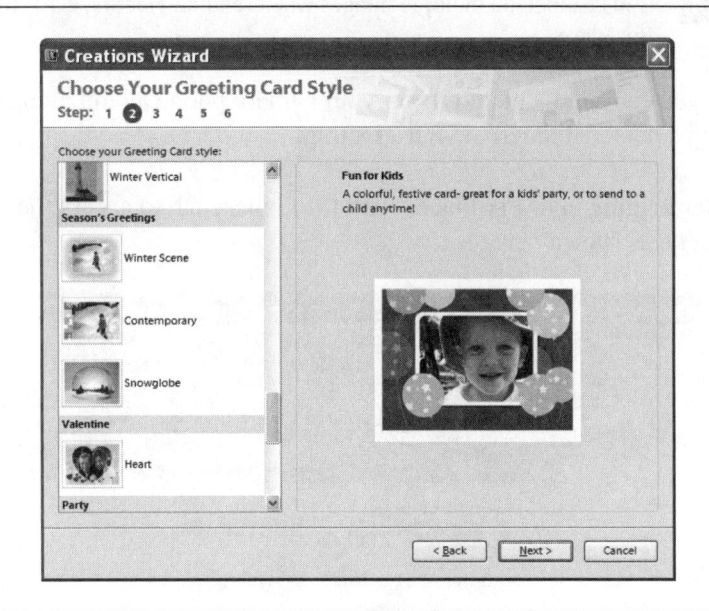

FIGURE 9-3 Adobe Photoshop Album's greeting card templates include designs for party invitations, holiday scenes, and Valentine's Day cards.

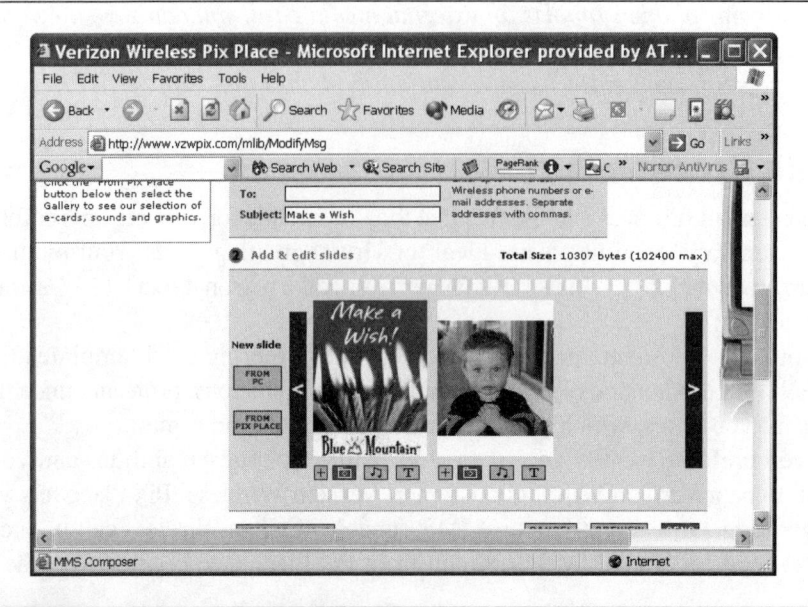

FIGURE 9-4 You can include multiple images when sending greeting cards from Verizon Pix Place.

part is that you can send a picture from your camera phone album along with the card, adding a personal touch to your greeting.

1. After logging in to Pix Place, click the Gallery tab to access the free image gallery, as shown here:

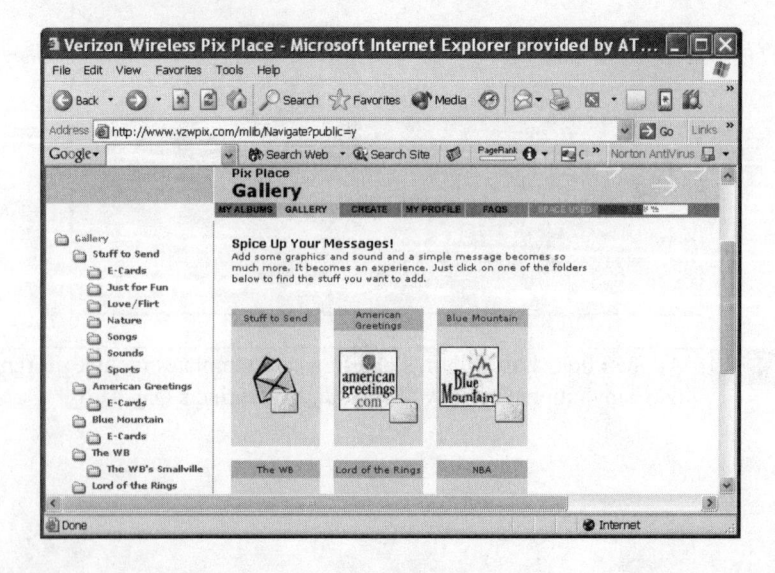

2. Choose the type of image you want (an American Greetings birthday card, for example), then choose the image. Click Send.

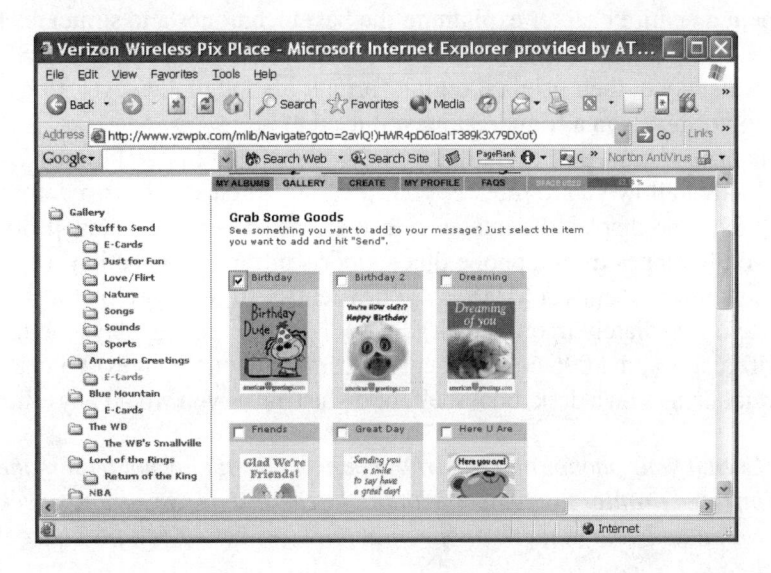

3. To add a picture from your album of uploaded camera phone images, click New Slide From Pix Place (you can also choose to add an image from your PC).

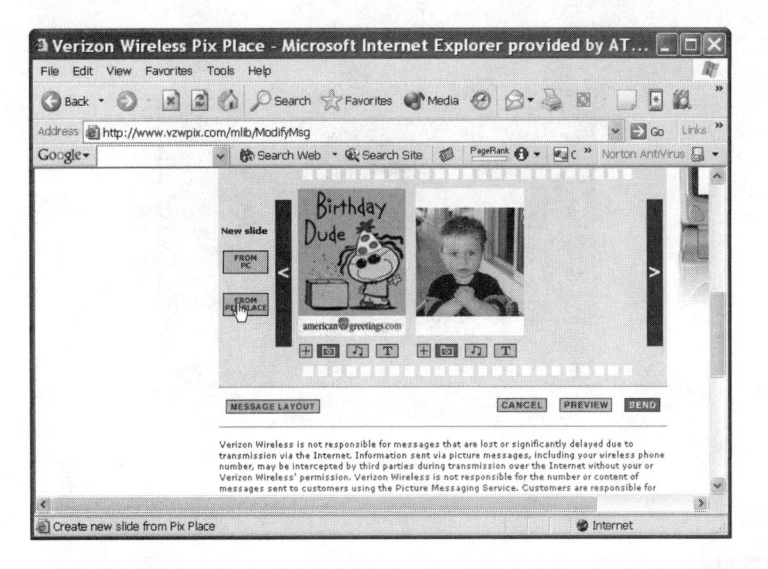

4. Enter the Verizon Wireless phone number or e-mail address of your recipient, then click Send.

Digital Frames

Yes, I spent an entire chapter explaining the best techniques and strategies for printing your camera phone images. But the truth is that these images are best suited for display in their original digital format. It's tough, however, to hang a collection of pixels in a frame. At least it used to be.

Nokia now offers a pair of digital frames—the Nokia Image Frame SU-4 and the SU-7—that allow you to transfer your pictures wirelessly from a compatible camera phone and display the images one at a time or as a slide show. Both frames store up to 50 images from a phone that supports infrared connections (the SU-7 also accepts images sent via MMS, so your friends can send you pictures that you can display immediately upon receipt). The 5.1-inch screen displays pictures at 320 × 240 pixels and 4,096 colors, ideal for camera phone images. You can display these virtual images on a desk, bookshelf, or nightstand as you would any other frame.

CAUTION *Even if your phone supports IrDA connections, it may not feature the proper infrared profiles to connect with the Image Frame. Be sure to check with Nokia and your camera phone manufacturer before you purchase the Image Frame.*

FIGURE 9-5 Show off your camera phone images digitally on Nokia's Image Frame.

Did you know?

Nokia Camera Phone Enhancements

Along with its stature as the top-selling camera phone manufacturer, Nokia is taking the camera phone phenomenon seriously by offering several add-on products. Along with Nokia Image Frames, the Finnish company offers the Image Viewer, shown next, which allows you to project your camera phone photos on to a TV screen or video projector.

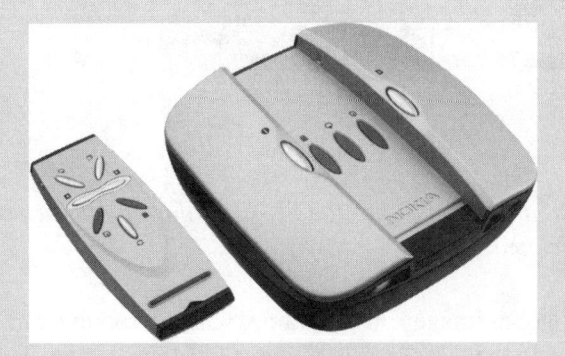

You transfer images to the Image Viewer from a Bluetooth-compatible phone that supports the proper profiles (such as Nokia's 3650 or 7610 models). Then you connect the viewer to a TV or projector with the RCA cord (be sure your TV supports RCA connections; most newer models do). Next, it's simply a matter of displaying your images one at a time or as a slide show. You can rotate images 90 degrees at the touch of a button and control slide show pacing with four- or eight-second intervals between images.

Although I've already reviewed several online storage options, Nokia's Image Album, shown next, provides a more immediate, physical storage option. The Image Album can hold up to 20GB of content (that's probably more camera phone images than you'll be able to capture), which you can view and organize on a TV screen through an RCA connection. You transfer pictures to the Image Album via infrared, Bluetooth, USB connection, or MMC or SD memory cards. Once you've stored the pictures, you can view them on a TV screen in thumbnail, full-screen, or slide show modes. From there, you can create your own folder structure, rename files, add comments, and adjust contrast and brightness levels—it's like having photo organizing software on your TV.

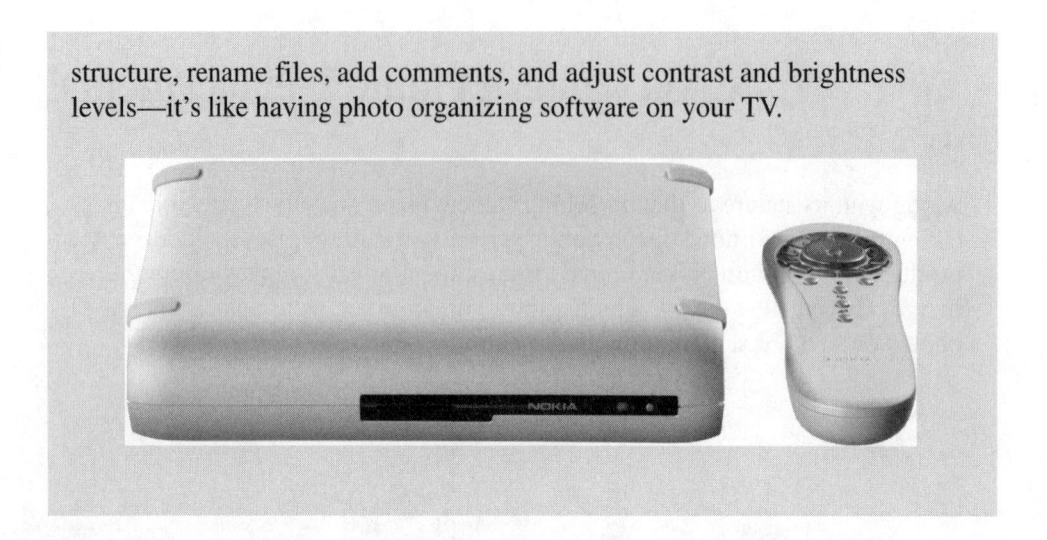

NOTE *If an MMS message sent to the SU-7 contains audio or text, those elements will be deleted.*

Once you've stored images on the frame, you can rotate them, adjust the brightness, and automatically rescale pictures to fit the screen. The Image Frame supports both landscape (horizontal) or portrait (vertical) viewing modes, allows you to create custom slide shows, and features an internal memory that keeps pictures stored on the device even when you unplug it.

Moving On

Using your cell phone to take pictures and instantly share them with others certainly qualifies as big fun, but that's not all there is. Some of the latest feature-rich handsets now feature integrated video cameras along with still photography functions. In the next chapter, I'll go over the basics of camcorder phones, including a look at some of the current models along with a few shopping tips.

Part IV

Get the Most Out of Your Camcorder Phone

Chapter 10

What Your Camcorder Phone Can Do for You

How to...

- Get familiar with your camcorder phone
- Identify technical terms
- Shop for a camcorder phone
- Use memory wisely

The idea of putting a camera inside a cell phone was so ingenious that it's hard to imagine another merger of technologies that's just as clever. Before you agree with me, let me introduce you to the camcorder phone. Still pictures are wonderful, but video brings those captured memories to life. Just as motion pictures followed still photography, video represents the next logical step in cell phones.

In this chapter, I'll explain why camcorder phones promise to be so popular, review some important technical information, and explore some of the available handsets with built-in camcorders.

Get to Know Your Camcorder Phone

It's not unusual to hear a certain technology referred to as a solution in search of a problem. Some people undoubtedly regard a camcorder as nothing more than a superfluous addition to a cell phone, but I don't think this is the case. Apparently, neither do you, and I've got the numbers to back me up on this.

By 2009, 31.1 million Americans will use video messaging services, and mobile video services are expected to generate $5.4 billion in annual revenue, according to market research firm In-Stat/MDR. The firm also found that 13.2 percent of U.S. wireless customers are "extremely or very interested" in purchasing video services for their wireless phones, ranking ahead of all other prospective mobile multimedia services, including gaming and music downloads.

Just as camera phones supplement film or digital still cameras, camcorder phones will supplement, not replace, traditional camcorders. That's because the ability to capture spontaneous moments and share them with others is appealing. Camcorder phones also allow you to view video from other sources on your cell phone, such as sites that provide streaming television broadcasts. However, the video quality doesn't come close to matching what you'd get with a $200 analog camcorder, to say nothing of a $700 digital unit. Also, if you want to send video clips to another phone, you'll face the same problems inherent with camera phones—mainly, network and phone compatibility. But as the technology improves, so will the potential applications.

Despite the camcorder features, these phones use the same lens as the camera on your phone, so there's no difference in appearance (you may not even know that your phone has video-capture capabilities).

> **NOTE** *You may be able to watch video on your cell phone even if it doesn't feature a built-in camcorder. Check your user manual or consult your carrier to find out if your handset supports video services.*

Terms You Should Know

You don't need to possess the skill or technical knowledge of Martin Scorsese to use a camcorder phone, but it is helpful to be familiar with a few basic terms that will appear from time to time.

Frames Per Second

Frames per second (fps) is a measure of how much information is used to store and display motion video. Each frame is a still image, and displaying frames in rapid succession creates the illusion of motion. The higher the fps, the smoother the motion appears. When you watch television in the U.S. or footage shot with a camcorder, the image is displayed at 30 fps. Currently, camcorder phones capture video at 15 fps, which is why the footage appears jerky.

QCIF

QCIF is short for Quarter Common Intermediate Format, which is a videoconferencing standard that specifies data rates of 30 fps at a resolution of 176 × 144 pixels. Though the term is commonly used to describe video footage transmitted over phone lines, it also applies to video captured by a cell phone. Current camcorder phones produce video at either QCIF or subQCIF (128 × 96) resolutions—in other words, video appears to be the size of a postage stamp when viewed on a computer screen.

Streaming Video

Streaming video is a sequence of moving images sent in a compressed form over the Internet and displayed by the viewer as those images arrive. The user doesn't have to wait for the entire file to download before seeing the video because the file is sent in a continuous stream and played as it arrives. Video content you receive on your cell phone from the wireless web falls into the streaming video category.

Buffer

A buffer is a temporary storage area. With streaming media, if the target device, such as a computer or cell phone, receives the data more quickly than required, it temporarily stores the excess data in a buffer before the file is played (this process is called *buffering*). If the data doesn't come through quickly enough, you'll notice gaps, or dead spots, in the presentation.

Bandwidth

Bandwidth is the amount of data, expressed in kilobits per second (Kbps) or megabits per second (Mbps) that can travel over a data network in a fixed amount of time. The greater the bandwidth, the more information that can be sent in a given amount of time. Video files require a larger amount of bandwidth than still photographic images, and the higher the video quality, the more bandwidth required. Most wireless networks operate at 40 to 60 Kbps, compared with an average of about 700 Kbps for cable Internet access and 450 Kbps for DSL Internet access. At those speeds, wireless networks are unable to support high-quality, full-motion video transmission, but carriers have been making strides in offering high-speed wireless networks on par with DSL (more on this later in the sidebar titled "Download and Upload Speed Differences").

MPEG-4

MPEG-4 is a video compression standard based on Apple's QuickTime technology designed to transmit video over low bandwidth networks. Camcorder phones support the MPEG-4 format.

QuickTime

QuickTime is a video and animation format developed by Apple Computer. Video created in QuickTime can be played on all Macintosh computers, as well as Windows-based PCs that have the QuickTime Viewer software application installed. QuickTime supports most computer video formats, including MPEG-4 and 3GPP.

3GPP and 3GPP2

Created by the 3rd Generation Partnership Project, 3GPP and 3GPP2 are standards for the creation, delivery, and playback of multimedia files over third-generation (3G), high-speed wireless networks. 3GPP and 3GPP2 files are based on the MPEG-4 standard, which makes them compatible with Apple's QuickTime file format (.MOV). 3GPP (.3GP) files travel over GSM wireless networks (such as

AT&T Wireless, Cingular Wireless, and T-Mobile), while 3GPP2 (.3g2) files are designed for CDMA networks (such as Sprint PCS and Verizon Wireless).

Issues to Consider

Just as camera phones have their own unique issues, so do camcorder phones. Tempting as it is, you just can't go around shooting video footage at will. You have to keep in mind memory concerns, battery life, and the inherent limitations that camcorder phones present.

Time and Size Constraints

You're understandably excited over the prospect of being able to shoot video with your cell phone. Because it's something you carry with you all the time, it's convenient, whereas you're not likely to lug around your standard camcorder except on special occasions that you planned to document ahead of time. However, unlike a regular camcorder, you can't, for the most part, use your camcorder phone to shoot footage for hours, or even minutes, on end.

Most camcorder phones limit the amount of video you can shoot to 15-second clips, so you have little margin for error in terms of getting the right footage. Also, while the video quality of today's consumer digital camcorders rival that of professional-grade images, the output from camcorder phones don't. That's largely because the main attraction of shooting video with your cell phone is the ability to share it immediately with others. Unfortunately, most wireless networks are unable to handle the trafficking of large video files. Like still images, the better the video quality, the more space it occupies.

> **NOTE** *Not all phones limit you to 15-second clips. Sony Ericsson's P900 features a video mode, which lets you keep shooting until you run out of memory. The downside is that you need to transfer those clips to a PC before you can send them to others. If you want to send a video clip directly from your phone, you'll have to shoot in message video mode, which limits recording to 11 seconds and produces clips less than 100KB.*

Depending on your phone, a full 15-second clip will take up between 90KB and 300KB. The Toshiba VM-4050, for example, takes video at 128 × 96 pixels in the QuickTime .MOV format, and a 10-second clip occupies about 195KB. The Nokia 3620, on the other hand, also captures footage at 128 × 96, but its maximum file size is just 95KB because it uses the 3GPP format, which uses more compression than QuickTime files.

Did you know?

Upload and Download Speed Differences

When cell phone makers began offering camcorder functions in their products, wireless networks were ill-equipped to handle trafficking large amounts of high-quality video. The 40 to 60 Kbps speeds of wireless networks are sufficient for voice and still images, but those files occupy a fraction of the space that video requires. The wireless carriers are working to catch up to the demands created by new features such as video sharing, but it's too soon to tell when these high-speed networks will be widespread and inexpensive enough for the average user.

Earlier this year, Verizon Wireless began rolling out its BroadbandAccess network, which promises 300 to 500 Kbps data rates over a cellular network, about what you get with a DSL modem. The problem is that right now, Verizon offers the service only to laptop users and charges $80 a month for unlimited connectivity. Eventually, the carrier will offer high-speed access in some high-end cell phones, but it hasn't made any announcements to this point.

AT&T Wireless and Cingular Wireless have been rolling out high-speed EDGE network access, which delivers data rates of 100 to 130 Kbps, although on a cell phone you'd get something close to 56 Kbps. The more users who access these networks, the less bandwidth can get through the system, just as only so many cars can move through a tunnel at the same time.

It's important to note that when carriers talk about data rates, they're referring to download speeds, which is the time it takes to move data from a location to your device (in this case, a cell phone). Those speeds are always faster than upload rates, which is the time it takes to move data from your device to another location (such as another cell phone). Verizon's BroadbandAccess service, for example, delivers upload speeds of about 40 to 60 Kbps. In other words, if you plan to share video with your friends, it'll take you a lot longer to send a file than to receive one (I'll explain how this can affect you financially in the next chapter).

These short, compressed video files look raw, jerky, and pixelated on a cell phone screen, and they're all that and downright miniscule on a computer monitor. When looking at such footage on a PC, the term "postage stamp" comes to mind.

Remember Your Memory

As I mentioned earlier, video files take up much more space than still images or even voice or other cell phone application files, which is one reason you're so limited in the amount of video you can shoot at one time. That also brings up memory-management issues—that is, how do you keep enough room to store pictures and everything else you need on your phone when you're gallivanting around town shooting video? One thing you'll want to check when considering a camcorder phone is whether it uses shared memory or dedicated memory.

With shared memory, video clips occupy the same space as contacts, appointments, messages, images, and ring tones. The more video you store on your phone, the less room you have for any other elements.

If your phone uses dedicated memory, your video clips are stored in a separate space. Even when you run out of room to save additional video files, you'll still be able to add additional contacts, ring tones, and so on. Whether your camcorder phone uses shared or dedicated memory, expect these devices to come with more onboard memory than standard cell phones or VGA-quality camera phones. Most of the older devices top out at about 3MB of storage, whereas you'll likely see a minimum of 16MB in the newer, feature-rich handsets.

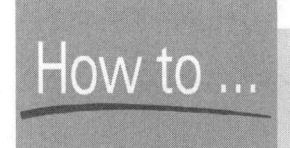

How to ... Save Clips to a Memory Card

Your camcorder phone may, by default, automatically store pictures and video clips in the handset's onboard memory. That makes little sense if your phone accepts a memory expansion card. Saving clips to a memory card is simply a matter of changing the settings of your phone's camera/video functions. The following instructions apply to the Nokia 3650, but the process is similar in other camcorder phones:

1. While in camera or video mode, click Options.
2. Select Settings, then choose Memory in Use.
3. Select Memory Card.

Every photo or video clip you save will be stored on the memory card until you change the settings.

Your best bet, however, is to find a phone that features a slot for memory expansion cards, such as Multimedia Cards (MMC), TransFlash (T-Flash) cards, or Secure Digital (SD). The Sony Ericsson P900, for example, features a slot for a Memory Stick Duo card. The phone, which comes with 16MB of onboard memory, can accept up to 128MB of total storage. If you use a 64MB card, for example, you can store more than 600 10-second video clips, or nearly two hours of footage.

Voices from the Community: Sprint Goes to the Movies

Camera phones are an extension of something that people already do. People have communicated with pictures for many, many years. We've made digital imaging accessible to the masses by making it more convenient. Digital cameras were dependent on the PC, what was called the Chain of Pain. The number one reason for returns of digital cameras was because people hadn't realized they needed to use it with a PC, which is something they didn't want to do. We knew that the primary use of a digital camera was sharing pictures via e-mail, and that printing was secondary. We tapped into the sharing aspect with camera phones and the Picture Mail service.

The appeal of moving pictures is an even richer way to communicate. We've made it convenient to do video. When you think about your video camera, it's a pretty labor-intensive process to get the video off the camera to your PC and get your media player going. And sending video clips over the Web? Good luck.

There will be an unprecedented use of video through cell phones. I coach a kid's hockey team and I've used it as a coaching aid. I videotape the players while they're going through their drills and show them what it is I'm trying to correct.

Video resolution will increase much faster than you can upgrade a network, but network bandwidths will improve. What we're most interested in is uplink speeds (how long it takes to send data from your phone). Some new networks may provide higher download speeds, but we're coming from the opposite direction.

—*Pierre Barbeau, General Manager of Mobile Imaging, Sprint*

CHAPTER 10:   What Your Camcorder Phone Can Do for You 225

As more camcorder phones and megapixel camera phones hit the market, you'll likely see memory card slots become more of a standard feature. With these, you'll be able to store pictures and video on the card without taking precious space away from your phone's basic features.

Shopping for a Camcorder Phone

Yes, it's true, the quality of the video you get with camcorder phones is essentially the same regardless of the model you choose, but there are still plenty of other issues to take into account, such as how much memory you'll need and what kind of battery life you can expect to get from your handset.

Look for More Memory

If you thought you had to keep track of how many photos you took on a camera phone, you really need to be mindful of the amount of video you capture. Some phones feature dedicated memory for pictures and video. The Toshiba VM4050, for example, allows you to store a fixed number of photo and video files on the handset, in this case 30, regardless of the picture and video settings. With other phones, however, it depends on how much memory remains on the unit.

The Nokia 3620, for example, comes with 16MB of onboard memory (that is, memory dedicated to the phone itself, not anything extra from an expansion card). In theory, that means you could store plenty of clips at about 95KB apiece. But since this phone uses shared memory, which means information such as your contacts, ring tones, messages, and graphics takes up space, you're not starting out with 16MB.

Ideally, if you like to download a lot of games and other apps, you'll want your phone to feature dedicated memory. Conversely, if you just want the ability to occasionally capture a quick video, shared memory is the best option for you. But as camcorder phones and megapixel-plus cameras become more prevalent, industry executives expect memory card expansion slots to become standard features in such high-end handsets. If that's the case, then memory will become less of a concern. Until then, you'll need to be mindful of how many video clips you've accumulated.

Working with Expansion Cards

Because it's likely that memory-card expansion slots will become standard in camcorder phones, look for a unit that currently supports this feature. Not only does this provide more space to save video and pictures, its portability means you can take your card anywhere and view your files on any device that supports the particular storage format. The good news is that there are several formats to choose from. The bad news is that there are several formats to choose from. If you plan to carry your video clips with you, you'll need to make sure the target device supports your particular card.

All of the following removable storage cards use flash-memory, which means data is erased and reprogrammed in blocks, and that it retains its data after power is removed. Also, all of these cards are small and all come in a variety of storage sizes, but there are differences in exactly how they work.

- **Memory Stick** Developed by Sony, this card (shown in Figure 10-1) is compatible only with the manufacturer's products, as well as Sony Ericsson cell pones. Memory Stick and Memory Stick Duo cards support a maximum capacity of 128MB, while the Memory Stick Pro can store up to 2GB of data. The Memory Stick is longer than other flash-memory cards, although the Memory Stick Duo is about half the size, more in line with other cards, and it comes with an adapter.

NOTE: *The Memory Stick with Memory Select Function provides up to 256MB of total storage.*

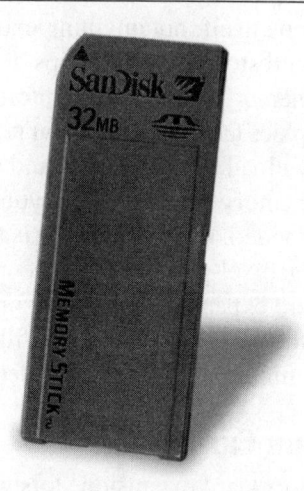

FIGURE 10-1 The Memory Stick is compatible only with Sony products.

CHAPTER 10: What Your Camcorder Phone Can Do for You   227

- **Multimedia Card (MMC)** About the size of a postage stamp, this card (shown in Figure 10-2) is slightly thinner, but also slightly less durable, than Secure Digital cards. Because it doesn't offer Secure Digital's data-protection features, MMC is less expensive. You'll find these cards in many Nokia models.

- **Secure Digital (SD)** This card (shown in Figure 10-3) features data-protection options not found in other cards. A slide-lock on the side protects data from accidental erasure, while cryptographic copyright protection keeps prying eyes away from your files. It also supports faster data-transfer rates than MMC. These factors contribute to a higher price than MMC cards.

- **TransFlash (T-Flash)** Designed specifically for mobile phones, the newest flash-memory medium, this card (shown in Figure 10-4) is also the smallest—approximately the size of a fingernail. Because it's so new, however, most memory-card readers (or devices, such as printers that feature memory-card slots) don't recognize the format. You can, however, purchase an SD adapter, which will enable you to use a TransFlash card with any device that supports SD cards.

FIGURE 10-2   The Multimedia Card is slightly smaller and less expensive than the Secure Digital card.

FIGURE 10-3 Secure Digital cards offer copyright protection not found in other removable flash memory cards.

FIGURE 10-4 The TransFlash card, designed specifically for cell phones, is the smallest flash memory card format.

Using Memory Card Adapters

Although sharing video is an important aspect of the camcorder phone experience (which I'll discuss in detail in Chapter 11), there's an easier way to get those files to your computer, especially if your phone allows you to go beyond the 15-second-per-clip limit. If your phone accepts flash memory cards, you can use them to transfer your video clips directly to a PC with a memory card reader.

You can purchase a standalone card reader that accepts all of the formats just discussed. SanDisk's ImageMate 8-in-1 Reader/Writer (shown in Figure 10-5) accepts eight different flash-memory card formats. You connect the unit to a PC via a USB 2.0 port (it's also backward compatible with the slower USB 1.1 ports on older PCs), insert a card, and transfer files to and from your PC. SanDisk also makes an ImageMate that connects to a FireWire (or 1394) port, which is faster than USB 2.0. Other companies that manufacture memory card readers include Kodak, SmartDisk, and Lexar.

If you use a Sony Ericsson phone that supports the Memory Stick format, you have the option of using a device that's slightly less obtrusive—a Memory Stick

FIGURE 10-5   SanDisk's ImageMate 8-in-1 Reader/Writer accepts eight varieties of flash-memory cards, including MMC, SD, and Memory Stick.

> **Did you know?**
>
> ## Beware of Battery Life
>
> Taking pictures with a camera phone is an extra drain on your handset's battery. Shooting video clips is a *real* drag on battery life. When shopping around for a camcorder phone, make sure it has a robust battery life rating, preferably more than four hours of talk time.
>
> If you're on a trip and plan to take lots of video footage (not to mention lots of still photos), it's a good idea to invest in a second battery. Better yet, buy an extended battery, one that provides more talk and standby time than the standard battery that comes with your phone. Extended batteries often provide two to three hours of more talk time than you'd get with a standard battery. It's best to purchase extra batteries through your carrier or cell phone manufacturer—be wary of third-party providers.

Reader Mouse. The mouse, which connects via USB 2.0, features a slot on the back of the unit to accept the Memory Stick. This way, you get a card reader without taking up additional space.

> **TIP** *Most Sony Vaio notebook PCs feature Memory Stick slots, so you can easily move clips between your camcorder phone and the computer.*

Choose a Model

The camcorder cell phone is a relatively new phenomenon, so there aren't as many units that offer video as there are that take still photographs. However, the available choices do vary in terms of features and execution. While the 15-second recording limit is standard, some phones will record less depending on how much sound you capture during the process. You'll also want to investigate how easily you can add such enhancements as text and voice messages and how easy it is to share your videos once you've captured them.

Next, I'll provide a brief overview of a few camcorder phones. This list isn't intended to be comprehensive, however, especially since more products are on the way.

Nokia 3620

This unit for AT&T Wireless, an update of Nokia's 3650 (shown in Figure 10-6), features an integrated camcorder that saves files in the 3GPP format, which is compatible with QuickTime and the RealOne Player. In fact, the RealOne Player is included on the handset, which lets you add music clips to your video recordings. It also provides a good experience for viewing streaming video content from news and entertainment websites.

You have to wade through several menu layers to get to the video recording functions. Also, while the Toshiba VM4050 records up to the full 15-second limit regardless of accompanying audio, the 3620 will max out at about 10 seconds if there's a lot of background noise in the scene you're taping.

Sending a video message involves the same process as sending a picture message. However, if you send a clip to another AT&T customer whose phone doesn't support video, the message is simply erased—that person won't receive any kind of text message, and AT&T doesn't feature a picture or video messaging site to view files like Sprint PCS.

FIGURE 10-6 Nokia's 3620 features Bluetooth, MMC expansion, and the RealOne media player.

How to Do Everything with Your Camera Phone

The 3620 does, however, feature Bluetooth and infrared support, so you can share video clips wirelessly with other Bluetooth or IrDA-enabled devices (such as PDAs). It also features a slot for a Multimedia Card, so you can add additional memory for storing your clips (the expansion card slot is, however, inconveniently located underneath the battery).

Samsung VM-A680

This stylish handset for Sprint PCS, shown in Figure 10-7, offers several video recording options you won't find on other units. You can use the camcorder with the cover closed, for example, and you can choose among brightness, color, and white-balance settings. The A680 also features a self-timer that delays taping for up to 10 seconds, so you can include yourself in the shot.

Like another Sprint camcorder phone, the Toshiba VM4050, the A680's talk-time battery life is uninspiring, rated at 3.2 hours. But it does take advantage of Sprint's Picture Mail functions and is well-received by reviewers as an attractive, well-performing cell phone.

FIGURE 10-7   You can shoot video clips with the Samsung VM-A680's cover closed.

Sony Ericsson P900

This high-performing GSM smart phone, shown in Figure 10-8, is designed for well-traveled business executives who need the P900's connectivity options. With features such as a high-resolution touch-screen display, Microsoft Outlook synchronization, and the ability to make and receive calls anywhere in the world, it's no wonder the P900 retails for $800.

Also included is a built-in camcorder that lets you shoot video in message mode, which limits you to 11-second clips, or video mode, which lets you shoot until you run out of memory. Fortunately, along with the 16MB of onboard memory, the phone accepts Memory Stick Duo expansion cards (you can expand up to 128MB of memory). Because the P900 uses a touch screen and stylus for input, it's easy to address your video messages.

Another eye-popping feature is the P900's rated talk time of 16 hours, which gives you plenty of leeway for shooting video footage without worrying about whether you'll be able to take that important call.

FIGURE 10-8   Sony Ericsson's P900 features video controls on its touch screen.

The P900's sticker price will keep most average users away, but its extensive features will appeal to business users looking for camcorder functions.

Toshiba VM4050

This Sprint PCS flip-style handset, shown in Figure 10-9, features a flash next to the lens that doubles as a movie light. The VM4050 tapes video clips for a full 15 seconds before automatically stopping, regardless of how much sound you capture during the recording process. The phone saves clips in the QuickTime .MOV format. Those 15-second clips are compressed to about 95KB on the phone; when you move them to your computer, they weigh in at about 200KB.

The VM4050 lets you store up to 30 pictures or video clips, and a meter helps you keep track of how much space remains on the unit. Sending video messages is a simple affair, requiring just a few clicks to send by e-mail or via **MMS** to other video-capable Sprint PCS phones (I'll go over how to send a video message in more detail in Chapter 11). You can also store video clips on Sprint's Picture Mail website along with your still photographs.

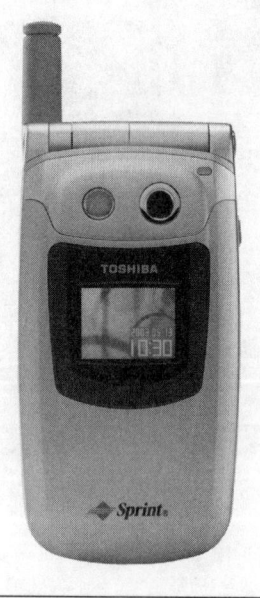

FIGURE 10-9   The Toshiba VM4050 saves movies in the QuickTime .MOV format.

Model	Carrier	Retail Price	Style	Talk/Standby Battery Life	Special Features
Nokia 3620	AT&T Wireless	$150	Candy bar	4 hours/ 8.3 days	MMC expansion slot; Bluetooth and IrDA enabled
Samsung VM-A680	Sprint PCS	$309.99	Flip	3.2 hours/ 9 days	Self timer
Sony Ericsson P900	Any GSM network (requires SIM card)	$799	Flip	16 hours/ 20 days	Continuous video recording mode; touch screen; Memory Stick Duo expansion slot
Toshiba VM4050	Sprint PCS	$329.99	Flip	3.3 hours/ 10 days	Camera flash also functions as video light

TABLE 10-1 Camcorder Phone Comparison

A few caveats to be aware of: Sprint rates the talk-time battery life at only 3.3 hours. Depending on your network coverage, you may get less than that, and any use of the camcorder will cut into that time, as well. Also, the VM4050 doesn't support any expansion cards, so after you reach the maximum of 30 pictures/video clips, you'll have to free up space by moving files to a computer. Finally, while this handset provides one-button access to the camera functions, you have to go through the main system menu to reach the camcorder.

Camcorder Phones at a Glance

There's as much variety in camcorder phones as there are in camera phones. Table 10-1 provides a quick overview of the models discussed earlier.

Moving On

Now that you know all about camcorder phones, it's time to shoot some video. In the next chapter, I'll discuss how to get good footage, how to share your video clips, where to find third-party content, and how to make a short movie, complete with soundtrack, using video-editing software.

Chapter 11
Capturing, Sharing, and Editing Video

How to...

- Shoot video clips
- Share video files
- Post video to moblogs
- Move clips to your PC
- Acquire video content from third-party sources
- Use video editing software

I recently watched two commercials from competing carriers touting their latest camcorder phones and video mail services. One commercial showed a man in the middle of a business meeting watching a clip sent by his wife. On his cell phone, the man sees his toddler-aged son throwing a ball against the living room wall and smashing a picture hanging there. The video as represented in the ad is crisp, clear, and professional looking. The other commercial involves a young man making salacious come-ons to a woman in front of the camera. The video is grainy and jerky, as if it were taken with a convenience-store surveillance camera. Let's just say one of these commercials is more accurate in its representation of cell phone video footage.

I'm not going to lie to you—you won't be screening home movies with the video footage you capture with your camcorder phone. While filmmakers have embraced low-cost digital video technology, don't expect to hear next year's winners at the Sundance Film Festival announcing that they shot their film on a Samsung A680.

Like camera phones, the point of a camcorder phone is to capture a spontaneous moment and share it with your friends. Also like VGA camera phones, camcorder phones come with certain limitations that you need to work around to capture the best footage possible.

In the following pages, I'll go over some tips and techniques for getting good footage. I'll also tell you how to share your video clips and how to view video from third-party sources.

Furthermore, although cell phone video isn't quite ready for prime time, you can still impress your friends by assembling your clips and creating a short movie, complete with soundtrack and special effects.

Shooting Video

At the most basic level, capturing video on a cell phone is no different than it is with a standard camcorder. You aim the lens and press a button to begin shooting and watch

CHAPTER 11: Capturing, Sharing, and Editing Video

the real-time footage on the display, and you can immediately review what you have captured on the phone's screen, which acts as a viewfinder. That's it for the similarities, although some of the differences do work in favor of camcorder phones.

Moving the footage to your computer can be less of a hassle with a camcorder phone, for example. And just try e-mailing a video you shot with a mini-DV camera—even with a high-speed connection, you and your recipient will be sitting around all day waiting for that file to transmit.

> **NOTE** *Yes, some home camcorders, such as the Sony DCR-HC85 MiniDV Handycam, feature an MPEG movie mode designed to capture low-resolution footage suitable for e-mailing, but I'd be surprised if many people actually use it.*

The only reason sharing standard camcorder video footage is difficult is because the quality of the footage is good. As I explained in the previous chapter, the better the video quality, the more space it occupies as a data file. So, just as you need to work within your camera phone's limitations, you also need to work with your camcorder phone's limitation.

Work with Strong Natural Light

Your cell phone's camcorder uses the same lens that operates the camera features, so the same rules regarding lighting apply. That is, the more light the better. Not only that, but the more natural light the better. Whereas many camera phones offer white balance adjustments for different lighting conditions (such as tungsten or fluorescent lights), most phones don't offer that option for the camcorder features. When the CMOS lens has to work hard to adjust for poor lighting, the subject ends up looking grainier than usual, as shown here:

However, if your only light source is indoor lighting, make sure it's bright enough that you can snap a picture without a flash. If you need a flash to take a picture, it's too dark to capture decent video footage with your camcorder phone.

> **NOTE** *Some camcorder phones, such as the Toshiba VM4050, feature a light that's designed to illuminate dim environments. The range of these lights is very small—about two or three feet—and they illuminate a small area, such as a face, not a whole body.*

Because the camcorder uses the same fixed-focus lens as your phone's still camera, make sure your subject is facing the direction of the light source. If the light source is coming from the back, not only will the subject appear in silhouette, but that will add to the graininess of your footage.

Get Close

I know, you thought I was through discussing the shortcomings of the fixed-focus CMOS lens, but this point bears repeating. With a fixed-focus lens, you have to get close to your subject. It's even more true with your phone's camcorder features. While distant subjects will lose detail in a still photo, those subjects can flat-out disappear when shooting video, as shown here:

Just to be clear, this applies when a person or small object is the focal point. If you're taking landscape shots, such as a skyline, you don't need to stand within a few feet of the buildings:

CAUTION: *Some phones offer zoom options with their camcorder features, but using them further degrades already shaky footage. Applying even a 2X zoom to a recording will render your video clip unwatchable.*

Let the Action Come to You

One of the reasons for the poor quality of camcorder phone footage is because the processor can only handle so much information. The more you move a camera while shooting, the more information needs to be processed in terms of determining the focal point and adjusting for lighting conditions, which means the processor needs to work harder, which further degrades the quality.

Also, because camcorder phones don't employ any kind of stabilization methods, any movement of your hand will cause the video to appear more jerky than *The Blair Witch Project*. If you must pan the camera to follow the action, do so as slowly as possible.

Using the Camcorder Function

Capturing video footage with your cell phone is as easy as taking a picture—it's simply a matter of pointing and shooting. About the only difference is that with most phones, you'll have to go through the menu to reach the camcorder functions instead of the one-click camera access button you find in the majority of camera phones.

How to ... Work with Audio

Your phone's camcorder will record sound along with video footage. Whereas a standard camcorder features a microphone designed to capture ambient audio, your phone uses the same microphone for phone calls to pick up audio during video capture. When used with the video functions, this microphone is ill-suited for blocking out certain ambient noises and acts more like a speakerphone than a boom mic, so you'll often hear an unpleasant cacophony of sounds unrelated to the subject of your video clip.

Keep in mind that when you're shooting video, the microphone is facing you, not your subject. If you wish to capture someone's voice, make sure they speak loudly. If other people are next to you, try to keep their sounds to a minimum, as their chatter or movements will show up loud and clear on the audio track. Also, keep in mind that the microphone is typically situated at the bottom of the phone, which is where you grip the handset when shooting video. It can be easy to cover up, depending on how you hold the phone. Anytime you move your hand—to pause a recording, for example—the microphone will record it as garbled noise.

Some phones let you record clips without sound, which is a good option if your footage doesn't involve someone speaking directly into the camera. Your other option is to replace the recorded sound with a different sound track in a video editor (I'll show you how to do this in the upcoming section, "Use Video Editing Software.").

To get to your phone's camcorder:

1. Click the phone's Menu button, then go to Video Camera or Camcorder (this is sometimes listed under the camera menu option).
2. Click Options, then Record.
3. Point the camera at your subject, using the screen as a viewfinder, then click Record or Start. Once recording has begun, you can use your phone's hotkeys to either pause or stop recording before the 15-second limit has expired.
4. After you've finished recording, use the hotkeys to either play the footage you just recorded or send the clip via e-mail or MMS.

Share Your Video Clips

Ah, this is the whole point, right? Capturing those precious, spontaneous moments and sharing them with your loved ones (or at least your well-liked ones). Sending video messages to your friends involves the same process as sending a picture message. It also involves the same limitations—that is, you can only send video messages to other phones on your carrier that support video clips (although the receiving phone doesn't necessarily have to feature a camcorder to be able to play back video clips). The details described next may differ on your phone, but the basic concept is the same:

1. Go to your phone's camcorder. Select My Videos or Saved Videos.

2. Click Options, then Send. If you want to send a multimedia message to an MMS-capable phone on the same carrier that can accept video clips, insert your recipient's phone number. Otherwise, enter an e-mail address or choose an entry from your phone's address book.

3. Depending on the phone, you may be prompted to include a voice memo and a text message. Include these as you wish, or click Skip to move to the next option.

4. Click Send.

Carriers provide different means of allowing you to watch video clips received as MMS messages on a cell phone. When you receive a message on AT&T Wireless, for example, you simply click the Open button to watch the video. With Sprint PCS, on the other hand, you'll receive a message with a long web link. After you select the link, you're taken to a web page where you download the clip onto your phone.

These options apply, of course, only if your phone supports video playback and uses the same carrier as the person who sent the clip. If you receive a video message from a Sprint customer and your Sprint phone doesn't support video playback, you'll get a text message with instructions to enter an e-mail address to which the file will be forwarded. AT&T Wireless, however, doesn't send any kind of message to recipients whose phones don't support video playback.

If you receive a video clip on a PC as an e-mail message from an AT&T Wireless customer, you'll simply receive a message with an attachment. Video e-mails sent from a Sprint customer include links to view the thumbnails of the clips. Clicking on a thumbnail will play the video in the QuickTime viewer (provided QuickTime is already installed on your computer). From the site, you can download videos to your computer (Sprint downloads all messages as compressed Zip files—see Chapter 4 for more information on Zip files) and send comments about the video to the sender's phone by clicking the Comments tab.

Sprint PCS Picture Mail

Of the three carriers that offer their own online picture messaging services, only Sprint PCS supports video clips. You can upload video files to Sprint's Picture Mail site just as you would photographs. You can also send video messages to other Sprint PCS video-capable phones or via e-mail. The only thing you can't do on the site is edit or enhance your clips the way you can still photographs.

NOTE *Although Verizon and T-Mobile didn't offer online video messaging services at the time of this writing, things change quickly in the wireless business. As video messaging becomes more commonplace, expect to see carriers beef up their online storage and messaging options.*

Once you've uploaded your clips to Picture Mail, you send a message following these steps:

1. Click Send Video next to the thumbnail of the clip you wish to send, as shown in Figure 11-1.

2. Enter a Sprint PCS phone number or an e-mail address in the To field. Or, select a name previously stored in your online address book.

3. Type a message in the Message field, shown in Figure 11-2.

4. Click Send.

When you receive an e-mail message containing multiple videos, you'll have the option to view all of the clips as a slideshow (that is, the Sprint site plays one clip after the other) or as thumbnails, as shown in Figure 11-3.

If you choose to view the clips as thumbnails, you'll see small images of each video available for download, as shown in Figure 11-4.

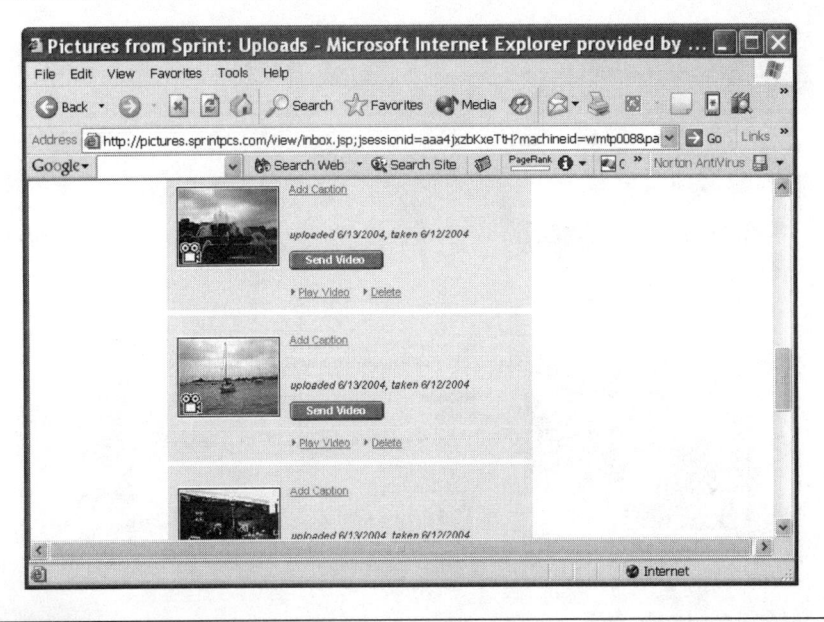

CHAPTER 11: Capturing, Sharing, and Editing Video 245

FIGURE 11-1 Click Send Video in Sprint PCS Picture Mail to begin sending a video message.

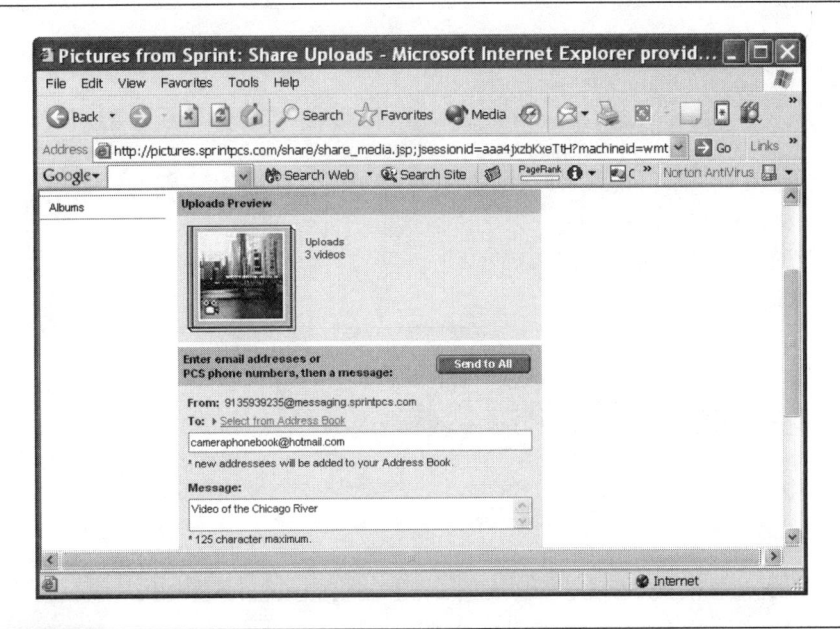

FIGURE 11-2 You can include a brief text message with your video message.

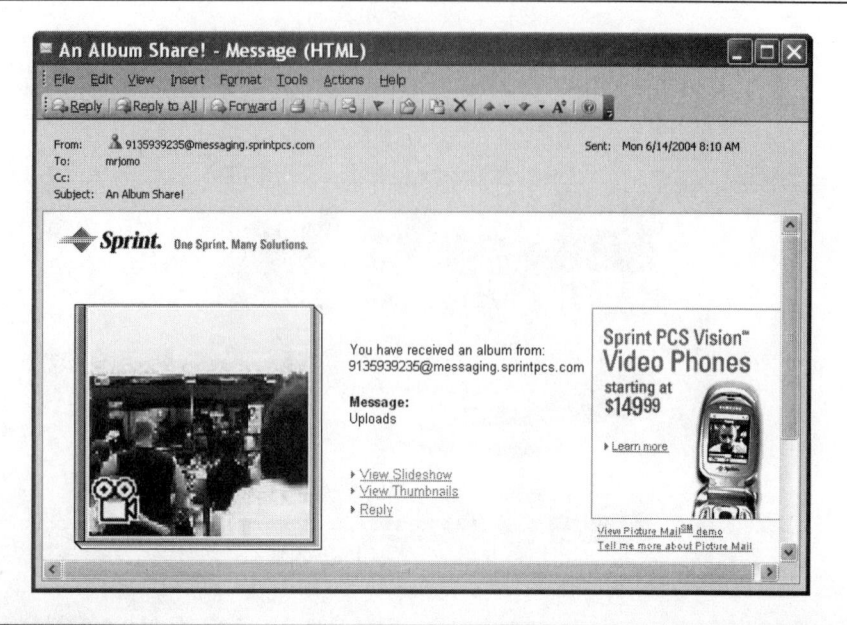

FIGURE 11-3 Recipients of Sprint Video Mail messages can view multiple files in a slideshow.

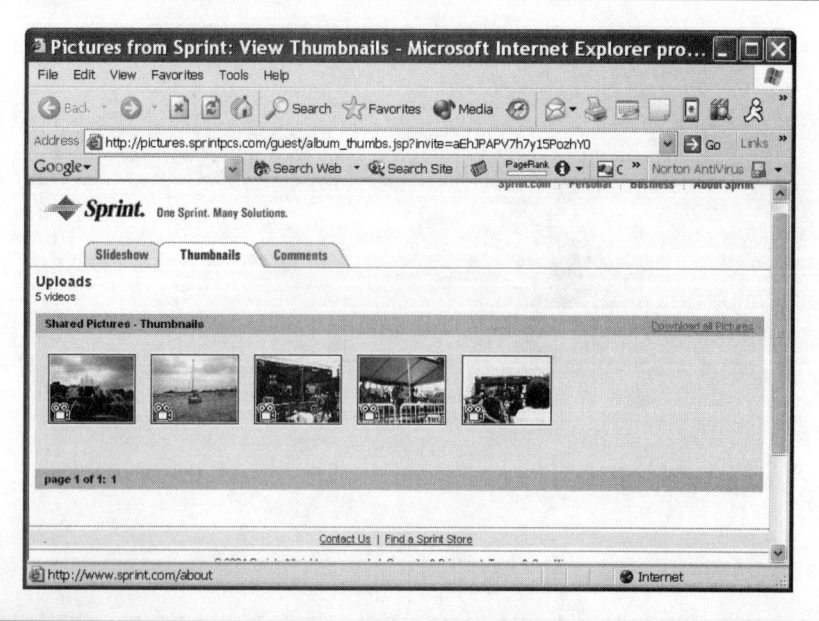

FIGURE 11-4 After receiving a Sprint video message, you can view each clip as a thumbnail image.

Sprint groups all of the videos into a single Zip file. After you choose to download all of the clips, click Save from the File Download dialog, then choose a folder to store the file:

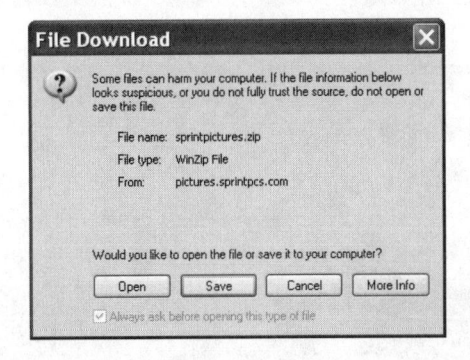

Textamerica

And you thought we were through with the whole moblog discussion. That topic *would* have been exhausted if not for Textamerica, which allows you to post video clips taken with your cell phone in addition to still photographs. The site accepts videos 1MB or smaller in QuickTime .MOV, MPEG-4, and 3GP formats (see Figure 11-5). A typical 15-second clip taken with a VGA camcorder phone will occupy between 200KB and 300KB, so this shouldn't be a problem. You post videos to the same address that you use to send camera phone pictures (see Chapter 8 for information on posting pictures to Textamerica). The only difference is that because of network traffic, videos may take up to several hours to appear on your site, whereas photos appear almost immediately.

Your video will appear in a small window and will play automatically after visitors click on the thumbnail, as shown in Figure 11-6. Visitors will need the QuickTime Player software installed on their PCs. Textamerica automatically places a link to Apple's QuickTime site below the clip window so visitors who don't have it can download QuickTime immediately.

NOTE *You can watch a video I posted to cameraphonebook.textamerica.com.*

Move Clips to Your PC

Unless your phone accepts memory expansion cards on which you can store hundreds of clips, you'll eventually need to transfer these files to your PC. Even if you have

248 How to Do Everything with Your Camera Phone

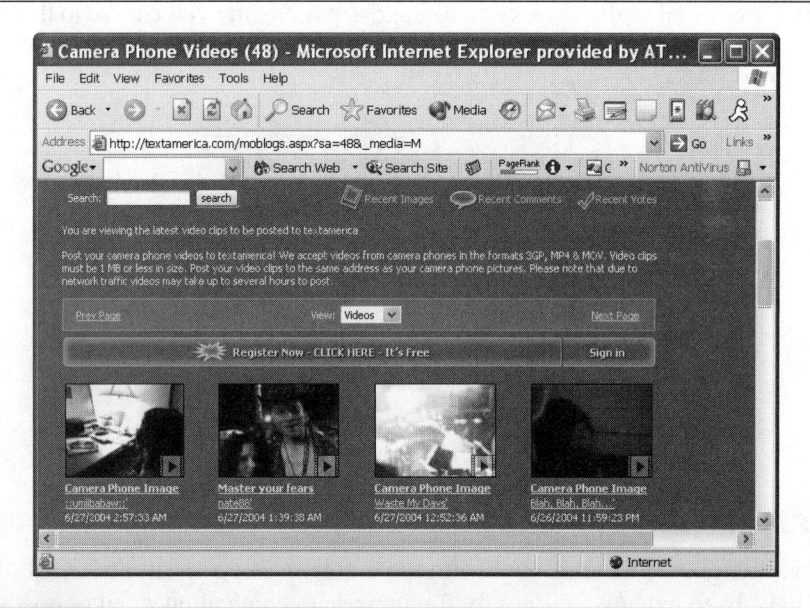

FIGURE 11-5 You can post short video clips from your cell phone to Textamerica.

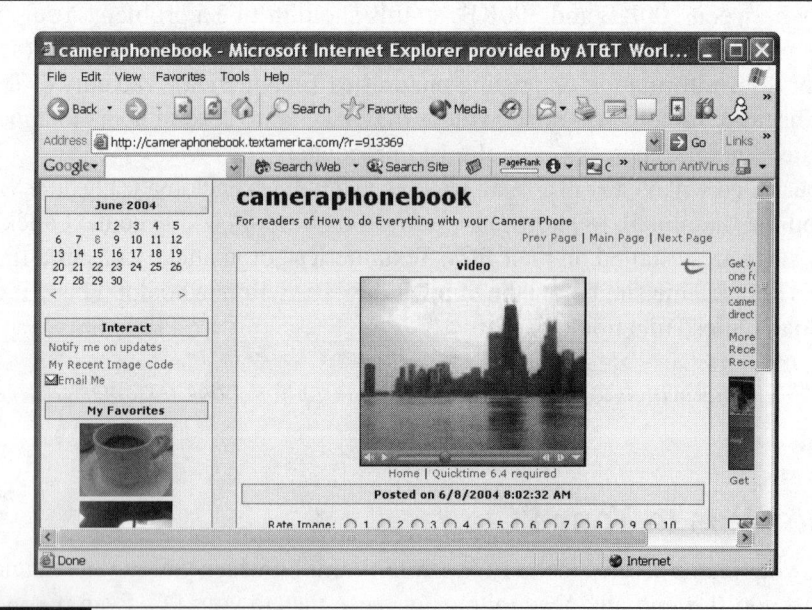

FIGURE 11-6 If QuickTime is installed on your computer, you can view video clips within a Textamerica site.

plenty of storage space, you'll still want to move them to your computer in order to perform such tasks as making short films.

E-mail

You can e-mail the clips to yourself, using the same steps described previously to send a video message. Unless you have a data plan that includes unlimited picture and video messaging, such as Sprint's Picture Mail, this can get expensive. A typical 15-second clip will take up between 90KB and 100KB. Even if you pay only 1 cent per kilobyte, that's up to $1 for each message (sent and received) depending on your plan, and those charges can quickly add up to a hefty surcharge on your monthly statement.

> **NOTE** *The clips I referred to above were shot with phones that include a VGA lens. Video clips taken with a megapixel camera lens will likely result in larger file sizes.*

Memory Cards

The flash memory card represents the best method for moving clips to your PC. It's the fastest, most cost-effective solution available, but the catch is that your phone must support expansion cards. If it does, make sure you save your video clips to the memory card. These are the steps required on the Nokia 3620, but the process is similar on whatever camcorder phone you use:

1. Go to the main menu, select Video Recorder, then click Options.
2. Under Settings, select Memory in Use.
3. Click Change, then select Memory Card.

From that point on, every video clip you record will be stored on the memory expansion card. When you're ready to move these files to a PC, simply insert the card into a memory card reader. Windows will recognize the card as an external storage drive and assign it a drive letter.

> **NOTE** *Because C: is typically assigned to the hard drive and D: is usually the CD/DVD drive, your memory card will show up as E: or higher. The exact drive letter assignment will depend on how many storage devices, such as a Zip or USB plug-in drive, you have installed on your computer.*

FIGURE 11-7 In Windows Explorer, select the files you wish to copy to a memory card.

From this point, you simply transfer the files through Windows Explorer. If you wanted to move your clips to a folder called My Videos, for example, you would use the following steps:

1. Click to select the file you wish to copy. To select several files in a sequence, click the first file, then select the last file in the sequence while holding the SHIFT key. To select more than one noncontinuous file, hold the CTRL key while making your selections (see Figure 11-7).

2. In Windows XP, click Copy This File from the File and Folder Tasks pane on the left side of the screen.

3. In the Copy Items dialog, shown in Figure 11-8, select the folder where you'll store a copy of the files, then click Copy.

Acquire Video From Third-Party Sources

One of the great things about working with video on your cell phone is that you don't have to do all of the work. There's plenty of video content available for your

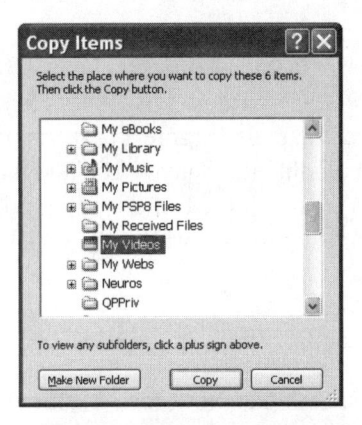

FIGURE 11-8 Choose the appropriate drive and folder in which to copy your video clips.

viewing pleasure, essentially turning your cell phone into a mini-television set. In fact, your phone need not include a video camera for you to be able to take advantage of this. Several phones, such as the LG VX6000, will let you download video content despite the lack of camcorder functions.

I'm sure you have a few important questions at this point, such as where do I find this content? How much will this cost me? Why do I want to watch video on my cell phone?

I'll answer the last question first. Why watch video on a cell phone? Because you can. Or, to put it less flippantly, it's all part of the convergence of computing, communication, and entertainment devices. Just as you can make phone calls and watch television through a PC, phones are becoming more powerful computing devices. Soon, industry watchers believe, there will be little distinction among these devices. Your TV won't be just a TV, your computer will no longer be just a computer, and your phone will no longer be just a phone. So whether you're in your living room or thousands of miles from home, you'll have access to all of this information.

The services described next use streaming video to deliver content to your handset. Because of the limitations of current wireless networks, these video feeds appear as little more than a series of still images with audio. If you're lucky, you'll get video playback at 15 frames per second, compared to the 30 frames-per-second transmission of broadcast television. Also, the quality of the video and audio depends on your signal strength and how much traffic is on the network. You may encounter audio drop outs, for example, if network traffic is especially heavy. As network bandwidth improves, however, expect the quality of the video to improve as well.

MobiTV

The MobiTV service for Sprint PCS customers includes 16 channels of programming, including CNBC, Fox Sports, CNET, and Discovery Channel. The company also plans to add more premium channels (Figure 11-9). As of this writing, 15 phones feature MobiTV support, including the Sanyo 8100 and the LG VI-5225. MobiTV's website (www.mobitv.com) features the full list of supported phones.

You'll need a phone that supports Sprint's PCS Vision service. To download MobiTV to your phone:

1. Go to the Menu, then click Downloads.
2. Select Applications, then Get New, then Multimedia.
3. Choose MobiTV from the list of applications.

Once you're logged on to the service, you can change channels just as you would on a standard television, except you'll have to wait a few seconds for Sprint's network to receive a signal. MobiTV costs $9.99 a month if you don't subscribe to

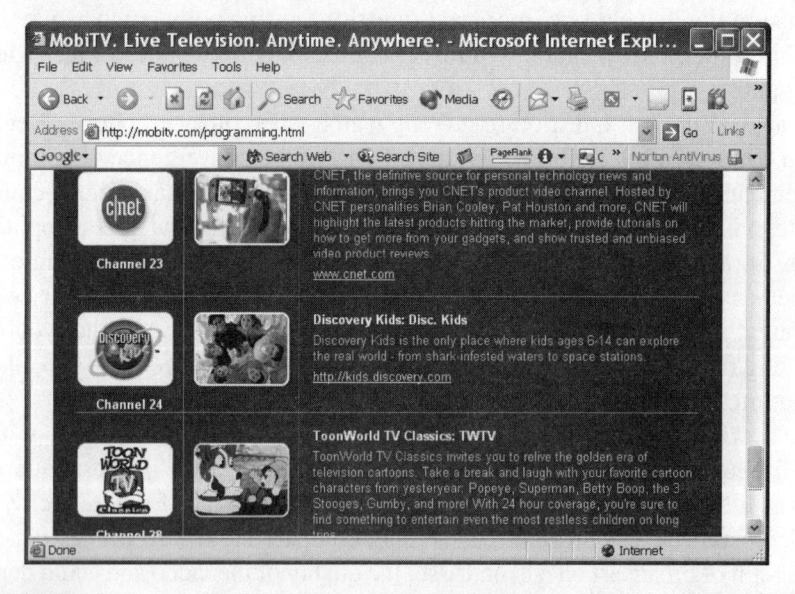

FIGURE 11-9   MobiTV offers 16 channels of programming to Sprint PCS customers.

PCS Vision, which itself costs $15 a month. If you subscribe to the PCS Vision Pictures Pack, you'll receive a $5 monthly credit for your MobiTV service. PCS Vision Premium Pack subscribers receive a $10 monthly credit.

> **NOTE** *These prices are always subject to change.*

RealOne

RealNetworks, the maker of the popular RealOne media player for PCs, also offers a mobile version that downloads streaming video for $4.95 a month to Sprint PCS and AT&T Wireless customers (see Figure 11-10). Fox Sports, ABC News, and the Weather Channel are among the programming available to subscribers. RealOne provides 90 different clips and four hours of new content each day.

Sprint PCS customers who use a Java-enabled phone can get RealOne by using the same steps just described for MobiTV; just choose RealOne from the list of applications. RealOne is built into the Nokia 3650 and 3620 handsets for AT&T

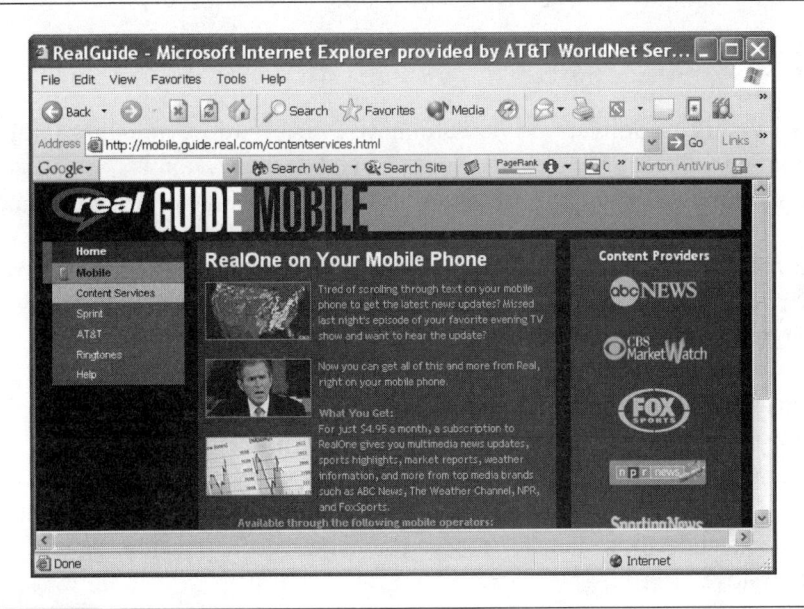

FIGURE 11-10 RealOne delivers video content to Sprint PCS and AT&T Wireless customers.

Wireless, as well as the Nokia N-Gage gaming device. The service is also available for those with subscriptions to the carrier's mMode service. Customers with other mMode-compatible phones can download the service through the mMode home page:

1. Select either the News, Entertainment, or Sports categories, then select RealOne for mMode.
2. Select Subscribe, then Buy to purchase a subscription.

NOTE *Java is a programming language developed by Sun Microsystems that enables applications to be downloaded to a PC or device via the Internet. RealOne is a Java-based application.*

CAUTION *AT&T Wireless customers pay usage fees on top of the $4.95 rate for RealOne, depending on how many kilobytes of data your monthly mMode plan supports. The extra fees don't apply to Sprint PCS Vision customers, who pay a flat rate for unlimited Vision access. If you access RealOne without PCS Vision, however, you will incur per kilobyte charges. RealOne notes that all of its content uses less than 300KB per clip.*

1KTV

The 1KTV service delivers on-demand news, information, and entertainment programming to AT&T Wireless, Sprint PCS, and Nextel customers, and its service should be available to Verizon Wireless customers by the time this book is printed. Along with its own original programming—1KTV News, Showbiz, Horoscopes, New Music, and Really Weird News—1KTV also offers Fox Sports, The Weather Channel, and movie reviews from *Variety* (see Figure 11-11). The company lists all compatible phones on its website (www.1ktv.com).

The service runs on cell phones compatible with the Java J2ME and BREW platforms (see explanation in "The Difference Between Java and BREW"). You subscribe to 1KTV through your phone's Internet options. The average show lasts between 60 and 90 seconds. Because the service transmits programming at a low data rate—between 1Kbps and 4Kbps—the experience is more akin to watching a multimedia slide show than TV programming, but at $2.95 a month, it is cheaper than alternative offerings.

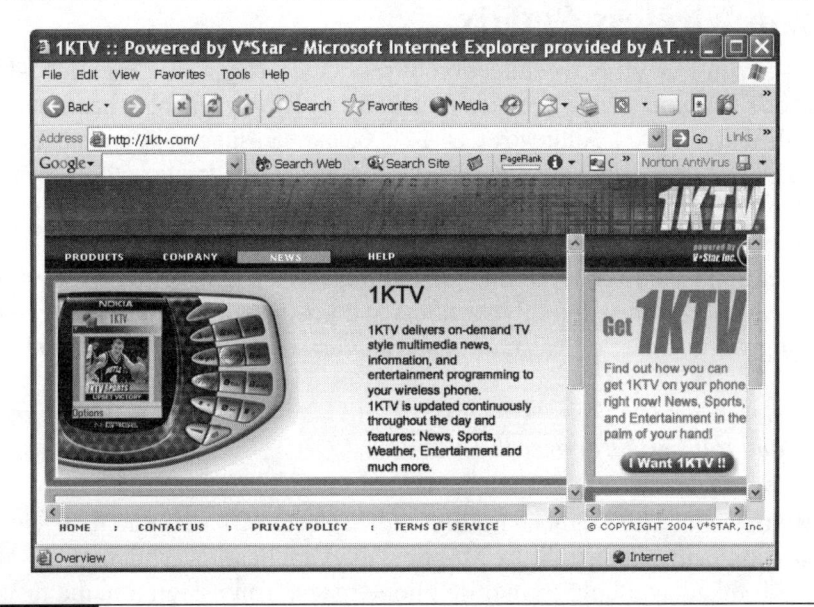

FIGURE 11-11 1KTV's video offerings include original programming.

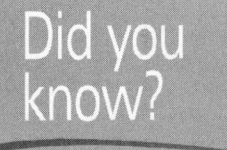

Did you know?

The Difference Between Java and BREW

For reasons I can't explain, two of the main operating platforms for wireless applications have coffee connotations. Java is Sun Microsystems' programming language designed for handheld devices and set-top boxes. J2ME (Java 2 Platform Micro Edition) is the wireless version of the platform, allowing developers to create applications for cell phones and other mobile devices. Both GSM (AT&T Wireless, Cingular, and T-Mobile, for example) and CDMA (Sprint PCS and Verizon Wireless) networks support J2ME applications.

BREW (Binary Runtime Environment for Wireless) is an open-source development platform, which means it's not owned by any particular company or organization. Instead, the source code—the building blocks of a program—is available to the public for use and modification. BREW applications are written specifically for phones that operate over CDMA networks.

Verizon Wireless GetFlix

Part of Verizon's Get It Now collection of services, GetFlix (see Figure 11-12), lets the carrier's customers view live video on their Get It Now–enabled handsets, which include the LG VX6000, Audiovox CDM-8900, and Samsung a610 and a670 camera phones. Unlike the previously mentioned services, which focus on delivering news and entertainment content, GetFlix is more personal in its nature. The service lets you view webcam footage on your cell phone, whether it's a public webcam, a camera you've set up in your home, or one that belongs to a friend or family member. If you have a webcam set up in your home and you want to keep tabs on what's happening while you're on vacation, you can view that footage on your cell phone.

> **NOTE** *A webcam is a digital camera, still or video, designed to capture images and transmit them over the Internet.*

GetFlix works with Logitech Mobile Video. Customers who purchase a webcam from the company can install the Mobile Video application, which makes their webcam footage available to mobile phone users. You assign a name to your

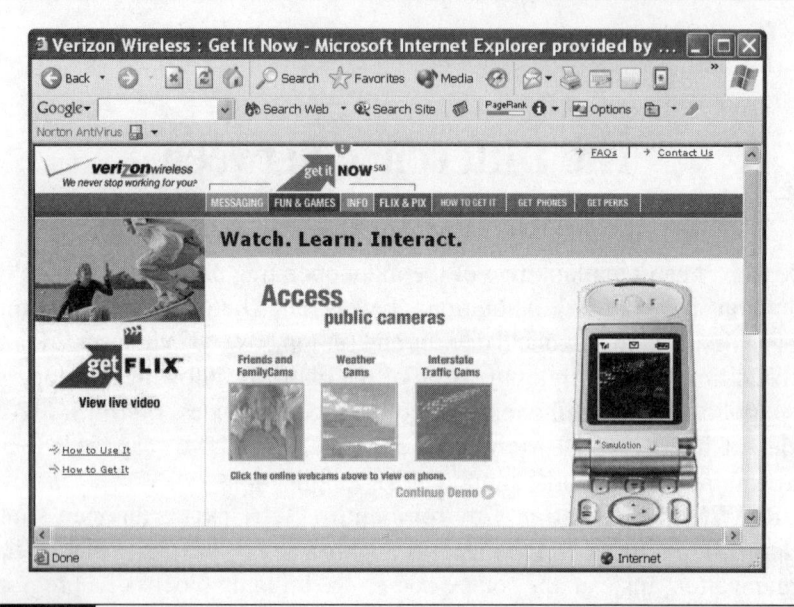

FIGURE 11-12 Verizon Wireless' GetFlix lets you view webcam footage on your cell phone.

Voices from the Community

The Tip of the Iceberg

Don't think of camera phones as camera phones only. Think of what they are evolving into: powerful multimedia recording and transmitting devices that offer still photography, audio and video recording, and streaming video/television reception. Think of camera phones with three, four, five megapixels and more, powerful digital zoom lenses, bright flashes, and sophisticated photo/video editing software. Within a few years, hundreds of millions of people around the world will be able to document everything that occurs around them.

An automobile accident, a train wreck, a tornado, a political rally, a visual abuse of power by the government, military, or police—everything can be recorded, stored, and sent around the world. Individual citizens will routinely beat professional reporters and photographers to the story. Law enforcement agents will be able to more easily identify suspects and wanted criminals.

But camera phones also can serve "the Dark Side." Government agents will be able to increase their surveillance on innocent civilians, pornographers will be able to more easily capture photos and videos of children and adults, and employees will be able to photograph and video-record confidential information.

The Dark Side exists with all technology, but it's not a reason for hand-wringing. It's a reason to truly understand the depth and breadth of the effects of camera phones and to develop appropriate policies to deal with the problems.

Camera phones will affect consumers and businesses in ways the original designers never thought. No longer will most people say, "If only I had a camera!" Camera phones will replace the few photos in your wallet or purse with an electronic album of hundreds of photos and videos stored inside the handset and on memory cards. Camera phones will be "memory joggers" as we store photos of products we're thinking of buying, locations we want to find again, people's faces we need to remember.

Businesses will see increased efficiency from the ability to better sell their products and receive information and advice. A real estate agent sends photos of a new home to potential buyers, a doctor in the field sends photos of a patient's wound to a colleague to obtain advice, a construction worker sends videos of problems on-site to a supervisor who is miles away. Barcodes and similar

> technologies that embed information could become extremely popular for camera phone users—both businesses and consumers—who will be able to obtain information or purchase products by snapping a photo of a barcode and sending it to a server.
>
> This is just the tip of the iceberg.
>
> *—Alan Reiter*
> *President, Wireless Internet & Mobile Computing*
> *Editor, www.cameraphonereport.com*

camera, which enables GetFlix customers to add it to their list of friends. When one of your friends has logged their camera on to the Internet, you'll receive an alert on your phone.

To sign up for GetFlix, which costs $5.25 per month plus airtime charges, do the following:

1. Go to your phone's menu, then click the Get It Now icon.
2. Select Get Apps, then click the Shopping Cart icon to browse the Get It Now shop.
3. Select the GetPix category, then the Logitech Mobile application.
4. Select a payment option, then download the application.

Logitech's Mobile Video Cam website (mobilevideo.logitech.com) includes a list of public webcams, including cities, scenery, and entertainment. If you have a Logitech webcam that you'd like to make available to your Verizon Wireless mobile phone, download the free Mobile Video software from the Logitech Mobile Video website (mobilevideo.logitech.com).

Use Video Editing Software

Yes, it's fun to get that jaw-dropping reaction from your friends the moment they discover that you can shoot video with your cell phone, but the satisfaction that comes from causing an acute bout of techno-envy is fleeting. Now that you have a collection of 15-second-or-less video files, you're probably wondering what you can do to make them a little more presentable. After all, 15 seconds is hardly enough to make a movie. Or is it?

Video editing software, for the most part, is designed for camcorder enthusiasts who want to add a little pizzazz to the footage they've collected. Some software programs, like Adobe Premiere, are sophisticated enough to create professional-level effects and transitions. Those products also cost about $700. There are also plenty of video-editing tools available for the novice user, but they're still targeted toward camcorder rather than specifically to camcorder phone users.

As camcorder phones become more popular, however, expect to see more tools designed specifically to meet those needs.

U-Lead VideoStudio 8

I tested one product, U-Lead Systems' VideoStudio 8, which includes features designed to handle the needs of footage captured from camcorder phones. With it, I was able to make a short film, complete with music soundtrack, cobbled together from a collection of short clips.

This $99 entry-level video-editing application is hardly the only program available for novice moviemakers—Roxio VideoWave Movie Creator and Apple iLife, which includes the iMovie application—are two of the better options. What separates VideoStudio from the pack is its support for video formats favored by camcorder phones. This application (shown in Figure 11-13) features built-in support for MPEG-4 files and, for an extra $30, you can purchase plug-ins (add-on software tools) to add 3GP support.

Working with the Wizard

In a nod to beginners, VideoStudio features a Movie Wizard when you start the program, which leads you through the process of selecting a video, adding text, selecting music, saving the file, and burning a disc (see Figure 11-14).

With the wizard, first you select the files you wish to insert. You can change the sequence of the clips by dragging a file to a different position in the Change Clip Sequence dialog, as shown here:

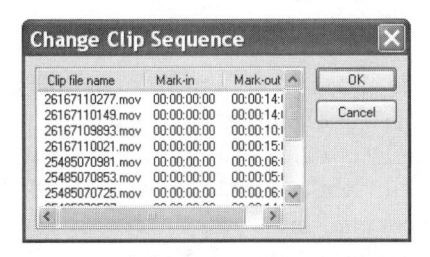

You can also do this after the clips are loaded into the timeline by sliding the thumbnail of the file to the position you want. Once you've put the clips in the proper sequence, click Next.

260 How to Do Everything with Your Camera Phone

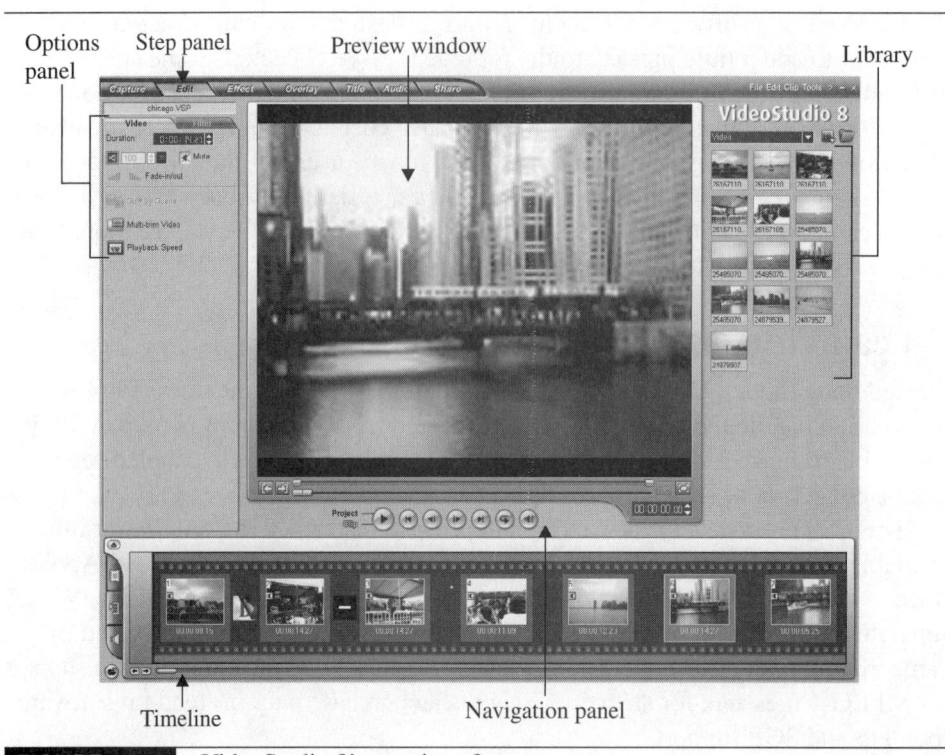

FIGURE 11-13 VideoStudio 8's user interface

In the next step, the wizard prompts you to add a title and background music to your video. To load background music, click the folder icon to browse through your system to find the music file you wish to add—VideoStudio supports the MP3 and Windows Media Audio (WMA) music file formats (see Figure 11-15).

TIP *Click the down-arrow button on the bottom left of the screen to access the title and music options.*

You'll notice a volume slide in this step. This controls the background music's audio level (see Figure 11-16). The more you slide the button to the left, the louder the background music selected will be. Moving it to the right will increase the sound captured with the video clip while decreasing the level of the background music. If someone is speaking in your clip, this is a good way to keep music in the background while keeping the focus on the dialog (just like they do in the movies!). If you only

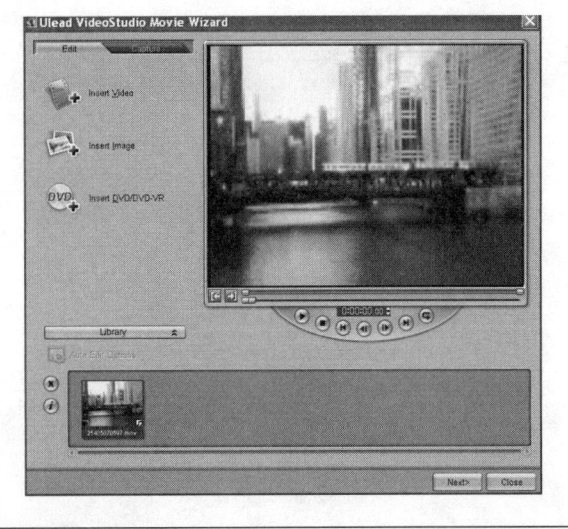

CHAPTER 11: Capturing, Sharing, and Editing Video 261

FIGURE 11-14 VideoStudio's Movie Wizard guides you through the movie-creation process.

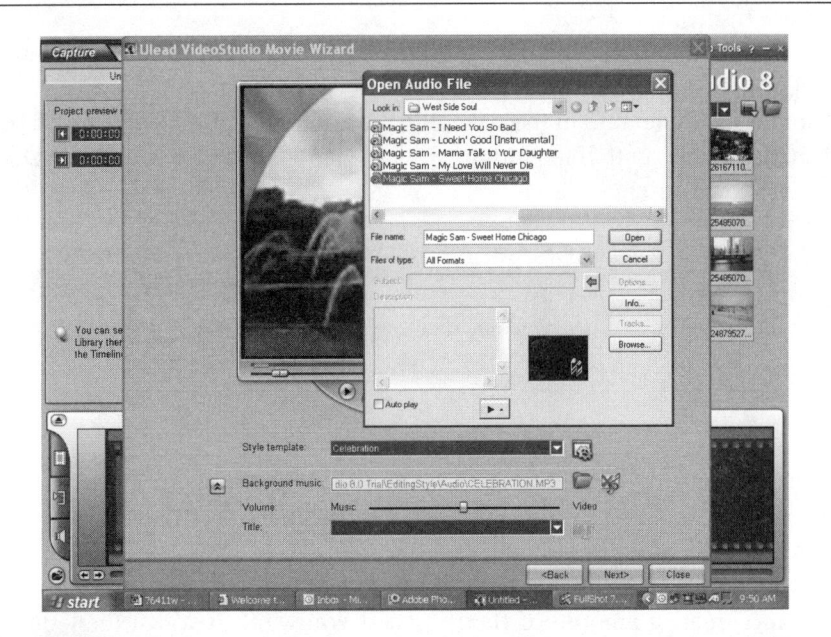

FIGURE 11-15 Load the background music of your choice in the Movie wizard.

FIGURE 11-16 The volume slide controls the audio level of the background music.

want background music, slide the bar all the way to the left, which will mute all of the background audio captured on video.

Another handy feature in the wizard is the ability to set the duration of your movie. Click on the button next to the Style Template menu to access the Duration dialog, as shown here:

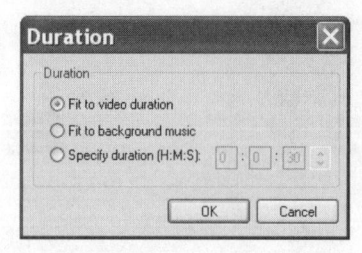

From here, you can set your movie to run at a specified length, or set the movie to run as long as the background music.

The wizard is a fine way to learn the basics of VideoStudio, but it doesn't provide the greatest amount of flexibility. If you want to adjust the length of individual clips, add transition effects between scenes, or fade the music in and out, you'll need to plunge headfirst into the program.

CHAPTER 11: Capturing, Sharing, and Editing Video   **263**

Making the Movie

In the interest of being thematically consistent, I decided to create a short movie about Chicago, one that the city's Tourism Bureau would be proud to show to visitors—that is, if it were shot on digital video instead of a Toshiba VM4050 camcorder phone. Still, the concept is solid. I took shots of some well-known landmarks, captured a few scenes from the city's annual blues festival, and—to show that Chicago isn't just concrete jungle—included a few scenes of the beach and boaters on Lake Michigan, for a total of 13 clips. For background music, I chose "Sweet Home Chicago" by Magic Sam (I know, not very original. At least I didn't choose "The Night Chicago Died").

CAUTION *Be careful about shooting public events such as the Chicago Blues Festival, which may have strict policies against taking video footage of the performers. See Appendix B for more information about privacy, security, and copyright issues.*

After launching the program, the first thing you'll want to do is click the Edit tab in the Step Panel at the top of the screen. In this window, you load the video files that you'll be working with into the program by clicking the folder icon at the top-right corner. Once the files are loaded, you'll see thumbnails of each clip in the Library.

Next, to assemble your movie, drag the clips to the timeline at the bottom of the screen (you'll see a Drag and Drop Video Clip Here box). You can rearrange the order of the clips even after you've moved them to the timeline. After you've assembled all of your clips, you'll see the length displayed in the Project Preview Range on the top left of the screen (see Figure 11-17).

Next, you can add transition effects between clips. VideoStudio comes with a wide selection of effects in several categories, including 3D, rotate, stretch, and peel. Click the Effect tab, then choose an effect from the drop-down menu in the Library. When you select a category, VideoStudio previews each effect in a thumbnail (see Figure 11-18). To add an effect, simply drag and drop the effect thumbnail in between two clips in the timeline. After you've placed the effect in the timeline, you can set the duration (typically one second or less), choose the color, and select the direction of the effect (you can set a peel effect, for example, to move from the bottom left to the top right).

To add a title to the first clip of your movie, click the Title tab, then double-click the movie window to type in your text. Use the tools on the left side to change the

FIGURE 11-17 After loading your clips into the library, drag and drop them to the timeline to arrange the sequence.

FIGURE 11-18 VideoStudio's transition effects

font, size, and color of the text. You can also make the text vertical and add animation effects to the text (Figure 11-19). In the timeline, you can change the entry and exit point of the title by dragging the clip or adjusting the length of the bar.

To add music, click the Audio tab in the Step panel, then click the folder icon in the Library to find a music file to load into the program (see Figure 11-20). After the music icon appears in the Library, click and drag it to the bottom row of the timeline (next to the musical notation).

For the movie I made, the video clips totaled two minutes and 17 seconds, but the song was more than four minutes. To edit the song to fit the video, I placed the cursor at the yellow end marker of the music bar, then dragged it back to match the spot where the video ends (Figure 11-21). Because I didn't want the music to end abruptly, I clicked the Fade Out button in the Options panel (you can also opt to fade the music in).

Neither did I want the background noise captured in the video files to be audible in the final movie. One way to eliminate background noise is to click the Storyboard View icon next to the timeline, select a clip from the timeline, then click Mute in the Options panel (see Figure 11-22). You can do this for each clip in the timeline.

FIGURE 11-19   VideoStudio's titling feature includes animation effects.

FIGURE 11-20 Drag music from the library and drop it in the timeline to insert a soundtrack file.

FIGURE 11-21 With the timeline, you can adjust the length of the music clip to match the movie.

CHAPTER 11: Capturing, Sharing, and Editing Video   **267**

FIGURE 11-22   To eliminate the background audio from your captured video files, select a clip in the Storyboard view, then click Mute from the Options panel.

TIP   *Make sure you save your work frequently. VideoStudio saves its files as "projects" in the native .VSP format. You'll be able to save your movie in a different format once you've completed your project. If you want to view your clips on a phone, save it as an MPEG file.*

If you prefer finer control over the sound, VideoStudio provides a couple of different methods for performing audio mixing. In Edit mode, click the Storyboard View icon next to the timeline, then select a clip in the timeline. In the Options Panel, you'll see the Clip Volume Control, which represents the percentage of the original recorded volume in a clip (from 0 percent to 500 percent). To reduce the background audio of a video clip, enter a new value in the Clip Volume Control (shown in Figure 11-23).

VideoStudio also features a Volume Rubber Band, a horizontal line in the middle of the track that's visible in the timeline when you click the Audio View button next to the timeline. You can use the rubber band to adjust the volume of the music or video track, as shown in Figure 11-24. With camcorder phone footage, however, you're less likely to use this feature, which is designed for detailed audio control for higher-quality video files.

FIGURE 11-23 The Clip Volume Control provides more detailed audio-level management.

FIGURE 11-24 The Volume Rubber Band lets you control audio levels at specific points in a video clip.

CHAPTER 11: Capturing, Sharing, and Editing Video 269

FIGURE 11-25 Video Studio lets you save movies in a format appropriate for online viewing.

Now that you've assembled your clips and inserted a soundtrack, it's time to export your movie to a format that anyone with a PC can view. Click the Share tab at the top of the screen to bring up the different exporting choices in the Options panel. After clicking the Share Video Online option, you'll see choices for saving your movie in varying qualities of Windows Media Video (.WMV) files, which formats your movie for playback in the Windows Media Player (see Figure 11-25).

If you want your video to be viewable in both the QuickTime and RealOne players, click Create Video File, shown in Figure 11-26, then select NTSC MPEG-2. You can also create a streaming video file for RealVideo (.RM) and Windows Media (.WMV) formats.

The Future of Video

Cell phone video is still in its infancy. It's likely that in a few years we'll look back at these times and scoff at how primitive the technology was. Industry watchers believe the following technologies will soon be coming to a cell phone near you.

FIGURE 11-26 Save your movies in a variety of formats with Video Studio.

Video Calls

Sometimes it seems as if the point of new technology is to make *The Jetsons* a reality. As faster 3G networks become widespread, expect to see phones that support two-way video calls hit the market. While making a call, you'll point your phone's integrated camera at yourself, while the person on the other end does the same. You'll be able to see each other in real time while holding a conversation. The EV-DO network, which Verizon is rolling out, supports video calls.

TV Tuners

The news and entertainment offerings you currently get on your cell phone will pale in comparison to cell phones with integrated TV tuners. Currently available in Japan, these tuner-equipped phones allow you to watch local broadcasts instead of a predetermined selection of channels. On tuner-equipped phone, the Toshiba V401T, even lets you record up to 12 minutes of footage, so it's like having a television and VCR in one tiny package.

Moving On

That's it for the main portion of the book, but there's still some unfinished business. In the following appendices, we'll take a look at what you can expect from megapixel camera phones, and I'll review the privacy and security concerns surrounding camera phones. I'll also detail the proper etiquette for using your camera or video phone.

Part V

Appendixes

Appendix A: Working with a Megapixel Phone

How to…

- Shop for megapixel camera phones
- Get the best images possible
- Crop your images
- Change the default image name
- Print your pictures

Although I've focused mostly on VGA-quality camera phones, I've mentioned megapixel camera phones several times throughout this book. The most obvious gain for consumers who purchase this type of camera phone lies in the larger images these devices provide, but there are other improvements as well, such as higher memory capacities and more direct methods for moving images to a PC. However, with these improvements in the technology come other issues that you'll need to address.

For starters, bigger images mean larger file sizes. With that in mind, you'll have to consider very carefully how many picture messages you plan to send in a month. Related to this issue is how you plan to move the pictures to a computer. Because you won't want to eat up valuable airtime e-mailing pictures to yourself, tools such as data cables, IR, and Bluetooth will be even more valuable.

In this section, I'll review the features you'll see in megapixel camera phones and why they're important to you, as well as discuss memory and messaging issues.

What to Look For

We always want something better. It's in our nature. The digital camera industry is working overtime to slake our lust for more megapixels, which is why today you can find a 6-megapixel camera for the price that a 3-megapixel camera cost just three years ago. Camera phones won't catch up to that level anytime soon, but it won't be long before they're on par with low-end digital cameras.

The first megapixel camera phones offered in the U.S. measure between 1 (1152 × 864 pixels) and 1.3 megapixels (1280 × 1024 pixels), compared with the 0.3 megapixels (640 × 480 pixels) you get with VGA-quality camera phones. Because megapixel images are much larger than VGA, as you can see in Figure A-1, you get much more image detail *and* the ability to crop parts of a photo while retaining more pixel information.

APPENDIX A: Working with a Megapixel Phone   **277**

FIGURE A-1   The picture on the left is a megapixel image; the photo on the right was taken with a VGA camera phone.

Along with better image quality, you'll notice how much more megapixel camera phones resemble real cameras (see Figure A-2), which is just as useful for the person being photographed as it is for the photographer (see Appendix B for more information). However, not all megapixel camera phones are created equally.

FIGURE A-2   Sony Ericsson S700's lens resembles that of a digital camera.

The Lens

When it comes to megapixel camera phones, the lens is the most important feature. In the first wave of these devices, most camera phones use the same CMOS lens found in VGA handsets. Although more megapixels mean larger images, the quality, as measured in color accuracy and image clarity, may only be slightly better than what you'll get with a VGA camera phone.

Camera phone manufacturers include CMOS sensors in their products because they're less expensive and consume less power than their CCD counterparts, which makes them ideal for small devices such as cell phones. Also, because camera phones were first designed to be a supplement to, not a replacement for, your regular digital or film camera, it made sense to sacrifice quality for price. However, these products caught on faster than anyone could have imagined. With so many people capturing moments they'd like to savor, image quality is becoming more important. Also, with megapixel camera phones on the market and multimegapixel phones around the corner, it makes little sense to continue to sacrifice quality.

Enter the CCD sensor. When a CCD sensor captures an image, all of the pixel is devoted to light capture, which results in a more uniform output. CMOS sensors, on the other hand, are less sensitive to light, which results in more noise (anomalies such as speckles and graininess), especially in low-light environments. Among the first batch of megapixel camera phones scheduled to be available in the U.S., only the LG 8000 (shown in Figure A-3) and the Sony Ericsson S700 include the CCD sensor.

FIGURE A-3 The LG 8000 includes a CCD sensor for higher-quality images.

So, should you wait until your carrier begins offering megapixel camera phones with the CCD sensor? Keep in mind that you probably won't see an abundance of CCD sensors until mid-2005. And given that many of the initial megapixel phones were released behind schedule, that's optimistic. For shutterbugs who aren't sure they're ready to take the plunge into the digital camera realm, camera phones with CCD lenses will offer a nice transition. If you're chomping at the bit and want better images now, go ahead and take a look at the current crop of megapixel phones, but if image quality is important to you, wait a while.

Memory Expansion

If you've made the switch from a VGA-quality camera phone to a megapixel model, it's a good bet that you're pleased with the decision. You have all the convenience you had before but with better images. Even more than before, you want to save those pictures to your PC, but the thought of e-mailing all those large files to yourself just doesn't sit well. Tools such as data cables and memory cards are more important than ever as more megapixel camera phones hit the market.

The first megapixel phones come with more integrated memory—usually between 5MB and 16MB—but even that will fill up quickly as you amass even a small collection of megapixel images. A typical high-resolution image taken with a Kyocera Koi comes in between 300KB and 385KB, which means you can use up all of your memory after about 42 pictures. That 16MB gets even smaller if it's shared memory, which means all your contacts, ring tones, and games eat into your available memory, leaving you with less room for photographs.

If possible, try to get a phone that accepts a memory expansion card, such as the Nokia 7610 (reduced-size MMC) or the Sony Ericsson S700 (Memory Stick Duo).

Data Cables

I've mentioned these before, but it's particularly relevant in this case. If you purchase a megapixel camera phone that doesn't accept memory expansion cards, it's in your best interest to invest in a data cable. With the larger file sizes that come with megapixel camera phones, you don't want to e-mail pictures to yourself to save them to your PC's hard drive—it's too time consuming and, if you don't have the right data plan, too expensive (see more information in the "Mind Your Messaging" section of this appendix).

Because people will want to store and print these higher-quality images, camera phone manufacturers are making USB cables available as part of the standard package with their megapixel phones. The Nokia 7610 and the Kyocera Koi both include USB cables as part of their standard packaging. The Koi also comes with the

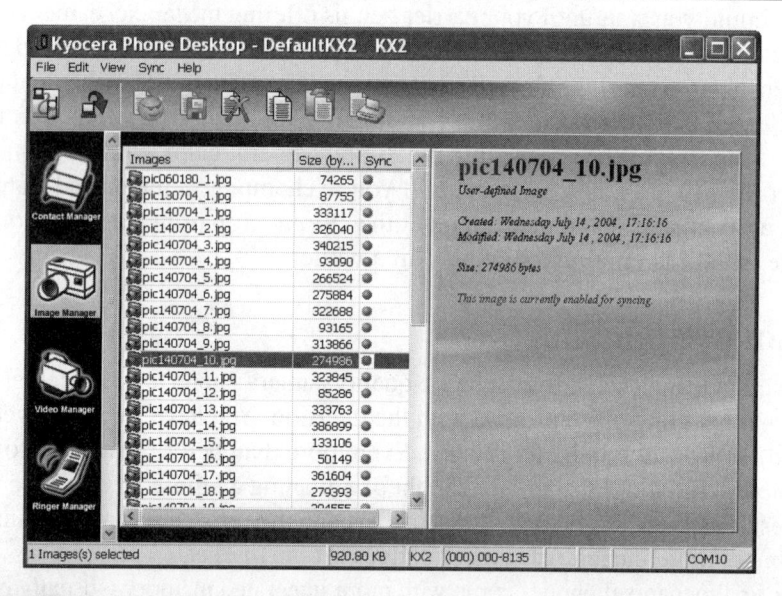

FIGURE A-4 The Kyocera Phone Desktop software lets you sync images between the Koi and a PC.

Kyocera Phone Desktop software, shown in Figure A-4, which lets you synchronize your pictures between your phone and PC. Check with your carrier to see whether the megapixel phone you want comes with a cable or if you need to purchase one as an accessory.

Consider an Extra Battery

Megapixel cameras require more processing power than their VGA brethren, which means your phone's battery will take a hit with extensive use of the camera functions. If you plan to use your megapixel camera phone for most of your vacation photos (which, given the image quality of these handsets, isn't farfetched), it's a good idea to invest in an extended battery if your phone supports it. This will provide more talk and standby time than the standard battery. If your phone doesn't support an extended battery, simply purchase a spare unit of the standard model.

Minding Your Messaging

Having those larger, better-looking images from a megapixel camera phone is undoubtedly a good thing. What's not so good is the amount of time it'll take to send those pictures as multimedia messages. Current wireless data networks are designed to handle small files. If you plan to send a lot of megapixel images directly from your phone, not only will you experience slow transmissions, you'll also end up with a bigger bill than you anticipated if you're not careful. Furthermore, the phone to which you attempt to send the images may not be able to receive them.

Picking a Data Plan

With file sizes of about 300KB, you won't want to send picture messages a la carte. Even at 1 cent per KB, that's an average of $3 per picture message. Sending megapixel images can be even more costly if you're paying for airtime as well. In this case, a carrier that lets you send an unlimited amount of pictures for a flat fee, such as Sprint's PCS Vision ($15 a month) is a more cost-effective option. Those high-speed wireless data networks are still just a gleam in your carrier's eye, so you'll be sending these large files over the same slow networks that you used to send VGA-quality photos.

Warning Your Recipients

Even if you have a great data plan, that may not be the case with your recipient. Carriers, for the most part, charge for each message sent and received. If your friends aren't counting on MMS being a big part of their cell phone experience, they probably won't appreciate having to pay $3 for a picture message. The best approach is to ask ahead of time whether someone would like to receive a picture message, as well as if it's okay to share pictures on a regular basis. A quick phone call, rather than a brief text message, is the best way to approach this. If you're not sure whether your friends are keen on receiving picture messages, then you shouldn't assume they want a text message, either.

> **NOTE** *AT&T Wireless customers can receive MMS messages from other AT&T customers for free.*

A Few Megapixel Models

Although several manufacturers delayed the release of their megapixel camera phones, there are still a few options at your disposal that offer their own unique approach. The following models are either widely available or should be available by the time this book hits the shelves.

> **NOTE** *In some cases, carrier information was not immediately available.*

Audiovox PM-8920

This handset for Sprint PCS, introduced in July 2004, was the first megapixel camera phone released in the U.S. The PM-8920, shown in Figure A-5, features an integrated 1.3-megapixel camera with a self-timer, 8X digital zoom, and a macro option for capturing objects at close range (ideal for pictures of flowers).

The PM-8920 includes 64MB of shared memory, which can handle up to 18 high-resolution images or 300 low-resolution pictures. What it doesn't include is Bluetooth or IR connectivity, although you can purchase a USB cable separately for direct image transfers to a PC.

Kyocera Koi

This 1.2-megapixel unit features a slider-style cover. That is, instead of flipping the cover open, you slide it 180 degrees counterclockwise, as shown in Figure A-6. Measuring 2.25 inches diagonally, the external screen is plenty large for use as a viewfinder to frame your shots. With a dedicated camera button on the left spine

FIGURE A-5　The Audiovox PM-8920 is the first megapixel camera phone in the U.S.

APPENDIX A: Working with a Megapixel Phone 283

FIGURE A-6 The cover of the Kyocera Koi slides, rather than flips, open.

of the cover, you can take pictures with the cover closed. You can use the jog shuttle button on the left spine of the phone's main body to navigate the menus and adjust camera settings with the cover closed.

You get 16MB of dedicated memory and a video recorder, as well. What you won't find are Bluetooth or IR support, so you can't beam your pictures wirelessly to a PC or handheld device that supports these features. Fortunately, the included USB cable and sync software provides a quick and easy method for moving images to your computer.

NOTE   *The Koi's sliding lens cover must be open in order to access the camera functions.*

LG VX8000

LG, the South Korean consumer-electronics giant, is making a name for itself in the U.S. with a line of stylish, feature-rich handsets. Its entry into the megapixel camera phone market, the LG VX8000 (see Figure A-3), was one of the industry's more anticipated releases.

The VX8000 is one of the first camera phones to include the high-quality CCD lens, so expect image quality to be stellar. Also noteworthy is that this handset will include support for Verizon Wireless' high-speed EV-DO network, so multimedia messaging and applications such as streaming video should zip right along.

As for the camera features, the VX8000 includes a switch to toggle between close-up and panoramic modes and 10 digital zoom settings. You also get USB connectivity, streaming music and video capabilities, and a video recorder.

Motorola V710

This 1.2-megapixel flip handset, shown in Figure A-7, features a 2.2-inch display, 16MB of memory, and camcorder functions. Where it separates itself from similar offerings is with its auto focus, rather than fixed-focus, lens, so you should be able to capture more detail in a greater depth of field.

The V710's Bluetooth connectivity means you can beam images wirelessly to other Bluetooth-enabled devices, such as handhelds or PCs that include the technology.

Nokia 7610

Another highly anticipated phone, this stylish candy bar-style handset (shown in Figure A-8) features a 1-megapixel CCD lens, a self-timer (with shutter delays of 10, 20, or 30 seconds), and a 4X digital zoom.

FIGURE A-7   The Motorola V710 includes an auto focus lens.

APPENDIX A: Working with a Megapixel Phone

FIGURE A-8 The Nokia 7610 can hold more than 200 high-resolution images on its 64MB MMC card.

The 7610 comes with a 64MB MMC expansion card, so there's enough memory to hold more than 200 high-resolution pictures or about 1,000 low-resolution images. The card can also store up to 10 minutes of video.

CAUTION *The Nokia 7610 uses a reduced-size MMC (RS-MMC) card, so it won't fit existing SD/MMC slots. You can, however, purchase an RS-MMC to MMC adapter for about $6.*

The 7610's integrated Bluetooth means you can beam your pictures wirelessly to other Bluetooth-enabled devices, such as the Kodak Picture Maker kiosks. Nokia also includes a USB cable for direct phone-to-PC image transfers as part of the standard package.

This phone is also designed to work seamlessly with Nokia's Lifeblog application, the carrier's photo diary application (see Figure A-9). With the Nokia PC Suite software, you can synchronize pictures stored on your phone and PC either wirelessly or via USB cable.

FIGURE A-9 Nokia's Lifeblog organizes your camera phone images by date.

Getting Great Pictures

Because megapixel camera phones deliver larger sizes and, in some cases, higher quality images, it's easier to get a good shot than it is with a VGA-quality device. The higher pixel density means the camera will capture greater detail and provide a larger print area. But that's no reason to start throwing all photographic principles out the window. Also, you'll want to get accustomed to some of the new and improved enhancement tools at your disposal.

Using the Highest Settings Possible

Although you may be taking pictures that measure a megapixel or slightly higher, that doesn't mean you're getting the best image. Along with resolution options, some phones, such as the Kyocera Koi, feature an image quality setting, which sets the compression. The higher the quality, the less compression used, which means a larger file size. Pictures I took at 1280 × 960 resolution at the highest quality were about

385KB in size, compared with about 100KB for most of the pictures I took at the lowest quality setting at the same resolution. Although the difference in quality may not be immediately apparent, it will become so when you attempt to edit or print your pictures.

Using Bright Light

Most of the initial megapixel camera phones feature the CMOS lens. So despite the higher resolution, you'll get your best results when shooting in bright, natural light, since CMOS sensors aren't as sensitive to light as CCD sensors. Although you may find short-range flashes and night mode settings on your megapixel phone, the resulting images aren't any better than what you'd get with the same features on a VGA camera phone.

In Figure A-10, I took the picture on the left at night using the Kyocera Koi's low light mode. As you can see, the image is much blurrier than the photo on the right, which was taken in standard mode. That's because low light (or night) mode keeps the shutter exposed for a longer period. When that happens, the slightest movement of your hand—such as pressing the button to take a picture—will cause blurriness.

Cropping Your Images

Because megapixel images contain more pixel information than VGA pictures, you have more room to work with for cropping and editing. In fact, you may find that you need to crop pictures taken with a megapixel camera phone more so than a VGA handset, especially when taking pictures of large, distant objects.

FIGURE A-10 The picture on the left was taken with Kyocera Koi's low light mode activated; the same shot in standard mode produced a better image.

FIGURE A-11 In order to get the sculpture in the background, I couldn't avoid capturing a piece of the wall and chain-link fence in the foreground.

Most digital cameras feature an optical zoom, which allows you to zoom in incrementally to eliminate unwanted foreground details. With camera phones, the digital zoom magnifies the shot at fixed intervals (2X, 4X, and so on). If you choose not to use the zoom, you'll often find that you can't shoot around certain objects in the foreground, as in Figure A-11.

Because this is a megapixel image, I had no worries about using an image editor to crop the top of the wall and chain-link fence out of the picture while still retaining much of the original detail, as shown in Figure A-12.

TIP *If you decide you need to crop your image further, undo the original crop and start over again. Each time you edit and save your pictures, they lose more information.*

Print Your Pictures

This is where the real fun happens. There's simply no comparison between the print quality of a megapixel image and a picture taken with a VGA-quality camera phone. True, prints from a megapixel camera phone don't have quite the sharpness and color accuracy that you'll get with even a low-end digital camera, but it's close.

FIGURE A-12 Cropping the fence from the picture resulted in minimal image degradation.

How to ... Change the Filename on Your Phone

Along with better images, megapixel phones offer more memory. You can store up to 200 high-resolution images on the Nokia 7610, which means you'll have plenty of room to store all the pictures you took on a weekend trip, for example. But when it comes time to move those images to your PC, you'll find yourself staring at unruly file names, such as pic150704_2.jpg. Yes, you can rename your files in Windows, but this can be tedious if you're transferring dozens, or even hundreds, of pictures at a time.

Instead, change the default image name that the camera phone uses to store pictures. If you're going on a trip to New York and you know you'll be taking lots of pictures, you can change the camera's default image name to New York. Subsequent pictures will contain the filename New York 001, New York 002,

290 How to Do Everything with Your Camera Phone

and so forth. The following steps apply to the Nokia 7610, but the process is similar among other camera phones that offer this option:

1. In camera mode, click Options, then Settings.
2. Select Default Image Name.
3. Enter a new name, then click OK.

Using pictures taken with the Kyocera Koi at the highest image quality, I was able to make a 4.8-inch × 6.4-inch print at a resolution of 200 ppi (see Figure A-13). The same image taken in VGA mode could only produce a 2.4-inch × 3.2-inch print.

FIGURE A-13 A high-resolution image taken with the Kyocera Koi can produce a quality 4.8-inch × 6.4-inch print.

> **Did you know?**
>
> ## What's Next for Megapixel Camera Phones
>
> Megapixel camera phones are certainly a big improvement over VGA-quality handsets, but the best is still yet to come, as indicated by products currently available in Asia.
>
> - **Multiple megapixels** 3-megapixel camera phones are already available in Asian markets. Casio introduced the first such unit, the 3.2-megapixel A5406CA. Consumers in the U.S. should see 2-megapixel models sometime in 2005.
>
> - **Optical zoom lenses** Samsung recently introduced the SPH-2300, a 3-megapixel camera phone with an extending lens that resembles those on standard digital cameras.
>
> - **Auto focus lenses** Instead of the fixed-focus lens, which sets the focus to a preset distance at which most objects will be in focus, auto focus lenses automatically focus on the object at which the camera is pointed by calculating the distance and adjusting its optics. This provides sharper detail in a greater range.
>
> Such features will bridge the gap between camera phones and low-end and midrange digital cameras. Furthermore, faster data networks, which will improve picture messaging capabilities, promise to make camera phones an attractive alternative to digital cameras. In the next two or three years, it's conceivable that many people will opt to use their camera phone as their sole camera.

Moving On

The final appendix of this book is a bit different from the rest of this book. It deals less with the "how to" aspects of your camera phone and examines some of the privacy, security, and legal issues surrounding these devices. Although this technology is still relatively new to the U.S., its impact has tremendous ramifications in terms of privacy fears—so great that even Congress has stepped in. Meanwhile, businesses are worried about corporate espionage, and schools are taking steps to stop cheating scandals before they begin.

And you thought your camera phone was a harmless little gadget to take along to your daughter's soccer match!

Appendix B: Privacy, Security, and Copyright

Camera phones seem to be everywhere, and that's becoming a problem. Because they resemble phones much more than cameras, it's difficult to tell when someone is furtively snapping a picture of you in an embarrassing or otherwise private moment, or whether they're simply checking their list of missed calls. An unfortunate aspect of human nature is the temptation to exploit tools that allow for secretive and invasive recording. Most of us don't partake in illegal or immoral behavior, but enough people do to cause trouble. True, some megapixel camera phones resemble cameras more than their sub-megapixel predecessors, which lessens the threat to a degree, but the majority of camera phone users have the sub-megapixel kind.

The problem has become so widespread that Congress has seen fit to intervene, not to mention the scores of public and private facilities that have instituted their own bans on camera phones. More and more businesses are concerned enough about security and intellectual property that they are implementing bans on camera phones on their premises.

Even where legal boundaries aren't clear, common sense, good judgment, and just plain decency should apply. After all, someone who has just tripped over a curb shouldn't worry over whether someone has snapped a picture of the embarrassing incident and is sending it around the Internet.

In this appendix, I'll review some of the privacy, security, and copyright concerns surrounding camera phones and study some of the legal ramifications of certain actions.

Privacy

Although the right to privacy isn't explicitly stated in the U.S. Constitution, it is generally understood to be one of our primary rights. Certainly, most people would like to believe that's the case. But it seems that with each new consumer technology comes a serious privacy concern. The fear of computer hackers gaining access to sensitive financial or medical information has been around for years. The day after Janet Jackson's "wardrobe malfunction" at the 2004 Super Bowl, TiVo reported that customers of its digital TV recorder replayed the incident more than any other previous event. For a few days after this revelation, there was a mini furor over the fact that TiVo *knew* this to be the case. The fact that the company is able to collect such data wasn't a secret, but many people were taken aback that their viewing—and re-viewing—habits were so closely monitored.

Now we have camera phones, which, as I hope I've explained well, are great tools for capturing and sharing spontaneous moments. Some of those moments, however, shouldn't be captured. For some Peeping Toms, "spontaneous moment" means snapping a picture up a woman's skirt or down her blouse. And with camera phones' instant access to the Internet, such pictures can circulate around the world in, literally, minutes.

Private Parts

For all the good uses people have found for camera phones—as an aid to thwart criminal activity, for example—concerns about more sinister uses have led some facilities to ban camera phones from the premises. Many health clubs, concerned about the privacy of their patrons in locker rooms, have implemented policies against their use.

But how enforceable are such rules? How can you tell when someone is legitimately using his camera phone or is engaged in suspect activity? Some facilities get around the issue by banning the use of cell phones altogether (see Figure B-1). But for other places that are potential fodder for voyeurs—shopping malls, sports arenas, beaches—a ban on cell phones may be unrealistic.

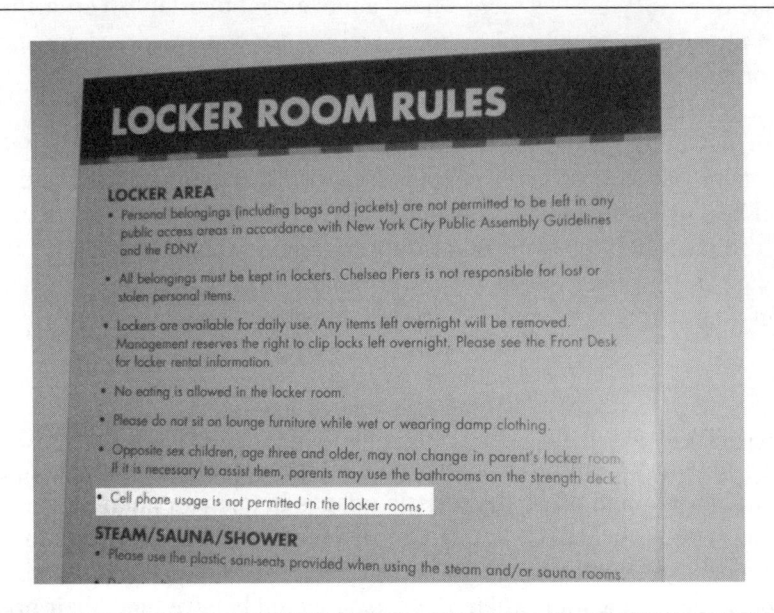

FIGURE B-1 Because it's difficult to determine when someone is using his camera phone for sinister purposes, some facilities ban the use of cell phones altogether.

Did you know?

A Matter of Courtesy

It's not just illegal or perverted activity that's cause for concern. Often, it's simply rude behavior that's most irritating.

Earlier this year, Sprint PCS ran a commercial advertising its Picture Mail service in which a woman surreptitiously snaps a picture of a man who is less-than-dainty while eating his pasta at a diner. She immediately fires a picture message off to her friend. I'm sure Sprint was simply attempting to show how fun and spontaneous picture messaging can be, but you could be forgiven for coming to the conclusion that the carrier was advocating secretly taking pictures of people in embarrassing situations and sharing them with your friends for a good, if mean-spirited, laugh.

Okay, this isn't exactly a national security threat, nor does it sink to the level of secretly photographing someone in the shower at a gym, but it still speaks to the issue of privacy. Just as there's been a movement to establish etiquette rules for cell phone users in general, some guidelines for camera phone enthusiasts are in order. Actually, there's just one important rule:

Ask permission from strangers before taking their picture.

You may think it's the same as taking a picture with a standard digital or film camera, but in those cases people know you're taking a picture (although it's still best to ask for permission first). When you whip out a camera phone, it's not immediately obvious that you're taking a picture, especially from a distance. You wouldn't want anyone sneaking up on you to take a picture without your permission, so don't do so to others.

Well, if private companies can't stop you, the government will. In May 2004, the House Judiciary Committee approved a bill that would outlaw the taking of "upskirt" photos and other voyeuristic images by camera phones. The bill, sponsored by Rep. Michael Oxley (R-Ohio), a former FBI agent, would make it illegal to videotape, photograph, film, broadcast, or record a person who is naked or in underwear at a location where the person would believe that "their private parts would not be visible to the public, regardless of whether that person is in a private area."

Violators of the Video Voyeurism Prevention Act would face fines and up to a year in prison. Although photographing or recording people in private places is already illegal in most states, several cases involving camera phone voyeurism have not been prosecuted because there hasn't been specific language on restricting taking compromising pictures of people in public places.

A similar bill, with the same name, previously passed unanimously in the Senate. As this book went to press, the bill was working its way through the full House of Representatives. While the Video Voyeurism Prevention Act would apply to federal property, several local legislatures are considering similar laws to outlaw such photography in their states and municipalities.

U.S. federal and local governments may be working fast in an attempt to keep up with technology, but they're not likely to go as far as Saudi Arabia, which has banned camera phones from the entire country because men have been using the devices to secretly photograph women.

Security

In certain contexts, from a security point of view, your camera phone may as well be a case of plastic explosives. These devices are small and quiet, which makes them easy to sneak in and use with little or no attention, and several units allow you to snap pictures with the flip cover closed, which makes it easy to capture images surreptitiously. While some professions undoubtedly will benefit from camera phones, others want nothing to do with them.

The Spy Who Robbed Me

The biggest fear in the business world is corporate espionage—that is, a competitor snapping a picture of a product or blueprint and using that information to undermine the company's efforts. This is troublesome for a wide range of businesses, from car manufacturers to fashion designers, that rely on a high level of secrecy during research and development. It's a fear that will only increase as the image quality of these devices improves.

The *Wall Street Journal* reported that aerospace and defense contractor General Dynamics allows employees to carry camera phones, but not visitors. Consumer products maker Kimberly-Clark, on the other hand, forbids both workers and visitors from bringing cameras into any of its buildings.

According to a survey by the International Security Management Association, an organization representing senior security executives, 30 percent of the companies responding have formal policies prohibiting camera phones on their premises, compared to 7 percent that prohibit normal cell phone use.

The survey, to which 135 chief security officers of Fortune 500 companies responded, found that there is more concern over outsiders using camera phones. While 23 percent of the respondents said their companies forbade employees from using camera phones on the premises, 29 percent banned their use by visitors, and 27 percent banned use from contractors on site.

Not all industry watchers are convinced these fears are justified. In a recent research report, Forrester Research analysts Carl Zetie and Martha Bennett wrote that camera phone policies are found most often in public areas where the risk of personal privacy invasion is high. "Enterprises must realize that camera phones are unlikely tools to be used in industrial or corporate espionage," the analysts wrote. "The camera phone threat in the enterprise is primarily one of casual, opportunistic, or thoughtless breaches of confidentiality rather than determined and systematic breaches."

Market research firm Gartner notes that while businesses are concerned that camera phones can compromise their security, "an outright ban of camera phones is shortsighted and hard to enforce." Instead, Gartner recommends businesses designate secure zones with tight restrictions and strict enforcement. In other workplace areas, clear guidelines should be established regarding what is acceptable.

Camera or No Camera?

It's tough to say whether fears of corporate espionage are real or overblown. What is clear is that cell phone manufacturers and carriers are beginning to take note and offering alternative versions of certain products. Sprint PCS now offers a version of palmOne's Treo 600, a PDA/cell phone hybrid, without the standard built-in VGA camera.

According to Sprint, companies concerned about the theft of sensitive information were wary of the popular smart phone because of the integrated camera. Other carriers, according to news reports, are considering similar moves. The one catch to the camera-less Treo 600 is that it costs the same as the model with the photography feature.

The Perfect Score?

Leave it to teenagers to find clever, if morally wanting, uses for technology. Schools are facing their own security concerns regarding camera phones: cheating students.

Students have previously used text messaging to pass along test answers to their fellow classmates. But entering all that information on an alphanumeric keypad can get tiring, and it's hardly subtle. Enter the camera phone. The Associate Press reported that Everett Alvarez High School in Salinas, California, banned all cell phone use after catching a student using a camera phone to photograph an exam and attempting to send it to a friend (not exactly a ringing endorsement for MMS).

The Owensboro, Kentucky Board of Education didn't wait for a cheating scandal to hit its schools. The board, according to a report in the Owensboro *Messenger-Inquirer,* revised its ban on cell phone use on school property to include camera phones, which students will not be allowed to use on school trips either, lest they take inappropriate pictures of other students. Other districts have taken similar preemptive measures.

Copyright

Just because you can take a picture of something doesn't mean you should. And just because you do take a picture of something doesn't mean that image properly belongs to you. Along with personal privacy and corporate secrets, one of the biggest concerns about camera phones regards copyright violations. This is a tricky subject, because what exactly constitutes an infringement on someone's copyright isn't always clear.

A copyright, according to the 10th edition of Merriam Webster's Collegiate Dictionary, is "the exclusive legal right to reproduce, publish, and sell the matter and form (as of a literary, musical, or artistic work)." In other words, you can't go out and publish your own version of, say, the latest Harry Potter book without permission from the publisher and author. Nor can you photocopy the entire book and curl up with the stack of pages every night before you go to bed.

Copyright law, for the most part, protects "fixed" works—that is, the creation is recorded in some tangible medium, whether in text, audio, or video format. Once a work is set on paper or recorded to tape or a digital medium, it is eligible for copyright protection. So why is it illegal to use your camcorder phone to record a few short video clips of performances from, say, the Chicago Blues Festival, especially when most of those performances weren't being recorded in any way?

Indeed, for years there were problems surrounding bootleg recordings of rock concerts. If the performers weren't recording the concerts themselves, they had no legitimate copyright protection. In 1994, Congress changed the law of unrecorded music performances as part of The Uruguay Round Agreements Act, which included a provision that prohibited the recording of live musical performances even when there is no other "fixation."

Did you know?

Money Isn't the Issue

Because copyrights are so intertwined with permissions and royalty payments, some people believe that as long as they don't charge any money for distribution of copyrighted material that they're safe from any legal ramifications. Not so.

You can't, for example, bring a video camera into a movie theater and tape the entire movie as it's projected on the screen, even if it's for your personal use and you have no intention of selling copies. Similarly, taking video footage of a concert or other live performance, even the short clips captured by camcorder phones, simply isn't legal. Yes, I know, it's not like you'll be able to use the tiny, grainy clips to sell bootleg DVDs on the street. If you get caught, that argument may lessen the punishment levied against you, but don't count on it to get you off the hook.

So when you're at any live event and you see signs that warn against the use of audio/video recording devices, be aware that you're not just dealing with the policy of the event planners, you're dealing with U.S. copyright law.

Fair Use

This is where things get a little muddied. Copyright law allows for fair use of protected materials. That is, the public is entitled to use portions of copyrighted materials for purposes of commentary, criticism, and research. If you're writing a book review, you have the freedom to quote portions of the book for explanatory or illustrative purposes without permission from the author.

Similarly, you are permitted to photocopy and distribute portions of copyrighted works for educational or personal use without securing permission or paying royalty fees to the copyright holder. Measuring fair use, however, is hardly an exact science. The law considers four main factors:

- The purpose and the character of your use
- The nature of the copyrighted work
- The amount of the portion taken
- The effect of the use upon the potential market

So what does this have to do with your camera phone? Bookstore owners in Japan have complained that customers armed with camera phones have been photographing magazine articles instead of buying the issue. The bookstore owners are upset that such an act cuts into their business, but what would be the legal ramifications in the U.S. if a camera phone user did the same thing?

I posed this question to a lawyer friend of mine, whom I'll call Beth (mostly because that's her real name). As lawyers often do, she told me that there's no clear cut answer. But this is copyright law, after all, so I'll cut Beth some slack.

The mere act of photographing a magazine article, Beth says, is akin to photocopying. So no, the act itself wouldn't violate copyright law. You could run afoul of the law, however, depending on how you plan to use the photographs.

There's a reason you don't find photocopying machines in bookstores. Because you're using a camera phone to avoid paying for a product, the bookseller would likely file a complaint for misappropriation of goods. If you did the same in a library, however, the issue becomes murkier. In that context, people copy articles all the time for academic research. Exactly how this would play out in court is difficult to determine because there haven't been any cases under this scenario to set a precedent. Also, it's impossible to track down every person who breaks copyright law.

The bottom line: it's best not to whip out your camera phone in your local Border's to photograph a magazine article. Even if it's not illegal, it's still not the right thing to do.

Be Fair, Have Fun

I hope you enjoyed this brief legal tutorial, and I hope these issues won't deter you from enjoying your camera phone to the fullest. Exciting technological developments are always on the horizon, and with them will come other issues to consider. I invite you to share your thoughts with me, whether it's an interesting use of a camera phone or a new philosophical dilemma that the technology has created. Just send a message to cameraphonebook@hotmail.com.

I also hope you've enjoyed this book. Happy shooting.

Index

Numbers

1/60 settings, using tripods with, 52
1KTV service, acquiring video from, 254–255
1xRTT network, Sprint's use of, 63–64
2.5G network, 1xRTT as, 64
3-megapixel camera phones, availability of, 291
3G wireless networks, significance of, 64
3GPP, relationship to camcorder phones, 220–221
4 × 6 pictures
    advisory about printing of, 162
    example of, 163, 165
    making, 165
50mm focal length, significance of, 55
450wbt Mobile Printer, features of, 160–161
525HD camera phones, display on, 17
640 × 480 resolution, significance of, 10–11
2,048 × 1,536 resolution, significance of, 27
3200 camera phones. *See* Nokia 3200 camera phones
3620 camera phone. *See* Nokia 3620 camera phones
3650 camera phones. *See* Nokia 3650 camera phones
7610 megapixel camera phones. *See* Nokia 7610 megapixel camera phones

A

à la carte options, considering costs of, 21
action shots, 59–61. *See also* images; JPEG images; photos; pictures; shots
address books, maintaining with Picture Mail, 134
Adobe Photoshop Album 2. *See* Photoshop Album 2
Adobe Photoshop Elements 2. *See* Photoshop Elements 2
Adobe Reader, downloading, 204
airtime minutes, advisory about, 39
Aladdin Digital Photo Center kiosks by Fujifilm, using, 171
"Album Share" message in Picture Mail, significance of, 136–137
albums
    creating, 199–203, 205
    sharing with Picture Mail, 135–137
antique or sepia effects, description of, 43
Apple iPhoto, managing images with, 94–95
arm, extending for self-portraits, 58
AT&T Wireless
    camera phones supported by, 20
    EDGE (Enhanced Data Rates for Global Evolution) network offered by, 222
    picture messaging services available from, 23
    prices for picture messaging services offered by, 145
attachments
    adding to e-mail, 151–152
    receiving, 152–153
audio
    quality of, 251
    using with camcorder phones, 242
audio clips
    adding to Paint Shop slide shows, 207
    adding to Pix Place messages, 141

audio levels, controlling in VideoStudio 8, 260, 262
audio mixing, performing with VideoStudio 8, 267–268
Audiovox camera phones, carrier for, 20
Audiovox PM-8920 megapixel phones, features of, 282
auto focus lenses, features of, 291
auto versus fixed focus, 56

B

background music, controlling in VideoStudio 8, 260, 262
background noise, eliminating in VideoStudio 8 movies, 265, 267
backlighting, avoiding, 54
bandwidth, relationship to camcorder phones, 220
batch processing, performing with Photoshop Elements, 103–104
batteries
    charging and recharging, 35
    life of, 230
    using extras with megapixel camera phones, 280
BBC (British Broadcasting Company), use of moblogs by, 194–195
Belkin
    purchasing Bluetooth printer adapters from, 160–161
    purchasing PC cards and USB adapters from, 71
black and white effects, description of, 43
The Blackout site, web address for, 194
blog, example of, 174
Bluetooth technology
    availability of, 14
    performing wireless transfers with, 71
    and printers, 160–161
    using to share pictures, 156
    using with Aladdin Digital Photo Center kiosks, 171
BREW (Binary Runtime Environment for Wireless) versus Java, 255

brightness
    adjusting, 52–53, 113–116
    setting preferences for, 41–42
Broadband Access network, capacity of, 222
buffers, relationship to camcorder phones, 220
buttons, placement of, 31–32
Buzznet.com moblog
    features of, 176–179, 190
    removing comments from, 192
    versus Textamerica, 183

C

caller ID. *See* photo caller ID
calls, receiving while in camera mode, 36
camcorder function
    accessing on cell phones, 242–243
    using with video, 241–242
camcorder phones
    becoming familiar with, 218–219
    capturing video with, 238–242
    memory considerations related to, 223–225
    and Memory Sticks, 226
    and MMCs (multimedia cards), 227
    Nokia 3620, 231–232, 235
    quality of footage taken from, 241
    Samsung VM-A680, 232
    and SD (secure digital) cards, 227–228
    with slots for memory expansion, 224
    Sony Ericsson P900, 233–234
    terminology related to, 219–221
    and T-Flash (TransFlash) cards, 227–228
    time and size constraints of, 221–222
    Toshiba VM4050, 234–235
    using audio with, 242
    using expansion cards with, 225–228
    using memory card adapters with, 229–230
camera attachments, buying, 15–16
camera mode, accessing, 36
camera phones
    abuse of, 297–299
    activating Bluetooth on, 71
    buttons on, 31–32

Index 305

card slots on, 34
deciding on options for, 21
versus digital cameras, 5
evolution of, 257
inexpensiveness of, 22
IrDA ports on, 35
lens on, 29–31
mechanics of, 4–5
menus on, 32–33
professional applications of, 8
prohibition of, 297–298
screen types for, 26–29
shopping for, 12–16
style considerations related to, 13–14
terminology related to, 10–12
types of, 9
uses for, 5–9
camera-phone brands
    Audiovox, 20
    Handspring (Palm One), 16
    LG, 17
    list of, 20
    NEC, 17–18
    Nokia, 18
    Panasonic, 20
    Samsung, 18–19
    Sanyo, 19
    Sony Ericsson, 19
    Toshiba, 19
candy bar displays, features of, 27–28
Canon photo printers, models and price ranges of, 162
car dealers, applications for, 8
card slots, using, 34
carriers
    choosing, 20–23
    list of, 20
categories
    creating in Adobe Photoshop Album 2, 85
    creating in Textamerica, 185
CCD (charged-coupled device) chips, purpose of, 4

CCD lenses
    in LG VX8000 megapixel camera phones, 284
    in Nokia 7610 megapixel camera phones, 284
    significance of, 29–30
    using with megapixel camera phones, 278–279
CD-R (CD recordable), comparing to CD-RW and Picture CD, 98–99
CDs (compact disks), moving files to, 96–97
cell phones
    banning use of, 295
    moving edited images to, 70
    sending pictures by e-mail from, 151
    watching video on, 251
Cingular Wireless
    camera phones supported by, 20
    picture messaging services available from, 23
    prices for picture messaging services offered by, 145
clamshell displays, features of, 26–27
CMOS (complementary metal oxide semiconductor) chips, purpose of, 4
CMOS lenses
    relationship to megapixel camera phones, 278, 287
    shortcomings of, 240
    significance of, 29–30
Comic Bubbles, adding with Picture Mail, 136, 138
comments
    adding in Buzznet, 177
    disabling in Mobog, 181
    removing from Buzznet and Textamerica, 192
community moblogs
    explanation of, 176
    pros and cons of, 192
    sending pictures to, 189
    suggesting with Textamerica, 188
    uploading pictures to, 190, 192
compressed folders, extracting files from, 73
compression, description of, 11
connections, considering types of, 13–14

construction workers, applications for, 8
contacts, linking pictures with, 198–199
continuous-action shots, taking, 59–61
contrast
    adjusting, 113–116
    setting preferences for, 41
copyright, overview of, 299–301
corporate espionage, significance of, 297–298
courtesy, demonstrating when taking pictures, 296
Creations, making with Adobe Photoshop Album, 199–205
Creations Wizard, using with Photoshop Elements, 209–211
crooked pictures, aligning, 108–109
cropping
    photos, 109–112
    pictures taken with megapixel camera phones, 287–289

D

Darkness setting, effect of, 53
data cables
    transferring images with, 69–70
    using with megapixel camera phones, 279–280
data plans, picking for megapixel camera phones, 281
data rates, significance of, 222
DataPilot program, using with IR USB cables, 4:4–4:5
depth of field, explanation of, 54–57
despeckle tools, using, 118, 120
digital cameras versus camera phones, 5
digital frames, overview of, 212, 214. *See also* frames
Digital Image Library
    adding pictures with, 92
    creating photo archives with, 97–98
    Keyword Painter feature of, 93
Digital Image Pro 9, editing images with, 106
digital zoom, significance of, 288
displays
    candy bars, 27–28
    clamshells, 26–27
    swivels, 29
D-Link, purchasing PC cards and USB adapters from, 71
download speeds, significance of, 222
dpi (dots per inch), significance of, 10
DVDs, moving files to, 96–97

E

e715 camera phones, internal storage space available on, 68
EDGE (Enhanced Data Rates for Global Evolution) networks
    data rates of, 222
    significance of, 64
edited images, moving to cell phones, 70
effects
    and resolution settings, 42–43
    setting preferences for, 42–43
electronic postcards, creating with camera phones, 5–6
e-mail
    adding attachments to, 151–152
    resolution concerns related to, 62–63
    sending pictures by, 150–153
    sending pictures with, 75–76
    sending video clips by means of, 249
Epson photo printers, models and price ranges of, 162
Epson PictureMate printer, features of, 159
EV-DO (Evolution-Data Optimized) networks, significance of, 64
expansion cards, using with camcorder phones, 225–228
Explorer, copying files to memory cards from, 250

F

fair use, relationship to copyrights, 300–301
Favorites lists, creating in Textamerica, 186–187
file formats, changing, 124–126
filenames, changing on megapixel camera phones, 289–290

Index

files
- displaying details in Windows, 82, 85
- moving to CDs and DVDs, 96–97
- renaming in Windows, 78–79

Fill Flash feature in Photoshop Elements, using, 115–116

filmstrip format, viewing photos in, 81

firewalls, relationship to Pix Place, 141

fixed versus auto focus, 56

flip phones
- locating lenses on, 31
- options on, 15
- with swivel displays, 29

focal length, explanation of, 55

focal points, finding for self-portraits, 58

folders
- assigning keywords with Microsoft Digital Image Library, 94
- moving pictures to, 78
- renaming in Windows, 77
- storing images in, 77–78

Forrester Research on camera phones and security, 298

fps (frames per second), relationship to camcorder phones, 219

frames, manipulating for shots, 49–50. *See also* digital frames

Fuji Film, web address for, 95

Fujifilm Aladdin Digital Photo Center kiosks, using, 171

Fujifilm.net
- features of, 150
- overview of, 168–169

Fun Frames, adding with Picture Mail, 136–137

FutureDial, web address for, 70

G

G4techTV moblog, significance of, 190

galleries, using with Buzznet, 178–179

gallery
- accessing, 37
- accessing on LG VX6000, 33

Gallery option, selecting, 37

Gamma Correction tool in Paint Shop Pro, using, 115–117

Gartner research on camera phones and security, 298

GetFlix, acquiring video from, 256, 258

glitter effects, description of, 43

greeting cards, creating with Photoshop Elements, 209–211

GSM smart phone, Sony Ericsson P900 as, 233–235

H

hand movements, minimizing when framing shots, 50

Handspring (Palm One) camera phones, features of, 16

Hewlett-Packard photo printers, models and price ranges of, 162

high and low resolution, using, 61–65. *See also* resolution

high-resolution display, example of, 27

high-speed setting, using with continuous-action shots, 60, 64

HP Photosmart 7000 printers, features of, 165

HP-450wbt Mobile Printer, features of, 160–161

I

icons, displaying images as, 82

Image Album by Nokia, features of, 213–214

image editors
- Adobe Photoshop Elements 2, 103–105
- features of, 102–103
- JASC Paint Shop Pro 8, 104–106
- Microsoft Digital Image Pro 9, 106
- printing pictures from, 163

Image Frames by Nokia, features of, 212, 214

image gallery
- accessing, 37
- accessing on LG VX6000, 33

image quality
- enhancing on megapixel camera phones, 15
- setting preferences for, 40

image size. *See* resolution

Image Viewer, features of, 213

image-management software
    Adobe Photoshop Album 2, 84–88
    Apple iPhoto, 94–95
    JASC Paint Shop Album 4, 89–92
    Microsoft Digital Image Library, 92–94
    online options for, 95
ImageMate Reader/Writer, using with camcorder phones, 229–230
images. *See also* action shots; JPEG images; photos; pictures; shots
    adding to Pix Place albums, 143–144
    associating with categories in Textamerica, 186
    creating panoramic images, 112
    cropping in megapixel camera phones, 287–289
    finding by keyword in JASC Paint Shop Album 4, 90–91
    in Pix Place Gallery, 144
    previewing in Pix Place, 142
    resampling, 122–123
    resizing, 119–123, 163
    resizing in Buzznet, 178
    rotating with Photoshop Elements, 108–109
    sharpness and clarity of, 10
    sizes of, 40
    storing in Windows, 77–78
    transferring with data cables, 69–70
    transferring with IR (infrared), 70–71
    viewing in Windows, 80–82
individual moblogs, explanation of, 174, 176
indoor lighting, using for video, 240
inkjet photo printers
    costs associated with, 165
    features of, 158–159
    setting print size with, 166
interior designers, applications for, 8
iPod moblog, sending pictures to, 189
IR (infrared), transferring images with, 70–71
IrDA ports
    advisory about sending files from, 153
    features of, 35
    and printers, 160–161

J

JASC Paint Shop Pro 8. *See* Paint Shop Pro 8
Java versus BREW (Binary Runtime Environment for Wireless), 255
JPEG Artifact Removal Tool, using with Paint Shop Pro 8, 105–106
JPEG graphics format, description of, 12
JPEG images. *See also* action shots; images; photos; pictures; shots
    degradation of, 109
    versus TIFFs, 124

K

KB (kilobytes)
    costs associated to, 62
    description of, 12
    and image quality, 40
Kbps (kilobits per second), relationship to high-speed wireless networks, 64
Keyword Painter feature, using with Microsoft Digital Image Library, 93
keywords
    assigning to folders with Microsoft Digital Image Library, 94
    deleting in Microsoft Digital Image Library, 94
    using with images in JASC Paint Shop Album 4, 90–91
kiosks by Kodak, using, 170–171
Kodak Mobile, web address for, 95
Kodak online print services, overview of, 167–168
Kodak Picture Maker kiosks, using, 170–171
Kyocera Koi megapixel camera phones
    features of, 282–283
    taking high-resolution images with, 290
    using image quality setting on, 286
    using USB cables with, 279–280

L

laser printers, advisory about, 158
law enforcement, using camera phones for, 7

Index

lenses
- features of, 29–31
- of megapixel camera phones, 278–279

LG 8000, CCD sensor in, 278

LG camera phones, features of, 17

LG VX6000
- assigning shortcuts to left navigation button on, 33
- sending pictures from, 37–38
- testimonial about, 33

LG VX8000 megapixel phone, features of, 283–284

Lifeblog by Nokia, features of, 193. *See also* moblogs; Nokia Lifeblog

lighting situations
- accommodating, 55
- adjusting color based on, 41
- adjusting for, 50–54
- for video, 239–240

lists, displaying images in, 82, 84

Looney Tunes characters, adding with Picture Mail, 136–137

low and high resolution, using, 61–65

low light
- avoiding, 51
- compensating for, 52

luminance value, adjusting, 113

M

megapixel camera phones
- Audiovox PM-8920, 282
- changing filenames on, 289–290
- costs associated with, 281
- cropping images with, 287–289
- and data cables, 279–280
- future of, 291
- Kyocera Koi, 282–283
- lenses of, 278–279
- LG VX8000, 283–284
- and memory expansion, 279
- and messaging, 280–281
- Motorola V710, 284
- Nokia 7610, 284–285
- picking data plans for, 281
- printing pictures taken with, 288, 290
- shopping for, 276–277
- using bright light with, 287
- using highest settings possible on, 286–287

megapixels
- description of, 10
- options for, 15

memory card adapters, using with camcorder phones, 229–230

memory cards
- relationship to printers, 159
- saving video clips to, 223
- slots for, 224
- types of, 34
- using with megapixel camera phones, 279
- using with video clips, 249–250

memory, managing for camcorder phones, 223–225

Memory Stick Reader Mouse, using with camcorder phones, 229–230

Memory Sticks, using with camcorder phones, 226

menu options, descriptions of, 32–33

messages, sending from Picture Mail, 244–245

messaging services, transferring pictures from, 71–76

microphones, positioning on camcorder phones, 242

Microsoft Digital Image Library. *See* Digital Image Library

Microsoft Digital Image Pro 9. *See* Digital Image Pro 9

MIPC (Mobile Imaging and Printing Consortium), significance of, 161

mirrors, using to frame self-portraits, 58

MMCs (multimedia cards), using with camcorder phones, 227

mMode home page, downloading RealOne from, 254

MMS messages
- sending, 33, 131
- sending and receiving with megapixel camera phones, 281

MMS (Multimedia Message Service).
    See also picture messaging websites
        description of, 11, 130–131
        resolution concerns related to, 62–63
Mobile Phone Tools package, using with
    Motorola camera phones, 69
mobile printers, availability of, 160–161
Mobile Video, relationship to GetFlix,
    256, 258
MobiTV, acquiring video from, 252–253
moblogs. *See also* Lifeblog by Nokia; Nokia
    Lifeblog
        Buzznet.com, 176–179
        examples of, 190–191
        explanation of, 174
        future of, 194–195
        Mobog.com, 179–182
        saving addresses for, 195
        Show Your iPod moblog, 189
        Textamerica, 175, 182–189
        types of, 174, 176
Mobog.com moblog
        versus Buzznet, 182
        features of, 190
        overview of, 179–181
        removing commentary from, 192
Motorola camera phones, using Mobile Phone
    Tools package with, 69
Motorola V600 camera phones, features
    of, 9
Motorola V710 megapixel camera phones,
    features of, 284
.MOV file, significance of, 208
Movie Wizard in VideoStudio, working with,
    259–262
movies. *See also* video
        advisory about shooting public
            events, 263
        making, 207–208
        making with VideoStudio 8, 263–269
MP3 music file format, VideoStudio 8's support
    for, 260–261
MPEG-4, relationship to camcorder
    phones, 220

multishot option, using with continuous-action
    shots, 59–61
music, adding to VideoStudio 8 movies,
    265–266
My Album. *See* T-Mobile
My Photo Gallery, subscribing to, 95
My Pictures folder, creating in Windows, 77–78
My Pictures option, selecting, 37
MyAlbum service, using with T-Mobile, 74

N

native file formats, significance of, 124
navigation buttons, location of, 32
NEC camera phones, features of, 17–18
NEC's 525HD camera phones, display on, 17
negative effects, description of, 43
news organizations, applications for, 8
Nextel, advisory about, 22
Nokia 3200 camera phones, candy-bar
    style of, 28
Nokia 3620 camera phones
        features of, 231–232, 235
        using memory cards for video clips
            on, 249–250
        slots for memory cards on, 68–69
        storage limitations of, 225
Nokia 3650 camera phones
        location of memory cards on, 34
        memory slot on, 17
        Mobile Printing Application for, 172
        saving video clips to memory cards on,
            223
Nokia 7610 megapixel camera phones
        features of, 284–285
        storage capacity of, 289
        using Lifeblog with, 193
        using USB cables with, 279
Nokia camera phones
        enhancements to, 213–214
        features of, 18
Nokia Image Frames, features of, 212
Nokia Lifeblog, features of, 193, 285–286. *See
    also* moblogs

O

Ofoto
- features of, 148
- online print services offered by, 167–168
- Print@Home feature of, 148
- using to share files, 147
- web address for, 95

OK button, snapping photos with, 32
Olympus photo printers, models and price ranges of, 162
online picture messaging, availability of, 74
online print services. *See also* photo printers
- Fujifilm.net, 168–169
- Kodak Mobile/Ofoto, 167–168

online storage, availability of, 14–15.
See also storage
optical zoom
- availability of, 291
- significance of, 288

Oxley bill, significance of, 296

P

P900 camcorder phones, features of, 233–235
Paint Shop Photo Album 4
- adding titles, comments, and keywords to images in, 90–91
- creating panoramic images with, 112
- creating photo archives with, 97
- creating slide shows with, 205–207
- features of, 89
- importing pictures to, 91–92
- making movies with, 207–208

Paint Shop Pro 8
- adjusting brightness with, 114
- cropping photos with, 110–112
- editing images with, 104–106
- resizing photos with, 121
- straightening pictures with, 109

Panasonic camera phones, carrier for, 20
panoramic images, creating, 112
paper, cost of, 166
paper size, choosing in Photoshop Elements 2, 164
PC cards, purchasing, 71

PCs (personal computers)
- moving pictures to, 68–76
- moving video clips to, 247–250

PDF file format, saving Photoshop Album Creations in, 204–205
people, lighting concerns related to, 55
photo albums
- creating, 199–203, 205
- sharing with Picture Mail, 135–137

photo archives, creating, 96–98
photo caller ID
- establishing with camera phones, 6–7
- resolution concerns related to, 63–64
- setting up, 198–199

photo paper, cost of, 166
photo printers. *See also* online print services
- accessories for, 161–162
- and Bluetooth/IrDA, 160–161
- choosing, 158–162
- concerns related to, 161–162
- costs associated with, 165–166
- vendors of, 162

photos. *See also* action shots; images; JPEG images; pictures; shots
- cropping, 109–112
- embedding in e-mail with SendPhotos Gold, 153–155
- enhancing with Picture Mail, 136
- moving to PCs, 72–73
- organizing on Buzznet, 178–179
- projecting with Image Viewer, 213
- resizing in Paint Shop Pro, 121
- searching in Adobe Photoshop Album 2, 86–87
- searching in Windows, 79–80
- sharpening, 116–118
- snapping with OK button, 32
- uploading to Kodak Mobile/Ofoto, 167
- uploading to My Album, 138
- uploading to Picture Mail, 132–133

Photoshop Album 2
- creating slide shows with, 205
- creating tags in, 85
- creating virtual collections in, 86–88

Photoshop Album 2 *(Cont.)*
  importing pictures to, 86–87
  making Creations with, 199–205
  searching photos in, 86–87
Photoshop Elements 2
  adjusting brightness with, 114
  aligning crooked pictures with, 108–109
  canceling crops in, 113
  choosing paper size in, 164
  creating greeting cards with, 209–211
  creating photo archives with, 96–97
  cropping photos with, 110–112
  editing images with, 103–105
  opening Image Size dialog box in, 119
Photosmart 7000 printers, features of, 165
picture buttons, locations of, 27–28
Picture CD, comparing to CD-R and CD-RW, 98–99
picture effects
  and resolution settings, 44
  setting preferences for, 42–43
Picture Mail service
  maintaining online address books with, 134
  sending picture messages from, 133–134
  support for video clips, 244–247
  uploading photos to, 132–133
  using with Sprint PCS, 72–73
Picture Maker kiosks by Kodak, using, 170–171
picture messages
  availability of, 23, 74
  costs associated with, 39
picture messaging websites. *See also* MMS (Multimedia Message Service)
  My Album, 138–139
  overview of, 132
  Picture Mail, 132–138
  Pix Place, 139–144
  prices associated with, 145
PictureMate printer, features of, 159
"Picture Share" message in Picture Mail, significance of, 136–137
pictures. *See also* action shots; images; JPEG images; photos; shots
  advisory about deletion of, 37
  aligning when crooked, 108–109
  costs associated with sending of, 21
  courtesy considerations related to, 296
  importing to Adobe Photoshop Album 2, 87–88
  importing to JASC Paint Shop Album 4, 91–92
  linking with contacts, 198–199
  moving to different folders in Windows, 78
  moving to PCs, 68–76
  moving with Picture Mail, 136
  printing from image editors, 163
  renaming in Windows, 78–79
  saving, 36–37
  sending, 37–38
  sending to community sites, 189
  sending to Mobog, 181
  sending to My Album, 138
  sending via e-mail, 63, 150–153
  sending with greeting cards, 209–210
  sending with Pix Place, 141
  taking for first time, 36
  taking in daylight versus dark environments, 165
  transferring wirelessly, 212
  uploading to Fujifilm.net, 168–169
  uploading to Pix Place, 139
  using Bluetooth for sharing of, 156
  viewing, 37
Pix Place, 74–75, 144
  adding audio clips to, 141
  advisory about firewalls, 141
  creating albums with, 143–144
  features of, 139
  limit of picture messages in, 139, 143
  logging into, 140
  New Slide option in, 142
  previewing images in, 142
  sending greeting cards with, 209–210
  uploading pictures to, 139
pixels
  description of, 10
  impact of, 116
  increasing density of, 163
.PNG format, significance of, 124

postcards, creating with camera phones, 5–6
ppi (pixels per inch)
    setting, 164
    significance of, 162
preferences, setting, 39–43
Print Preview feature, using, 165
print size
    changing, 120, 122
    determining, 166
Print@Home feature of Ofoto, description of, 148
printers. *See* photo printers
printing kiosks, using, 170–171
printing, resolution concerns related to, 65
printing technologies, emergence of, 172
prints
    adjusting size of, 162–165
    buying from Kodak Mobile/Ofoto, 167
    ordering from Fujifilm.net, 168
privacy, overview of, 294–297
professional applications of camera phones, examples of, 8
.PSD format, significance of, 124
.PSP format, significance of, 124
PSP (Paint Shop Pro). *See* Paint Shop Pro 8
Public Keyword, creating for Buzznet galleries, 179–180

Q

QCIF (Quarter Common Intermediate Format), relationship to camcorder phones, 219
QuickTime player, downloading, 208
QuickTime, relationship to camcorder phones, 220

R

real estate agents, applications for, 8
RealOne, acquiring video from, 253–254
Remember Me option in Picture Mail, effect of, 133
resampling images, 122
resolution. *See also* high and low resolution
    description of, 10
    lowering, 162
    result of making changes in, 121–123
    setting, 163
    setting in Ofoto, 167
    setting preferences for, 39–40
    significance of, 13
    and special effects, 44
RS-MMC cards, using with Nokia 7610 megapixel camera phones, 285
RUNpics, subscribing to, 95

S

S700 megapixel camera phones, features of, 277
Samsung camera phones, features of, 18–19
Samsung e715 camera phones, internal storage space available on, 68
Samsung SCH-a610 camera phones, clamshell design of, 27
Samsung SPH-a600 camera phones, lens on, 29
Samsung SPH-a620 flip phones
    features of, 14
    lens on, 29
Samsung VM-A680 camera phones, features of, 9, 232, 235
SanDisk ImageMate Reader/Writer, using with camcorder phones, 229–230
SanDisk TransFlash memory card, benefit of, 160
Sanyo camera phones, features of, 19
Save for Web feature, using with Photoshop Elements, 103
SCH-a610 camera phones, clamshell design of, 27
SD (secure digital) cards, using with camcorder phones, 227–228
Secret Word feature in Textamerica, explanation of, 184
security, overview of, 297–299
self timer, using for self-portraits, 59
self-portraits, taking, 57–59
Send Album option in Picture Mail, effect of, 136

Send Picture Message option, effect of, 33
SendPhotos Gold program, features
    of, 153–155
sepia or antique effects, description of, 43
services. *See* wireless services
Settings option, effect of, 33
Sharpen filters, using, 117–118
shopping, using camera phones while, 6
shortcuts, changing, 33
shots, framing, 49. *See also* action shots;
    images; JPEG images; photos; pictures
Show Your iPod moblog, sending pictures
    to, 189
shutter lag, explanation of, 59
shutter speed, significance of, 52
Siemens SX1 camera phones, features of, 9
sites. *See also* websites
    creating on Buzznet, 178
    creating on Textamerica, 183–185
Slide Show Player, sharing slide shows with,
    207
slide shows
    creating with Paint Shop
        Album, 205–207
    viewing in Buzznet, 177
    viewing with Sprint Video Mail,
        244, 246
Snapfish Mobile
    features of, 149–150
    web address for, 95
SnapMedia program, features of, 70
Soft Keys, purpose of, 32
Sony Ericsson camera phones, features of, 19
Sony Ericsson P900 camcorder phone, features
    of, 233–235
Sony Ericsson S700 megapixel camera phones,
    features of, 277
Sony Ericsson T610 camera phones, features of,
    14, 28
Sony Memory Sticks, using with camcorder
    phones, 226
Sony photo printers, models and price ranges of,
    162
sounds, adding from Pix Place Gallery, 144

soundtracks, adding to Paint Shop slide
    shows, 207
special effects
    and resolution settings, 42–43
    setting preferences for, 42–43
specks, eliminating, 118, 120
SPH-a600 camera phones, lens on, 29
SPH-a620 flip phones
    features of, 14
    lens on, 29
Sprint PCS
    camera phones supported by, 20
    and MobiTV, 252
    moving photos to PCs with, 72–73
    picture messaging services available
        from, 23
    prices for picture messaging services
        offered by, 145
Sprint Picture Mail. *See* Picture Mail service
storage, increasing, 34. *See also* online storage
Straighten tool, using with Paint Shop Pro, 109
streaming video
    downloading from RealOne, 253–254
    relationship to camcorder phones, 219
subjects
    framing in shots, 50
    proximity of, 55–56
swivel displays, features of, 29
system menu, accessing, 36

T

T610 camera phones, features of, 14, 28
tags, creating in Adobe Photoshop Album 2,
    85
"talking postcards," testing, 131
text messages, character limit of, 181
Textamerica.com moblog
    associating images with categories
        in, 186
    The Blackout site on, 194
    versus Buzznet, 183
    creating categories in, 185
    features of, 190

U

logging into, 183–184
overview of, 182–189
removing comments from, 192
support for video clips, 247–248
T-Flash (TransFlash) cards, using with camcorder phones, 227–228
third-party online services
Fujifilm.net, 150
Ofoto, 146–149
Snapfish Mobile, 149–150
thumbnails
displaying, 37
displaying in Digital Image Pro, 107
displaying in Pix Place, 141
viewing in Picture Mail, 244, 246
viewing in Windows, 82–83
TIFF images
versus JPEGs, 124
saving files as, 125
tiles, displaying images as, 82–83
timeline in VideoStudio 8, adjusting length of music clips with, 265–266
timer, using for self-portraits, 59
titles, adding to VideoStudio 8 movies, 263, 265
T-Mobile
camera phones supported by, 20
My Album service available from, 74, 138–139
picture messaging services available from, 23
prices for picture messaging services offered by, 145
Toshiba camera phones, features of, 19
Toshiba VM4050 camcorder phone
digital zoom feature of, 57
features of, 234–235
storage limitations of, 225
touchup tasks, performing with Digital Image Pro 9, 106–107
TransFlash memory card, benefit of, 160
travel chargers, using, 35
tripods, relationship to exposure settings, 52
TV tuners, future of, 270

U

U-Lead Systems' VideoStudio 8 editing software, features of, 259–269
Unsharp Mask option, effect of, 117
The Uruguay Round Agreements Act, significance of, 299
USB adapters, purchasing, 71
USB cables, using with megapixel camera phones, 279–280
USB ports, using with data cables, 69
User Buzz page, accessing in Buzznet, 179–180

V

V600 camera phones, features of, 9
V710 megapixel camera phones, features of, 284
Verizon Pix Place. *See* Pix Place
Verizon Wireless
Broadband Access network offered by, 222
and GetFlix, 256, 258
moving images to PCs with, 74–76
picture messaging services available from, 23
prices for picture messaging services offered by, 145
VGA (video graphics array), description of, 10–11
VGA-quality camera phones
setting print size with, 166
taking pictures with, 162–163, 165
video. *See also* movies
acquiring from third-party sources, 250–254, 256, 258
capturing, 238–239
future of, 269–270
getting close for, 240–241
letting action come to you, 241
quality of, 251
reasons for watching on cell phones, 251

video. *See also* movies *(Cont.)*
    using camcorder function for, 241–242
    working with strong natural light, 239–240
video calls, future of, 270
video clips
    adding titles with VideoStudio 8, 263, 265
    adding transitions with VideoStudio 8, 263–264
    moving to PCs, 247–250
    saving, 209
    saving in Picture Mail, 247
    saving to memory cards, 223
    sharing, 243–250
    size constraints of, 221
    Sprint PCS Picture Mail's support for, 244–247
    Textamerica.com moblog support for, 247
video editing software
    overview of, 258–259
    VideoStudio 8, 259–269
video messages, sending from Picture Mail, 244–245
Video Voyeurism Prevention Act, explanation of, 297
VideoStudio 8 editing software
    exporting movies from, 269–270
    features of, 259–260
    making movies with, 263–269
    Movie Wizard in, 259–262
    saving work in frequently, 267
View Gallery option, effect of, 33
virtual collections, creating in Adobe Photoshop Album 2, 86–88
virtual photo albums
    creating, 199–203, 205
    sharing with Picture Mail, 135–137
Vision service, support for, 252–253
VM4050 camcorder phone
    digital zoom feature of, 57
    features of, 234–235
    storage limitations of, 225

VM-A680 camera phones, features of, 9, 232, 235
Voices from the Community
    An Editor's Picks, 9
    A Family Affair, 34
    Helping the Bride, 145
    For Her Fans, 190–191
    Never Miss a Precious Moment Again, 60
    Printing Developments, 161
    Sprint Goes to the Movies, 224
    The Tip of the Iceberg, 257
Volume Rubber Band in VideoStudio 8, using, 267–268
.VSP format, significance of, 267
VX6000
    assigning shortcuts to left navigation button on, 33
    sending pictures from, 37–38
    testimonial about, 33
VX8000 megapixel phone, features of, 283–284

W

watermark effects, description of, 43
web log, example of, 174
webcam, explanation of, 256
websites, 258. *See also* sites
    Adobe Reader, 204
    Belkin, 71, 160–161
    Bluetooth printer adapters, 160–161
    Canon photo printers, 162
    DataPilot, 71
    D-Link, 71
    Epson photo printers, 162
    Fuji Film, 95
    FutureDial, 70
    Handspring (Palm One) camera phones, 16
    Hewlett-Packard photo printers, 162
    JASC Paint Shop Pro 8, 105
    Kodak Mobile, 95
    LG camera phones, 16

Index 317

Mobile Printing Application for Nokia 3650, 172
Mobile Video Cam, 258
MobiTV, 252
Motorola Mobile Phone Tools package, 69
My Photo Gallery, 95
NEC camera phones, 18
Nokia camera phones, 18
Ofoto, 95
Olympus photo printers, 162
   optimizing pictures for posting to, 103
   QuickTime player, 208
   resolution concerns when posting pictures to, 61
RUNpics, 95
Samsung camera phones, 19
Sanyo camera phones, 19
SendPhotos Gold program, 155
Show Your iPod moblog, 189
Snapfish Mobile, 95, 149
Sony Ericsson camera phones, 19
Sony photo printers, 162
T-Mobile's My Album, 138
Toshiba camera phones, 19
Verizon Pix Place, 139
WinZip, 73

white balance
   adjusting, 52–53
   setting preferences for, 41–42
Windows
   renaming files in, 78–79
   searching for photos in, 79–80
   storing images in, 77–78
   viewing images in, 80–82
Windows Explorer, copying files to memory cards from, 250
WinZip, downloading trial version of, 73
wireless networks, speeds of, 222
wireless services
   choosing, 20–23
   list of, 20
WMA music file format, VideoStudio 8's support for, 260–261

Z

Zipped files, extracting, 73
Zoom & Trim feature in Ofoto, description of, 168
zoom
   avoiding, 57
   significance of, 30–31

INTERNATIONAL CONTACT INFORMATION

AUSTRALIA
McGraw-Hill Book Company
Australia Pty. Ltd.
TEL +61-2-9900-1800
FAX +61-2-9878-8881
http://www.mcgraw-hill.com.au
books-it_sydney@mcgraw-hill.com

CANADA
McGraw-Hill Ryerson Ltd.
TEL +905-430-5000
FAX +905-430-5020
http://www.mcgraw-hill.ca

**GREECE, MIDDLE EAST, & AFRICA
(Excluding South Africa)**
McGraw-Hill Hellas
TEL +30-210-6560-990
TEL +30-210-6560-993
TEL +30-210-6560-994
FAX +30-210-6545-525

MEXICO (Also serving Latin America)
McGraw-Hill Interamericana Editores
S.A. de C.V.
TEL +525-1500-5108
FAX +525-117-1589
http://www.mcgraw-hill.com.mx
carlos_ruiz@mcgraw-hill.com

SINGAPORE (Serving Asia)
McGraw-Hill Book Company
TEL +65-6863-1580
FAX +65-6862-3354
http://www.mcgraw-hill.com.sg
mghasia@mcgraw-hill.com

SOUTH AFRICA
McGraw-Hill South Africa
TEL +27-11-622-7512
FAX +27-11-622-9045
robyn_swanepoel@mcgraw-hill.com

SPAIN
McGraw-Hill/
Interamericana de España, S.A.U.
TEL +34-91-180-3000
FAX +34-91-372-8513
http://www.mcgraw-hill.es
professional@mcgraw-hill.es

**UNITED KINGDOM, NORTHERN,
EASTERN, & CENTRAL EUROPE**
McGraw-Hill Education Europe
TEL +44-1-628-502500
FAX +44-1-628-770224
http://www.mcgraw-hill.co.uk
emea_queries@mcgraw-hill.com

ALL OTHER INQUIRIES Contact:
McGraw-Hill/Osborne
TEL +1-510-420-7700
FAX +1-510-420-7703
http://www.osborne.com
omg_international@mcgraw-hill.com